GETTING IT STRAIGHT

Villains Talking

Freddie Foreman
and **Tony Lambrianou**
with **Carol Clerk**

PAN BOOKS

First published 2001 by Sidgwick & Jackson

This edition published 2002 by Pan Books
an imprint of Pan Macmillan Ltd
Pan Macmillan, 20 New Wharf Road, London N1 9RR
Basingstoke and Oxford
Associated companies throughout the world
www.panmacmillan.com

ISBN 0 330 49013 3

Copyright © Freddie Foreman, Tony Lambrianou and Carol Clerk 2001

The right of Freddie Foreman, Tony Lambrianou and Carol Clerk to be identified
as the authors of this work has been asserted by them in accordance
with the Copyright, Designs and Patents Act 1988.

All rights reserved. No part of this publication may be
reproduced, stored in or introduced into a retrieval system, or
transmitted, in any form, or by any means (electronic, mechanical,
photocopying, recording or otherwise) without the prior written
permission of the publisher. Any person who does any unauthorized
act in relation to this publication may be liable to criminal
prosecution and civil claims for damages.

1 3 5 7 9 8 6 4 2

A CIP catalogue record for this book is available from
the British Library.

Typeset by SetSystems Ltd, Saffron Walden, Essex
Printed and bound in Great Britain by
Mackays of Chatham plc, Chatham, Kent

This book is sold subject to the condition that it shall not,
by way of trade or otherwise, be lent, re-sold, hired out,
or otherwise circulated without the publisher's prior consent
in any form of binding or cover other than that in which
it is published and without a similar condition including this
condition being imposed on the subsequent purchaser.

This book is dedicated to the memories of

Donald Clerk, Charlie Kray and Geraldine Charles

20081829

MORAY COUNCIL
LIBRARIES &
INFORMATION SERVICES
364.37

Contents

Acknowledgements

The authors would like to thank the following people, who willingly gave their time and encouragement during the preparation of this book: Janice King and Wendy Mason-Lambrianou for their love and support; Jamie Foreman for his invaluable advice; George Foreman for remembering so many amusing stories; Karen and Adam Lambrianou for their love; Prince and Guy for their loyalty – to Prince, RIP and thank you from Tony; Robert Smith and Gordon Wise for the opportunity, and for their belief; Maria Jefferis for her friendship and hours of tape transcription; Carol's husband, Nigel O'Brien, for his love, ideas and tireless help; and their daughter Eve for her inspiration.

The Authors

Tony Lambrianou on Freddie Foreman

The first time I met Fred was in early '64 at his pub, the Prince of Wales, in the Borough. The firms north and south of the water never really mixed then. Fred had an independent firm. We all knew of each other, but we didn't tend to cross sides often. You didn't go on other manors.

Fred's always had a respected name. He was known as a game man. He kept his business very tight to his chest.

When we all went down after the Kray trials, we became friends. I've always found Fred a very likeable, easy-going man. He's a good listener.

Freddie Foreman on Tony Lambrianou

Tony and myself got to know each other during the trials, sitting in the dock for all those months. Where I came to know him better was in Leicester Prison. We spent a couple of years there together. And then when I got moved to the Scrubs, Tony came down after a couple of years, so we met up again. We used to play against each other at football.

We had a certain rapport. I was a hard person to get to know in those days. I was a very private person, a bit secretive, and I didn't have too much to say to anybody. I'm more friendly and open today than I was then. But I liked Tony because he was a genuine guy, and we got on well together.

I've really enjoyed working with Tony and Carol, our co-author, on this book. It was a good excuse for going down memory lane while getting pissed once a week in my own kitchen, without having to worry about travelling home afterwards.

But I must apologize for my terrible language. If any of my family had such a foul mouth, I'd 'wash it out with soap and water', as my mum used to say. My only excuse is that I really did do a bit of method acting, as my son Jamie would call it, and got right back into my old character.

This book has taken me back to all the madness and mayhem of the old times, and looking back, it's a wonder that I never lost my marbles totally and ended up in the fucking funny farm. Oops! Apologies – I'm at it again!

I hope this will help people to understand a little more about us. I'd like everyone I've yet to meet not to judge me or anyone like me until they've spent good, quality time with us, maybe a night around the dinner table, or a friendly drink in our company. What is perceived as the stereotype gangster is often far from the real person.

Maybe people will be able to accept that lives don't always take the same path. But as we travel along, hoping to achieve success, I'm sure we all strive, in one way or another, to gain respect.

My family, my extended family and great friends . . . we share a special bond of mutual respect, unequivocal loyalty and, most important, love. I'll cherish it always.

Foreword

Freddie Foreman made his first high-profile court appearance – at London's Old Bailey – at the tender age of sixteen, on an affray charge. He would see the inside of that building on another four occasions as he built a career spanning more than three decades.

The most fearless – and feared – criminal in Britain, involved in murders and major robberies, Freddie Foreman returned to the dock in the Old Bailey's legendary Number One Court after the murders of Jack 'The Hat' McVitie, Frank 'The Mad Axeman' Mitchell and Tommy 'Ginger' Marks, and in connection with the Security Express robbery.

Tony Lambrianou, like Freddie, turned to crime in his teens to escape the poverty endured by his Geordie mother and Greek-Cypriot father. He rose quickly to the top of his profession as a criminal, joining forces with the Kray twins as their empire expanded across London. He had served various minor prison sentences by the time he came to court over Jack McVitie.

Freddie, from south London, and Tony, ten years younger and from the East End, might never have become the close friends they are today were it not for Reggie Kray's murder of McVitie at a party in October 1967.

Tony witnessed the killing and drove away the body. He took a hair-raising ride through the Rotherhithe Tunnel into the manor ruled by Freddie Foreman, who collected and disposed of McVitie. Amazingly, neither man knew of the other's involvement until the case came to court in the famous Kray trials.

Now retired from crime, both Freddie and Tony have carved out new careers in the media. They have published their memoirs and are regularly called upon by journalists and authors. They have appeared on countless TV and radio programmes, as well as helping researchers as consultants.

Freddie is pursing his ambitions to write for TV and films, while Tony, now living in Kent, has become a keen gardener and traveller. Both are involved in charity work and, along with other villains of the Sixties, they have made a recording debut with trip-hop star Tricky on his album *Product of the Environment*.

Recently, over a drink or three, Freddie and Tony realized that they had rarely discussed their past: they had never compared notes about the parts they each played after the murder of McVitie. And as they talked on, they discovered that they still had a great deal to ask each other, and to explain, after all these years.

Suddenly, it was important to get this down in writing, to explain how it really was in the old, lawless days of sharp suits and shooters, and to separate the fact from the fiction that has grown up around the legend.

Freddie and Tony asked me to record a series of conversations during which they revisited the past with a realism and emotion unknown in previous accounts of the era.

The meetings took place in pubs and, more often, at Freddie's home in north-west London – in the study, in the elegant sitting room and, cosily, around the kitchen table – where his partner Janice was on hand with a ready welcome and a bottle of something dangerous.

The drinks flowed into the night and there was revelation, outrage, argument, laughter and the occasional tear as Freddie and Tony travelled right back to the heart of their former selves, getting it straight, exploding the romantic myth of the London gangster and arriving back at a place, today, where they can testify that their notoriety has been as damaging to their lives as it has been beneficial.

Here, then, are the conversations – exactly as they happened.

Carol Clerk
London, December 2000

THE
GANGSTER
YEARS

1

The Sixties Villain: Having What It Took

Conversations in the study and in the kitchen at Fred's home in north-west London, 12 October 1999 and 7 December 1999

WHAT'S IN A NAME

Tony You were always known in our circles, Fred, as 'The Undertaker' or 'Brown Bread'. In the Sixties, people wouldn't mention your name, but we knew who they were talking about. Everyone knew.

Fred Because I'd done a couple of things where people went missing and, um, they were never found.

Tony You had a fearsome reputation. Make no mistake about it. You didn't upset Freddie Foreman.

Fred 'The Undertakers', 'The High Executioners' . . . that's how they referred to us in the criminal world, but we didn't, at the time, know. Nobody ever said it to our face.

It was just the way people looked at you. But it wouldn't have been a compliment to us, cos it's like saying, 'Oh, you're fucking murderers.' That's dangerous talk, isn't it? Because you wind up with the Old Bill coming to you about it – 'Why are they calling you that?' – and next thing you know, you're at the Old Bailey.

I think Patsy O'Mara was the one who actually started it, calling me Brown Bread. He was on the firm with me. He was a good worker, Patsy. And he used to phone up the pub or club and he'd say, 'Is Brown there?' You know, Brown Bread for Fred. But then Brown Bread went on to say, 'You're dead.' This was from the late Fifties.

One of our pals, Staffie, he used to ask, 'Is Uncle there?' I was

Uncle Fred to some people, Brown Bread to other people. I had all these different fucking names.

The newspapers named me 'Mean Machine' when I was in Spain. The only Mean Machine I know is Roy Shaw [a notorious villain also known as 'Pretty Boy' Shaw]. They got me mixed up with him. He was a bare-knuckle, unlicensed fighter, and I used to go to those fights. Why they called me that, I don't know.

Tony Did you know just how powerful you were at the time, Fred?

Fred Well, I knew when my pal Alfie Gerrard and myself used to walk in different places, people would go, 'Oh, fucking hell, *they've* just come in.' I didn't feel menacing at all. I just felt that we had a bit of respect where we went, and we was treated right.

Tony (*Laughing*) That's an understatement. It's like the [Kray] twins. No one ever referred to them by name. It was, 'They're around.' Or, 'The other people are about.'

Fred See, that's the way it was. But I know Terry Murphy said, 'Fucking hell, never mind about the twins coming in, when Fred and Alf used to walk in, people used to fucking crap themselves.' It surprised me, cos we were just being ourselves.

Even now, people think you go in and take over and you twist people's arms, you nick money out of their pockets and won't pay for nothing and you smash up pubs and terrorize 'em and ill-treat women and throw booze in their faces or whatever. They expect you to act like a complete idiot thug, the way gangsters are portrayed by the media.

Tony Exactly true.

Fred We're respectful to women. We put them on a pedestal. Never having any sisters, I always was in awe of women. Cos with five brothers, a girl had to be treated with respect if she was coming round the house. And your mother, you treated her that way, and all the women you come in contact with over the years.

So back then, we were just keeping ourselves to ourselves, we never fucking went and caused trouble anywhere. Course, if there was a row it was a serious row. It ain't gonna be a punch on the chin, you know. They'd wind up fucking hurt, and the comeback – they couldn't handle the comeback next day if something went off.

Tony They *worried*.

Fred You just want to be treated with respect. It's not anything you demand off anybody. It's not wanting to be treated any different to anybody else. If you go round saying, 'You gotta respect me,' and you give them all that shit, then who's going to respect you?

The understatement is always better in a way, isn't it? I mean, if I was gonna do anything . . . if you was insulted and something really went off, you wouldn't start making threats saying, 'Oh, I'm gonna do this and that, I'm gonna kill you.' You just go back the next day and do it. And they know that. You don't have to fucking tell them what you're gonna do.

Tony Number-one rule. Don't brag about it. Go and do it.

ALL THAT BUSINESS WITH THE KRAYS

Tony I knew a lot about you before I met you – 'Just don't bother him.' You had to be connected up to be introduced.

Fred I didn't want to meet anybody who I didn't know or didn't come through the right channels.

Tony It came through recommendations.

Fred Yeah. The twins used to recommend somebody and then I would go and meet them. They might have some business. Cos if the twins got any work put to them, and they used to get quite a bit, and they couldn't really handle it, like a major robbery or a bit of sophisticated crime, someone who could cut open a vault or a safe, or do a bank or an armoured car or rob a gold bullion dealer's, if they wasn't capable of doing it themselves, they used to refer it to me.

Because of the name and reputation that the twins had, everyone went to them thinking they could get these things done, which they could, but I was the one who carried them out. The elite little firm who could go and do these things were with me. So they liked to keep me quiet, didn't they?

People always seem to think I'm an East End boy and a henchman for the Kray twins, which I really resent. I'm a south

Londoner. I wasn't fucking one of the Kray firm at all. And the judge even said that in the trial. I had my own people, my own firm.

I was backing the twins up and they knew that I was behind them. They done favours for me over the years, they put work my way, and they really helped me in one particular situation, which was the Battle of Bow in 1961.

I knew they was heading for stardom in one way or the other and that they was gonna become a name. But I knew what the future sort of held for 'em. I thought they'd either be killing someone or they'd be dead. They were reckless. They thought they could walk on water.

Tony   You said something to me one day in Leicester Prison: 'Had they got seven years apiece a few years earlier, it might've educated them a bit.'

Fred   It would've done them a lot of good. It would've given them a little taste of what it's all about.

Tony   They didn't have that, did they? But, anyway, it was a one-off firm. I think they got to the stage where they thought they was untouchable. And people knew, obviously, you was a friend. That was the big ace. I don't think it would have got as big as what it did if they hadn't had you.

Fred   People would have moved on 'em and joined forces.

Tony   Yes, I think that would have happened.

Fred   Their enemies didn't fancy taking on me as well as them.

Tony   That's right. It was too powerful.

Fred   They thought that if they moved on them, that I would come in, I'd be the counter-attack, iron a few out. And I would have done. We was that close, that friendly, that if anybody attacked the twins' firm, then I was duty bound to join in and fucking help them out.

Tony   That's loyalty. One thing the twins wanted was loyalty. But with your firm, there was common sense there.

Fred Well, all we was concerned with was going out and getting money, whereas the twins' firm got money through violence and intimidation and extortion.

Tony Yeah, yeah. It had to be that. The twins' firm was different from yours, Fred. The twins had to have that violence.

Fred They did a lot of the violence themselves.

Tony Let's not take it away from them, they did it themselves.

Fred We was very different. Different crimes, different criminal activities. There was more money in what we did. Bigger, major crimes, and they carried a lot more bird – banks, burning open vaults, robbing security firms and armoured vehicles, you know. Nothing petty.

Tony I was working in the Midlands for quite a while, getting money out of the clubs as an 'agent', and what we needed from the twins, because wherever you went in the country, people knew of them, was

Fred . . . their name.

Tony Fear was the key to that. Cor, not much. *Not much.* If Reggie gave someone a right-hander, ten people would jump on the man after he went down. A lot of them festered on the violence, like Scotch Jack Dickson, and this is what sickened me at our trial, the finger-pointing – '*Him*, he done it, he done it.'

Fred Those were the grasses who rolled over.

Tony And they were the very people who committed a lot of the violence. But I've gotta be honest about it. The twins would come in the Regency [club] and people walked out. When you've got people frightened . . .

Fred We didn't trade on fear in that respect, but, yeah, if anybody crossed our path . . .

Tony Do two things, in my eyes. Keep that shut. And never point the finger. That meant a lot to me.

Fred Well, you done fucking fifteen years for keeping your mouth shut.

Tony We all threw a lot away, you know. People say to me, 'Do you regret what you've done?' I don't regret it because I done it. But I would never put myself in that position again.

GETTING ON THE FIRM – HOW YOU QUALIFIED

Tony I must say this about [the Krays' henchman Albert] Donoghue. At that time, he was game.

Fred I liked him. I used to say to the twins, 'Send him over to pick me up if you wanna have a little meet.' He used to come over in the car and I'd jump in with him and I'd meet the twins somewhere out in the back of nowhere. They used to find all these different gaffs, didn't they? They'd find one pub and use it for a few weeks and then change the meet to another.

He was very quiet, he never said too much, and I liked him, Donoghue, for that reason.

He'd come over, he'd give me whatever money the twins were sending on a cut-up from the West End, the Colony Club and places like that, like, two or three grand, we'd have a couple of drinks and off he'd go.

He says in his book that he would've liked to have got on my firm, but no way. Nah. Cos I had my own firm and I had proved, trusted people and they had a pedigree. They'd been tested.

Tony You could have the best.

Fred He [Albert] wasn't tried and tested, as far as I knew. If you fucking buy a pair of Church shoes, you wear 'em and wear 'em and they last you for years. It was like your quality people, you know. If they've been nicked, they stood up and they never fucking rolled over. They never put their pen to paper and tried to do a deal with the police. They kept their mouths shut.

Tony That's all you want, that you didn't wind up in court. I got nicked for three people in 1965 for a robbery. I was the only one that went down for it. Before that, in '63, I got eighteen months, and that was for other people as well. I got out of them both on appeal.

My [brother] Nicky done a borstal for someone. He took the rap for young Danny Farley. He said, 'I'll take it, make sure I'm looked after in the nick and I'll do your time for you.' If you can get someone out of it, then you do it. My Nicky done the time, but the people didn't want to look after him, and I made a noise about it, Fred. I went round there.

The day Nicky came out of borstal, we went to a party at the Astoria Club to see Danny Farley. My Nicky dragged him out and walloped him. And it turned out to be a party for the law, the CID. Next day I got a visit from a copper – 'What was the problem last night?'

Fred If you went out to work to earn some money, you'd have people round you who wouldn't leave you if you was in trouble, and you all got nicked together. You couldn't have anyone who was gonna panic and drive off and leave you roasting on the pavement. He had to have strong nerves and be solid and he had to stand his ground and stay and die with you.

He did his job sensibly and he didn't overreact, which is another important thing. You didn't want anyone who was gonna be trigger-happy and start shooting people. That was just as bad in our game.

On many occasions, I went out with a gun and I knew what that gun was there for. If you come into problems when you was leaving the scene of the crime, then you'd have shotguns for that reason, and you never produced them otherwise. That was a last resort, to get away if your liberty depended on it.

You had to respect the gun. We had more respect for the gun than the average person in the street in the early Sixties. You pull a gun on 'em and they'd still come at you and they wanted to tackle you and they wouldn't do as they were told. It wasn't like in America, where if you pulled a gun, they knew they'd wind up dead. It's only after years and years that a few people got fucking bowled over, got blasted, that they began to respect the shooter like they do today.

It was not a plus to be violent. The best work, the way we considered it, is when it went smoothly with the least amount of violence necessary and nobody got really hurt and went to hospital, because that made the case even worse. If anyone did get arrested later on, they got more bird because of the injuries. If you could get it as sweet as possible without injuring anybody, that was a good bit of work. Other than that, it was a bit of a failure.

It was surprising the number of robberies we did and nobody got really hurt. They never went to hospital with fractured skulls and gunshots in the leg, which happened a lot afterwards. Some robbers got fucking nutty with it. They used to get the money and then go back and shoot the guard in the legs. Or as they'd drive away from a bit of work, they'd have a pop and let one go at somebody who'd fucking run into the scene. They did it just for the violence's sake.

Years ago, it wasn't all armed robbery. We took, like, sticks. In the late Fifties, coming into the Sixties, there was no shooters. We used to just ram the car or the lorry or whatever's going to the bank to collect the wages. The cashiers used to bring out trays with all the wage packets lined up, and we used to stop 'em.

We used to have, like, pickaxe handles but nobody really got hurt. They was just for the body, if anywhere, not the head. You'd get the fella who'd want to put up a fight thinking it was his own money, not the firm's money, the have-a-go hero, and they used to get a whack. They couldn't mind their own business.

But then the police started using guns and that's why we had to start using them ourselves. The changing face of it was the Battle of Bow. It started with a raid on the Coutts bank van. One of the firm was shot dead by armed guards in the back of the van. They had two guns on board, which the firm never knew about. So robbers took the guns with them after that.

It was more self-defence than anything else. And if the police came after you, you'd blow their radiator out. We used to get out and fucking blast their windscreen or whatever, not intending to kill any coppers, but to stop 'em from arresting you.

There was very, very few policemen actually shot in those days. It was a hanging offence, and people didn't shoot coppers or anyone else. They'd go in a bank and they'd blast the ceiling, make a few holes, just to give people a scare. It was intimidation, really.

I mean, it would've been a terrible disaster if you killed somebody on a robbery, which Joey Martin, a good friend of ours, did on one job. He never intended to kill anybody. He let one go and he tried to keep it down low, but the guy wound up dying.

Joey got sentenced to life and a recommendation of eighteen years. And when I saw him, he'd already done twenty-eight years. It wasn't a premeditated killing, but the Home Secretary kept him in there for thirty-three years, like Ronnie and Reggie. The authorities are getting their revenge and this man was shafted really and truly by them shiny-arsed bureaucrats up at the Home Office.

Another thing we did, which other firms didn't – we'd commit a crime, and as soon as we come off the work, we'd get rid of the motors and change our clothes completely cos of the forensic. Then we'd go to one person, 'Right, you take the money back to the safe house and back to your business as quick as you can. Get in the betting shop, in the back door, and be on the board, chalking up the winners and the fucking losers on the race. And the Old Bill come in, they'll see you chalking up on the board.'

And someone else will be sitting in his office, another will be in his restaurant, another one will be at his launderette. You know, you ain't left your place of work all day.

And the money would go off with that one person, and we'd know by the scream in the paper how much was there. No one was worried about anybody getting sticky fingers. The money would be intact and when it came to the cut-up, everybody got their whack.

Tony What we wanted from a man was basically the same thing. He did his job and everything was above board and no strokes were pulled.

Fred And the people who'd put up the business to us, they'd get their whack, so they couldn't start screaming that they hadn't been paid. Everybody got treated right.

And no big bosses saying, 'Right, you do this, you do that.' It was very democratic. When you discussed these bits of work, you decided who was gonna do what.

You all knew your strengths and weaknesses, who was gonna be the getaway drivers, strong-willed and wouldn't pull away, staying there till the fucking last second and wouldn't move, whatever was going on around you. There'd be fucking bullets flying and, you know, hundreds of people running about, but they'd stay there and wait till you was ready to come away.

And then you'd have the people who was good on the pavements doing their job, and they could move about and have a row, and was agile and athletic enough to handle any situation.

Tony If you was at the heavy game, it came through recommendations, a lot of it. You'd hear about drivers or someone who was a good man up-front, whatever. Armed robberies in the Fifties, Sixties, Seventies . . .

Fred (*Laughing*) Every week there was one going off, weren't there? I mean, we went for the big time, big prizes, big money.

Tony   But you didn't get on one of them firms just by enjoying it.

Fred   No, you couldn't go up and ask to be on it. You had to be invited. You had to have a bit of credibility and done your apprenticeships before you was accepted. Also, you had to be very strong to be able to carry all those gas and air bottles on your shoulders, up ladders and across rooftops . . . Those bank jobs were like a commando assault course.

A lot of criminals enjoyed the money but they liked the notoriety more. We wouldn't be interested in that sort of person. I mean, they wanted the glory and if something went in the newspaper about the job, they would let everybody know that they'd done it by the way they was spending their money and behaving.

When we was recruiting people to the firm, you knew that they played their cards very close to their chest and never divulged anything. They never broadcast what they've done and what they haven't done. If they got money, they wouldn't act silly with it, going out and buying new Jaguars, and treating all the people in the bar, and flaunting their wealth. They kept their money to themselves and spent it privately, in the home and on their children's education and holidays.

They had good wives and family, stable people. They're the sort that you *had* to work with, that you had respect for. Your credibility had to be really tip-top to be on the firm.

And this was to be the proper criminal, to go out and commit fucking crimes where it wasn't just the committing of the crime, it was your behaviour after it took place.

You'd pick up the paper the day after a crime and the other firms, when nothing had happened, they'd go, 'You know who's had that – Foreman's firm. They've had this, cos we ain't heard nothing about it. Nothing's come to light.' We ran the tightest ship in London.

You had to have all these qualities. I personally always kept myself very fit because I thought, I owe it to myself and to my family. If you get nicked, that's it, they're the ones that are gonna be without money, without a father, and your wife's gonna be without her husband. I owed it to my own personal self to be 100 per cent fit so that if any situation arose, I'd fucking get out of it one way or the other.

I used to encourage the firm to do that. That's why I opened a boxing gym. They used to come up and work out. But we didn't socialize much. You wanted them to go and do their own thing and go with their own company, their own people, so they [the police] couldn't put you together.

DRESSED TO KILL

Tony Everybody was suited and booted. Everybody wore suits, shirt, tie, highly polished shoes. I remember when the mohair suits came in – sharp, very smart. Before that, people used to wear blue serge.

Fred We used to wear that back in the late Fifties, didn't we?

Tony What was the other one? The chequered one?

Fred Prince of Wales check.

Tony Dogtooth was another one.

Fred Yeah, and chalk stripe, to make you look taller and slimmer. You know, we still go to places now when we all get together, and everyone's turned out with the suits, collars and ties. Our sort of people have still not lost the dress code.

Tony I was over at your brother's, at that pub the other week . . .

Fred At the Hope, yeah.

Tony And everyone had a suit on. I just popped down there and I was casual and I didn't fit.

Fred You didn't feel right, no.

Tony You feel better when you look your best. A good haircut. You know, present yourself. Cos that's half the battle. Once you put the suit on, you become a different person. I do, anyway.

People see what they wanna see. Presentation is part and parcel of what it's all about. Certainly, it took me a long way.

Fred Appearances count for a lot, don't they? If you look poor and you got no money, you don't earn no money. Nobody's gonna trust you.

Tony Exactly right.

Fred You had to look like you were getting a good living, give a bit of confidence. Just your attire made you look wealthy, even though you might've only had a tenner in your pocket.

Tony A lot of the men used to always have a nice raincoat on, always a navy-blue raincoat, cos it always fitted the part.

Fred A gaberdine mac.

Tony And a lot of them used to wear the Crombies, which I liked the style of.

Fred The shape at the back with the half-belt.

Tony You had to have a Crombie.

Fred I used to have a guy come over and measure me and fit me. I never went to the tailor's. He used to bring all the samples of material, and I would pick 'em. I had so many suits made it was ridiculous.

I was built in such a way that I couldn't get anything off the peg. It would be too short here, too big there, fit me here and then it would be too long there. Like today, you can go in Marks & Spencers and you can get a different pair of trousers to fit the jacket, but you couldn't do that those days. So nearly everybody had their suits made who had any money. We all did.

Tony And we all had certain tailors we went to. I remember the Krays used to use Woodsy.

Fred East End used Woodsy down in Aldgate. The south Londons used to use Heimy Harris.

Tony Oh, the Elephant, he was.

Fred And who was the other one? Levy?

Tony Levy, Shoreditch.

Fred I finished up with this Hungarian tailor who used to make suits for fucking royalty, and he took the spivvy look off and made it more classy. I didn't want exaggerated shoulders and stuff like that. I wanted them nice, to make you look slim all the time. Cut down on the padding, make it more natural, your shape. And I even had a geezer who used to make my shoes. This guy used to go to Paris to make shoes for General Eisenhower, Commander of the British Forces in Europe. He finished up the President of the United States, General Eisenhower.

Tony Even today, people say to me, 'I like the suit you're wearing, where did you get that?' I still always get them made. There's very few who do it.

Fred The materials used to be out of this world. They were expensive, woven with silk threads. Beautiful. I'd like to have a few of those suits now. Unfortunately, my [wife] Maureen, every time I got nicked she used to give all my fucking suits away.

Tony (*Hearty laughter*) Do you remember what they said at the Old Bailey, that the defendants looked smarter than the jury? The way we were dressed, that was exactly the style of the time. It was just coming in then with the short, squarer shoulder, but slightly in to the hip.

Fred Not so exaggerated with the padding.

Tony Even the barnet, Fred. Like, it matched the clothes you were wearing. And we look at each other now and we've put on a little bit of weight here and there, and a few years have gone by . . .

Fred I wear clothes for comfort now.

Tony Yeah, I've noticed that with you, Fred.

Fred I fucking do, I have to (*laughing*).

Tony But we were known for our look. I thought it was one of the smartest periods of time that I ever knew.

Fred And the women were very well turned out.

Tony Beehive hair, the heavy black make-up . . .

Fred And the high heels and suspenders.

A GROUPIE'S PARADISE

Tony One thing you have to understand about Reggie – he weren't a bad-looking boy, but he never knew how to handle women. He was very shy. I always remember the time on the boats, Victoria Park. The twins used to always go over there, Fred. You remember, Victoria Park, little boat in there, little meeting place they had?

Fred Did they?

Tony Yeah. Ronnie had this thing about going there, having a cup of tea in the morning in the park. Nice. One day me, my brother Nicky, Reggie and a couple of birds that we'd been in the pub with were in the boat. And I watched Reggie chat one of them up and the girl was right keen, but he didn't seem to have a clue, Fred. Nothing detrimental about him. He was very shy with women.

　　I mean, he had many opportunities. A lot of women did fancy him. He didn't take advantage of it that much. But *I* did (*laughing*).

Fred Trust you.

Tony Not always, but, I mean, obviously, it was there for the taking.

Fred Lecherous bastard!

Tony I mean, we all did. They [the Krays] was well known in the area at that time.

Fred It's all this fascination about power and ruthlessness. Women like a bit of danger, a bit of fear, I suppose.

Tony They love it.

Fred It's like little girls when you chase 'em, and they get frightened and they giggle. My [daughter] Danielle, I used to put funny masks on and chase her all round the house, hiding under beds and behind curtains. She loved it. It's all exciting. I chase my [partner] Janice round the house. She giggles and laughs like a little girl (*laughing*). Some foreplay, innit?

Tony Gawd almighty! It's hard enough to keep 'em once a week! But, no, being truthful about it, it does attract women. I mean,

Charlie [Kray] loved the ladies. He used to be here, there and everywhere, but not the twins. Ronnie liked girls. Reggie, it was always very businesslike with him, very polite. Both of them were above board in women's company.

Fred   They wouldn't swear.

Tony   Reggie did love his wife, Frances. I knew her when she was a girl. He was very loyal to Frances, weren't he, Fred?

Fred   Didn't he love her!

Tony   Oh yeah. He didn't play around when he was with her. Never ever.

Fred   He didn't play around, really, at all.

Tony   It's funny, one night at a party at Manor House, there was a couple of birds there, and Ronnie went off with one – I was surprised at that, Fred [Ronnie having a reputation for homosexuality] – and she has her arm round him and he said to me, 'I'm not impartial to a woman.'

Fred   He was bisexual?

Tony   Yeah.

Fred   Oh.

Tony   People get it wrong on him. He always used to say, 'What I do in my life is my business.'

Fred   I could see a woman finding Ronnie amusing and funny. He was a bit of a charmer, really. He had some nice little turns of phrase, and he would really look after somebody. I could see a woman liking that.

Tony   Who was the mother and daughter who was around at that time?

Fred   Oh, Janette . . .

Tony   Janette and her daughter!

Fred   Didn't they have a club in Chelsea? Down at the World's End, King's Road?

Tony That's right. Ronnie was always out with them, the mother and the daughter. And he used to go back to their flat, regular. Whether anything was going on there . . . I mean, you've gotta remember, they were very smart men, which was attractive.

Fred They had that bit of aura about them, a bit of power, which girls get turned on by. When they used to turn up anywhere, there was always loads of girls about.

Tony Oh, a lot of attractive girls around. The opportunities were there for everyone. It happened. I mean, yeah, *I* slipped in.

Fred And I suppose by getting with one of the firm, the girls were establishing theirselves. Albert [Donoghue] done quite a few.

Tony Cor, yeah . . . But I remember one, she was going out with Eddie Futrell out of Birmingham. She left him because she fancied me.

Fred So it's down to you that she left him.

Tony Well, she went on to do great things. She became a chief croupier in the White Star Shipping Lines boats.

Fred I used to get into a bit of trouble myself. Cos when I had my pub, they'd come up and they'd slip their telephone number in my top pocket and I never even knew. And Maureen used to go through my suits and find them. I mean, when you're a club or pub owner, they always wanna know the guvnor. And, of course, you was always very smart, and you were generous and you used to send them over bottles of champagne and take them to clubs in the West End and have a nice car. You was a good catch, I suppose.

Tony Yeah.

Fred Not a good catch when you got nicked and they had to come visiting you, but while the good times lasted, then the girls was all for it. And you never just had one, you had three or four on the go, all at once.

When you live on the edge like we were, you don't know what's in store, what's gonna happen from one month, one day to another, and you live life to the full. You work hard and you play hard. Not like you was gonna leave your wife, not when you've got young kids. When they're grown up, it's a bit different if you fall in love with somebody, but at that stage you was loyal, though you messed around. It's one of those things that goes with the territory. It's the image. You're surrounded with girls. When you run a business, you've got fucking dozens of 'em, ain't you? You're spoilt for choice. It was a perk of the job.

Tony   I still bring it on today. I always wear a suit like I did in that time, it's the way I dress, and it attracts a lot of women. I get it all the time, and I'm fifty-eight now.

Fred   But you don't bite.

Tony   I don't bite on it, Fred.

Fred   Well, me neither. I mean, women's looks and conversation and the eyes . . . you know when they're sort of making a play. Even at my late age, I get certain girls come on to me a little bit, but I can't be messed about.

Tony   No, that's right.

Fred   Years ago, when I was in my thirties . . . you're rampant, you're running around and your dick runs your fucking life, so you just follow where it goes – although I wasn't *too* bad.

Tony   As a young man you're chasing it all the time. Now I'm not. But I see the funny side of it. I see a kick out of it that I can still do it. My [wife] Wendy used to get the hump about it, but she knows I'm not gonna get involved. My loyalty is to her. At the end of the day, I go home with her. I don't want their phone numbers. But it happens more today than what it did then.

Fred   I haven't noticed it *that* much lately. (*Laughing*) But I'm fucking ten years older than you, ain't I?

2

Pubbing and Clubbing

*Conversation in the Prince of Wales Pub, Lant Street,
London SE1, 2 May 2000*

*Fred returns to the pub he ran from 1963 to 1968, scene of countless jolly-
ups – and of his arrest after the murder of Jack 'The Hat' McVitie.*

Fred   To me, it looks the same. Obviously, there have been a lot
of changes over the years, but I still remember this as my front
room. That's what it becomes when you live above the pub, which
I did. I like it. It looks great. It's still got that welcoming feel about
it – warm colours and woodwork and panelling, thick carpet, good
service, nice music. It's a proper place to have a drink, a real pub.
It's got the same old atmosphere about it.

It's all the one bar now. We used to have two. This was the
saloon, and down the other end was the public bar. You could just
walk through. We took away the dividing doors, and we just had a
glass partition jutting into the room a little bit from the main door.

This brings back a lot of very good, very fond memories.
There's my stool over there in the corner, where I used to sit at
the bar. George Raft [the Hollywood film star] sat where we're
sitting now.

Down at the far end, behind the bar, is where the water used
to drip down the walls when I flooded the shower upstairs, standing
with my foot on the plughole. They'd say, 'Oh, Fred's having a
shower again.'

I'm looking round the pub and there's about ten people here
who all know me. They're customers that used to be in here thirty-
five years ago. And I'm still buying them drinks!

Johnny Furminger [one of those customers]   You're a gentleman and
an officer! Me and my wife Sandra used to come in. I remember
[footballer] Bobby Moore being here with his wife, Tina. And the
Krays. They always used to buy us a drink.

Fred They used to come in firm-handed. They used to bring about thirty people, just on social visits.

As I pulled up outside on the corner today, I remembered how I used to park my old red Mercedes there, and how I was arrested getting into it one day. This was over Jack The Hat. A dozen coppers swooped down on me, and that's when my time here came to an end.

But we had some great times. I think of Sunday lunchtimes – they used to be packed right out. It was a happy pub. It was everyone's pub. Marriages were made here.

When I took over the pub, we set a trend in giving people good, class service. I was one of the first. I put nice, soft carpet down all over the floor. It cost me a lot of money, this carpet. Nice velvet drapes [now replaced by Venetian blinds], big bunch of flowers behind the bar, pretty-looking, young barmaids serving the drinks, and soft lights. All the other pubs had big, neon lights, and if the girls had a spot on their faces, it showed up.

Tony That's right.

Fred We had these little wall lights with red bulbs to tone it down. Pull the curtains over, shut the rest of the world out, and this was your little vacuum of pleasure. It was like a club in here.

Tony It *was* like a club. What you did was bring the West End into south London. You had it all done out in red.

Fred You'd have a big, silver bowl full of ice, and you had your lemon and your orange and them sort of little things that you'd get in a West End nightclub, but not in pubs at that time.

And I used to go down to the A1 Stores in Walworth Road, run by some Jewish friends of mine, and they used to give me all the top records. They'd say, 'This is the latest one out, it's going to be a hit,' or, 'This is a new record from America,' and I used to come back and stick 'em all on the old jukebox, so when the kids came into the pub, they'd all jump about and think it's lovely.

And all the local customers, they had to go. They'd want their pint filled to the fucking top, and they used to walk across to put it on the table and spill half of it all over the fucking carpet.

Tony (*Laughter*)

Fred I'd say, 'Oi, fucking watch that, that cost a lot of money, that carpet.' So I told the bar staff, 'Look, don't fill the glasses right up. If they want to top up afterwards, give them a little bit more.' And I told the locals, 'Don't fucking spill it all over my carpet.' And they were all . . . (*impersonates rumblings of discontent*). 'I gotta get rid of these fucking mugs,' that's what I used to say. And that's what I had to do. Get rid of all the locals. Cos I didn't want them.

Tony (*Laughing*) If I remember it right, Fred, you didn't throw them out at first.

Fred Well, that's when I fucking took the dartboard down. It was over there in what used to be the public bar. They used to say to me, 'You gotta soak the dartboard, guvnor. You gotta put it in that tin bath in the cellar and soak it overnight.'

And I laid on sandwiches and food for 'em on their darts nights, you know, the fucking sausages on a stick and all that sort of thing. Up this end of the bar, we're having a little laugh and a chat in the corner. A few of my pals were spending money, buying drinks at a tenner and £12 a round, and these fucking mugs are spending, you know, two bob of a night. And they used to shout out, 'Silence up the end there! Quiet! Man on the mark!' Cos the geezer's up there at the dartboard, taking a fucking shot. 'Man on the mark!' Oh, you can imagine, can't you?

I said, ''Ere, it's finished, no more fucking "man on the mark" bollocks,' and the dartboard went in the dustbin. They came in the next day – 'Where's the dartboard gone? Where's the fucking arrows?' I said, 'You'll find them outside in the bin.'

They was all in their forties, fifties. They were very rough. I mean, one guy, he was like the local tough guy, bully type, street fighter and all that, all scarred up. And he held the door one night as I went to come into the pub and he went, 'Are you a member in here?' He was one of them comedians, you know. And I'd just about had enough of them.

I hit the fucking door with my shoulder and he went flying from the door to the bar. He landed up at the foot of the bar, smashed into it and done his arm. 'What you done that for?', you know. This cunt won't even let me in my own pub!

Anyway, he wound up with his arm in a sling. I said, 'Go down that pub down the road. Don't use my pub any more. I've had enough of all you locals.' And I built a different atmosphere in here.

Tony What I liked about it, you were guaranteed a good night's entertainment.

Fred Girls wasn't interfered with. They could come out, three- or four-handed, and not be hit on by geezers or be molested in any way. They knew that they could have a comfortable little chat and a drink on their own, and if they wanted to accept a drink from somebody else down the bar then they'd accept it, but if they didn't want to, no big deal. There was no pressure put on 'em. It was nice and comfortable, and they loved the music.

We used to have the best service and I must admit that I nicked John Doyland, a gay fella, off the twins to come to work for me. He used to be with them in the Double R club.

Tony Yeah, I know him well. Fair-haired fella. He was very nice.

Fred I loved him, young John. He was a nice kid. And he was a great designer. He designed all my flats and houses. He used to go out with Maureen and buy all the furniture and wallpaper, and he was so particular in what he did. He didn't design this particular pub, but when he came over, he liked what I'd done and he added a few little touches of his own. He put a big bouquet of fresh flowers up here, in the corner of the bar, just to give it that little touch of class. He'd come down to the bar dressed in lovely suits with the collar and the tie and a carnation in his top pocket.

Tony Don't see it no more.

Fred And cufflinks and things. He used to look immaculate behind the bar and it was like showbiz, you know, cos we had little spotlights on the barmaids and the staff. It was like they were performing. And he could serve twenty people in one call. He would remember everybody's drink. He could do the work of two, three barmaids. He could, honestly.

And he'd give the customers' hands a little squeeze when he'd give them their change back if they was good-looking boys and all that, and that's how he used to perform. He had a little dog, Pinkie.

Tony Wasn't that a poodle, Fred?

Fred Poodle, it was dyed pink.

Tony He used to take it round the clubs with him sometimes.

Fred Yeah. And when he was here, he used to leave the dog upstairs with my two boys, Jamie and Gregory, who were only little at the time, and the stories they'd tell me of what they did to that poor little dog I can't repeat.

Tony (*Laughter*)

Fred The dog used to be hysterical when John come up the stairs after the pub closed. He used to take a flying leap into John's arms. If that dog could talk, you know what I mean . . .

Tony They're very highly strung, poodles. We had one for sixteen years.

Fred I hate to think what they did get up to with him. You know what two boys are like . . .

Tony Who was your worst-ever customer, Fred?

Fred One particular geezer who came in who was a wrong 'un and I chased him down the road and pulled the shooter out on him, threatened to blow his kneecaps off.

Tony (*Laughter*)

Fred I said, 'What you doing in 'ere?' He thought he could walk in because he didn't know that we knew what he'd done. He'd got a geezer nicked with a lorry-load of chemist's aspirins and stuff like that in his lock-up.

I said, 'Go home.' I took the drink out of his hand and put it down on the fucking counter. I said, 'Go on, fuck off now. You can't come in here.' I see him go out, and I've walked outside as well after a minute or two. He's got the engine running, the car lights are on, he's put a raincoat on and he's walking across the road back to the pub.

He's gotta be tooled up. Anyway, I hit him straight on the chin before he could do anything, you know, and he run back past his car and up towards the pub that Johnny Ward had later.

Tony Yeah, yeah.

Fred I chased him up there and then he turned round in the road and he stopped this car coming towards him. He was trying to drag the driver out to get in, to get away, but the driver drove off and left him cos I come round the corner.

Tony (*Laughter*)

Fred And then he run to the other pub on the next corner, opposite the car place, Ford's Despatch.

Tony Where the funeral director's is.

Fred That's right, opposite the funeral director's, Alf Smith's. And that's when I caught him (*laughing*). He went in the door of the pub. He run in through the curtains and I come in behind him. I could see the geezers' faces, they was lifting their pints up to their lips and they stopped in mid-air. I just caught the back of his fucking coat by the collar, and dragged him back out again.

Tony Out he comes. Out he comes.

Fred (*Still laughing*) And I've pulled him out in the street and as I threw him on the floor, I got my .38 out the back of my trousers and I'm gonna give it to him. And my pals Ronnie Everett and Alfie Gerrard come running up. They'd seen me go out and they tailed me. I'm just gonna do it and they went, 'Put that away! Put it away!' And I never did him. I let him go. Well, there was too many witnesses. And I only lived down the road here, in the pub. There was a rush of blood to the head cos he was a grass, and that's what made me do it, really. I wasn't thinking straight.

Tony Was you always tooled up?

Fred Oh yeah. That period . . . well, I mean, my brother had been shot on his doorstep, hadn't he? This was years later, but there was wars going on, weren't there?

Tony There was a lot of different firms around. You never knew what was gonna happen . . . especially when you started getting round all the pubs and clubs.

Go back, say, from '59 onwards when I was a member of the Pen club down Spitalfields. Jimmy Nash [one of the six, infamous Nash brothers] got done for a murder there in 1960, and he got acquitted of it – rightly so, as well.

At that time, right, the West End, it was more coffee bars, that type of thing. You had the Pigalle, you had the Society, you had the Stork, you had the Talk of the Town and other showrooms.

You started to get in the backstreet drinking clubs, the shebeens. There was a lot of 'em popping up at the time. They had all the boys using them, with different firms going to different ones, just drinking. There was one shebeen there, the City Club in the City Road. I mean, the fights in there that no one ever got to hear about . . .

You'd get a man come out on a Friday night and go over to a few of the boys and get into our company and, of course, they didn't know how to behave. Because in the criminal fraternity, you knew how to behave in each other's company.

There were classier, more tightly run places, like, for example, the Regency club in Stoke Newington. It was a restaurant with three clubs on different floors. The one downstairs was for us. Lenny Peters used to come into the middle one – remember Peters & Lee, Fred?

Fred   Oh, yeah.

Tony   I mean, it was a nicely run place, and the twins started a lot of that off with the Double R club, and the Kentucky. They brought a style into it.

Then, in the early Sixties, clubs started opening in the West End, and some of the boys were going in to look after them, places like the Brown Derby and the Starlight. It was at the top of Oxford Street, down the side of where Lilley & Skinners is. And if I remember right, the Starlight was the first to put a bit of a casino in the place as well.

Fred   Me and Micky Regan put tables in there. You couldn't have gambling in pubs, but in clubs you could. And Jack The Hat robbed the Starlight, didn't he? He held it up.

Tony   He done it.

Fred   Inadvertently, his actions led to me getting the pitch down there. It was a great big, basement club and they had a few tables. Jack had his own little firm around him, and they went in there masked up. They nicked the money from behind the bar and the blackjack table, and they got all the guys who were there at that time to drop their trousers.

Tony   That's right, yeah.

Fred   You'd have to fucking kill me before I'd drop my trousers. But that's what they did with people. You know, they bullied them. It was to disarm them.

Tony   Well, it's a bit difficult to move about with no trousers on.

Fred   You can't do much, can you? And it's humiliation. To have that done to you – you've gotta fucking kill 'em, ain't you?

It's a fucking out-and-out liberty to put them on the spot when they're with wives and girlfriends, to make a man drop his trousers, facing masked people with shotguns.

Anyway, that's how I come to put my tables in there with Micky Regan. We had these gambling tables, we had 'em in clubs like Oscars in Albemarle Street, and we also had the franchise for the Newmarket horseracing game. And we put it in all the clubs in the West End, Mick and I, and that used to be a great little money-earner. Well, of course, after that episode with Jack The Hat – who was the guy used to run the Starlight, the little fella?

Tony   Barry Clayman.

Fred   Right. Well, the twins turned round and said to him, 'You need someone down there looking after you.' Cos whoever was supposed to be looking after him at the time wasn't really doing it, and Jack obviously didn't respect it.

So the reason that they pulled me and Mick in, with our tables, was to look after it. Once we put the tables in, it was our place. If anyone wants to come and rob it, they do that at their fucking peril. And there was no more trouble there.

Tony   That was the first time gambling came in. It was the very early Sixties, and you had the changeover going on then. The gambling was legal. You had to be licensed and that, but they were the first, Fred, the Krays, to start to use that type of club. And that was how the club scene really started.

Barry Clayman went on to work in showbiz. Cos I remember The Rocking Berries rehearsing down there when the groups were coming through in the early Sixties. They had The Walker Brothers – Scott Walker, brilliant singer – The Pretty Things, remember them, the group? The Small Faces were another group who used to get down there.

Fred I had The Small Faces down in the basement of my boxing club at the Borough, not all that far from here, cos I turned it into a recording studio. And Cat Stevens used to be in the gymnasium there, working out. He's Muslim now, but he used to come in here afterwards and have a drink.

Tony Just thinking about those days, the late Fifties, early Sixties, reminds me of something. A lot of people had American cars, didn't they? Chevrolets, Cadillacs.

Fred Oh, you'd get them quite cheap. They left them here, didn't they, at the American bases.

I used to go to this big American base called Douglas House in Bayswater Road, at Lancaster Gate. I was introduced to the guy in there who ran the whole fucking show, from the knife and fork and the tablecloths to everything that was used in that place, to set up some business for us. And I used to go in there and have T-bone steaks.

Tony Whatever you wanted.

Fred Which was something that you never saw in those days. They had the best of everything. And they had dance nights there. You'd have Ted Heath and his orchestra playing, and they're fucking jiving and jitterbugging, all the birds, and they actually had a dartboard. I took a couple of the firm in with me, Micky Regan and Big George Cahill, and we wound up with these Yanks, playing darts, having bets on the dartboard.

Tony It's not their game, darts, is it?

Fred No. We fucking ironed the Yanks out. Douglas House was like four buildings all in one. It was massive. We was like strangers in there, really, but we was mixing with the American servicemen, having all the best grub and things that you couldn't get anywhere else in London.

Tony You was privileged there, Fred. But, really, all our lives revolved around the pubs and clubs. I remember when the twins took over the Carpenter's Arms in Bethnal Green, and they had it exactly the same as this pub, when you had it, Fred. The red seating, the red carpet, the red drapes . . .

Fred They all copied it.

Tony Do you know, Fred, this is amazing. I went to the Carpenter's Arms recently to do a TV interview and that pub has not changed. It's exactly as I remember it. It was incredible – the atmosphere in there was electric. It was like going back into the past. You know, when it hits you.

I remembered that Saturday night when my [brother] Chris and I met two brothers from west London, Alan and Ray Mills, in the White Bear in Aldgate. We were gonna introduce them to the twins.

We went over to the Carpenter's Arms. And as I was sat there, doing this TV interview, it all came back to me . . . where Ronnie stood, and where Charlie was . . . Violet [the Krays' mum] and all the firm were there. I remembered us leaving and how it was touch and go whether we went to the Regency or whether we went over west London. The Mills brothers had never been to the Regency, so we went there. And that was the night that Reggie murdered Jack The Hat. That's where that story really starts.

3

Guns: Mad, Bad
and Dangerous to Know

Conversation in Fred's kitchen, 8 March 2000

Fred   The first gun I ever owned was an army .45 – a massive, heavy, bastard gun. There was a lot about in the Forties after the war.

Tony   The British service one, it had the ring on it.

Fred   Yeah, the ring on the bottom. I was about sixteen. And my mother found it in my wardrobe with a bundle of notes, which came to about fifty quid. That was a lot of money then. You're talking about 1948.

My mother assumed that I'd used the gun to get the fifty quid, but it came from something else. At that time, I never had used the gun. But it was in the culture. I had to have one because everybody else did. I could not be seen without one. But it was so stupid, keeping it in the fucking wardrobe.

I mean, they had capital punishment in those days. And my mother said, 'You know what'll happen to you. You'll be hung.'

It was fucking terrible. She was worried sick. 'Get that out of the house,' and all that. Oh, I got it out. I had a friend . . .

You can always find somewhere. Wrap it up, put it in a fucking tin box, a bit of greaseproof paper and stick it down in a garden shed somewhere.

Tony   We buried ours in gardens.

Fred   We used to hide them in sheds on the allotments – that's where we used to put all our crooked bits and pieces.

And I took this .45 out once when I made an attempt to hold up a little post office, and it got fucked up. There were two of us, but some people came in and we run out. Really, it was a bravado thing at that age.

Tony Yeah, it was. We first started getting ours when we were kids. A pal of ours worked for a famous gun manufacturer. His job was making them! Course, he smuggled bits out, so we had ready access. But, you'd know, Fred, it was easy to get guns after the war years. The Yanks that were still here sold untold arms.

Fred There was loads of guns here at that time, but through the Fifties and going into the early Sixties, the fucking guns that was on the street was unbelievable. I had an arsenal of guns. I had a real arsenal.

Tony We always had them around us. They was always available. Oh, unlimited. But I never liked a second-hand gun, because it can cause you a lot of problems.

Fred You don't know its history. It could have been used several times by other people. You get nicked with it and you're in deep shit.

Tony I've gotta be honest here – I've sold 'em, second-hand ones, but it's a thing I don't like doing. Each gun is like a set of fingerprints. A firearm spins. A shotgun don't do that – it pumps. But when a bullet hits a barrel, spinning, it leaves a certain mark. New ones are totally different. They've got no trace on them.

Fred People used to bring me guns all the time, and I used to buy loads. If I wanted to get 'em now, I wouldn't have a fucking clue where to go, but in those days, people would come to *you*. I had a special flat for the armoury. A friend of mine had died, and I kept the flat going in his name. The landlords never knew that he was dead cos the rent was paid regular.

Tony Keep it all above board, yeah.

Fred I bought Tommy guns, I bought Belgian FM rifles, I had a Sten gun which was fitted with a silencer – a naval gun it was. I had single-shot rifles that were for marksmen in competition. I had loads of them. And, course, a lot of guns used to come adapted with the short barrel.

Tony When they saw a barrel off a shotgun, they're doing a very dangerous thing. That can rebound on you, Fred.

Fred Oh, yeah.

Tony If the barrel is cut too short and you fire it, that can blow up in your hands.

Fred They used to cut the fucking stock off.

Tony Just to make them smaller.

Fred So you could carry them on a bit of rope under your raincoat.

I had a lot of long-barrelled guns. The Belgian FM gun was thirty rounds with two different magazines. That was a lovely gun. Brand-new. And I was gonna use that one time . . .

Tony (*Hearty laughter*)

Fred I was in the back of the motor, all ready to go to work. It would've been like the Valentine's Day Massacre all over again, but it turned out a friend of mine was there who shouldn't have been, and so I had to cancel it.

And then I had the small Berettas and the old Saturday-night specials, the .38 Colts, the little short-barrelled ones. Oh, I used to like the little .38. It used to fit in the back of your trousers. And I liked the revolver. It's more reliable than the automatic, because the automatic jams. I know it's got the safety on it, the revolver, but I always used to take the first bullet out just in case it was fired accidentally.

We went on some business one time. We was looking for certain people, me and Alf [Gerrard], and he was sitting behind me in the back of the car. I've got this gun under my seat. As we were getting out the car, I went under the seat for this automatic. I went to put one up the spout. It went *click*, *click*, and it fucking went off. Alf had moved over to climb out the other side of the car, and the bullet went through the back of my seat right into the place where Alf had just been sitting.

Tony *Cor!*

Fred I loved Alf like a brother. I've never met another man like him. He was a one-off. (*Laughing*) So that's how dangerous guns are. You know, I could've fucking killed my own pal.

Tony Shotguns are bad as well. Hair triggers . . .

Fred Hair triggers are dangerous. A load of people shot themselves, didn't they? [William] Hickson, who got nicked with me on
the Security Express robbery, shot himself in the foot in a robbery.
He got twelve years, didn't he?

Everyone then was tooled up. If you went to certain places, you
used to carry a tool. You'd take one if something had gone off the
night before and it was possible you might meet up with the
people. You'd say, 'Well, if we're going over there, we'd better be
tooled up.' As one geezer, Bobby Mason, used to say, 'Tools on
board!' So, of course, he got the nickname Tools On Board.

I used to be tooled up when I had my club, the 211 in Balham,
in case of any trouble. There were these geezers one night who
smashed a girl and broke her jaw.

Tony Not funny, that.

Fred They was about a dozen-handed. They went out and I
followed them across the road. The one who'd done it had a
pickaxe handle in his hand. I told him to drop it as I went towards
him. It rattled on the fucking pavement. I gave him a couple of
whacks with the pistol first, marked him up, and then I put the gun
to his shoulder, pulled it and, bang! He dropped down like a fucking
log.

My pal Mick was battering another guy who was dancing like
Cassius Clay, all round the fucking road. He wound up going
through the hedge. He landed face down in the garden. We went
round there, kneeled on his back, and I put the gun behind his ear
and fucking blasted his ear off.

The guy I shot in the shoulder – I didn't want to kill him, just
hurt him badly. But when they examined him in hospital, they
found that the bullet had hit the shoulder blade and richocheted
round the body. It did a zigzag, and it came out around the waist
on the same side that it went in.

Tony He was lucky it didn't hit a vital organ.

Fred You can kill someone even when you set out not to. You
might think, 'I'm only gonna shoot him in the arse,' but if you hit
the main artery, they bleed to death. There was the guy who got
shot in the pub in East Street, off the Walworth Road. He was
going over the counter – one of the young Brindles, wasn't it?

PULLING THE TRIGGER

Fred I can't remember how many times I used a gun, really. I fired quite a few, but most of the time, it was only to frighten people, in the ceiling or the door or something like that. I don't want to make [ex-cop] Nipper Read look like he's telling the truth, do I, when he talks about me doing seven murders in that book by Martin Fido [the then recently published *The Krays: Unfinished Business*]!

Tony I'll tell you about shooting. It's a spontaneous reaction. It's in the heat of the moment.

Fred Well, unless you're going out deliberately to fucking do somebody, yeah. If you intend doing it, you're just gonna get on with it. I wouldn't say anything goes through your mind before you fire. You just do it.

Tony I've been there when people have been shot, but I never pulled the trigger myself.

Fred You gotta be glad about that.

Tony I'm gonna say I am. Yeah. If I'd had to, I would have done it, without a shadow of a doubt.

I saw a man shot in front of my eyes, twice, with a .38. Not dead. He was shot in the stomach. This was in a club in north London. It was an argument over nothing, and next minute, a gun was pulled and it went bang. You get that burning smell with it. The first bullet hit him and it didn't even make him move, Fred. I couldn't believe it. He stood there and ordered a drink. And the geezer gave him another one. And the man walked out with them two bullets in him.

How would you describe it, Fred? Shock. (*Softly*) It did scare me at the time.

Fred I look back over my childhood and what happened to me. We had a hard life, but my parents did a great job in feeding and caring for us, even though I had rickets when I was two. Times were hard for a young couple bringing up five sons in the Thirties. Then my four brothers went to war and left me alone, aged seven. I was sent away to strange people and places — a feeling of rejection, loneliness, despair for a seven-year-old, and it had an effect on me.

The next five years were unreal, full of bombs, death and disruption. It must have shaped my mental outlook on life, to be able to withstand any danger or problem that presented itself.

I don't lose any sleep over things, you know. I suppose I might have a bit of a Jekyll and Hyde personality. I'm not a really great worrier about my actions.

If you have to use a gun in the course of business and it's done correctly and you've not jeopardized yourself or left yourself out on a limb, then you can feel, not satisfied with what you've done, or proud of it, but you didn't worry. It was just in your working fucking life in those days. That's how I looked at it. I'm talking about thirty years ago; I'm not talking about the present.

Tony It's different.

Fred As you get older, you mature and you soften. You're not so aggressive, and the old testosterone's not racing round your body like it were when you were younger. You're not chasing your dick around and all that.

Tony It's very interesting to look at it like that.

Fred You're more laid-back, more mellow. You think a bit more before you do anything now, so all that is in the past. I was definitely a suitable case for treatment in those days. I look back and I say, 'What the fucking hell was I doing all these things for?' Maybe they was right when they threw me out the army and wanted me to go for fucking shock treatment. Maybe I needed it, you know.

Tony I don't think so, no.

Fred I must have had a little bit of a nuttiness in me. It was cold and calculated, but I wasn't hurting the ordinary man in the street. I wasn't hurting somebody over a silly row. I wasn't hurting people who I felt didn't fucking really deserve it.

Tony That's right.

Fred It hit him in the lower region and he died because they couldn't stem the flow of blood. But the old scores were settled at a later date . . .

Tony My mate happened to be there, Fred. A Scotch fella. He was training to be a publican, and he was a barman there that night. Two men walk in, and they shot one of the Brindles. He stopped two bullets, Fred.

When they questioned my mate about it, he saw nothing. He didn't want to know. He was so scared. It was not his argument, he just happened to be there. And I can introduce you to the man to this day.

Fred You can kill someone with a punch, just by hitting them on the fucking chin. I've give many a man a backhander, a slap, rather than fucking hit him on the jaw. I know people who've hit a man on the chin and wound up doing life, you know. Cos the geezer's head hits a fucking sharp object, or the pavement, and if he's got a thin skull, it's like cracking an egg with a spoon, innit?

Tony It's a murder charge.

Fred Yeah, yeah. But then, looking at it the other way, you can shoot a guy five or six times and he's still fucking alive.

Tony That's how it works. You know, you can blast them with a shotgun – doesn't mean to say you're going to kill 'em.

Fred Some guns you could fire at people and never touch them. You couldn't hit a fucking barn door with an army .45. There's such a kick on it. I used to have a big, old warehouse down in the bowels of the earth and I did a bit of practice shooting down there. The fucking noise I used to make (*laughing*). Fucking machine-guns going off, bullets flying everywhere . . . and they used to richochet as well. I tried, and I couldn't hit the fucking door with a .45. If you hit someone with one of those, it was by luck more than judgement.

But the most important thing to remember is that if you use a gun, you're endangering yourself as much as anyone else. Look what happened to 'Scatty' Eddy Watkins, my old mate 'Duke' Osbourne and me.

That all started when I had an interest in a spiel in the Old Kent Road with my pal Ronnie Oliffe. Duke was one of the punters and, years before, he'd been the twins' armourer. He held all the shooters for them. Now he was doing a bit of cannabis smuggling from Pakistan.

I thought, Good luck, it's only a bit of puff. It was the Pakistani Black, which was a good smoke in those days.

One day in 1979, he phones me up. They've got a big, articulated lorry, it's already gone in and out of Belgium, they've come out of Kent and now they're being followed by customs officers and God knows what.

He said, 'Fred, I've gotta get this off the road and into a safe place.'

I said, 'OK, I'll see what I can do. Where are you now?' He's at Blackheath. I said, 'Pull up there where the coffee stall is, where all the lorries can park easily.' So when I drove up there, there's Duke and Scatty Eddy standing by the lorry. They said, 'We're surrounded. They're all over the place, around the Heath.'

I said, 'Thanks very much for letting me walk into it.'

The lorry looks empty. The cannabis is all under the floorboards and behind the walls.

I said to Eddy: 'The only thing you can do now is drive down the Blackwall Tunnel. I'll go first and get to the other end. When you get to the last fifty yards, pull the lorry across the road, block it, get out, and run out of the tunnel. Then I can take you away. They won't come on us cos they think there's tools on board.' And there was.

Tony Course. Yeah.

Fred So I go to the end of the tunnel with Duke, and we're waiting for Scatty Eddy to come through. He doesn't. I said, 'I bet he's gone down to the Rotherhithe Tunnel by mistake. Let's try and find him, see if we can get him away.'

We wound up driving to the BT yard that they were taking the lorry to in the first place. I changed in the car, put on a duffel coat and a hat. I walked across to the traffic island to get to the yard, and then Duke came running up, calling out: 'Fred, come back, come back! They've just gone round the island and there's motor bikes with the aerials up.' They were customs officials. They're right up Eddy's arse and we can't get near him.

He [Scatty] drives into the car park. I said, 'We've gotta assume he's nicked now.' They're just waiting for him to get out. They chase him, he pulls out a gun and he shoots a customs officer dead.

We've drove off, me and Duke, and we don't know this has gone on. I go back to my old nan's and have a cup of tea and a bacon sandwich. Well, it's all over the television – customs officer shot dead in Aldgate. I spat the tea out. I nearly choked on the bacon sandwich.

They arrested Scatty Eddy, and now they're looking for everybody else involved in it. They nicked quite a few people. Duke and myself are badly wanted.

We swapped manors. I went to north London and he went to an address in Bermondsey. Then he was moved out to Hackney Marshes. He was holed up over there in a back room, and about three weeks before Christmas, he took an overdose. The boys who were looking after him found him stiff as a board, dressed in his suit. He'd left a letter covering everybody else's arse. We thought a lot of him. He was a good friend. Poor old Duke.

They carried him out and laid him on the football field and phoned the police.

Now they was looking for me, cos they saw me up on Blackheath and got me on cameras.

I had to leave my home, my businesses, everything that I owned and go on my toes. I went to Spain first, and from there to America to start again.

My son Jamie followed me out to Allentown [Pennsylvania], cos they wanted to arrest him. If they had him in custody, that would encourage me to come back and say, 'Release my son.' He'd been seen driving me over to Duke's house in Sutton. And that's all he'd been doing – driving.

When I did come back from America, four years later, I was arrested and put in Winchester Prison as a Category A prisoner. I was charged with importing cannabis. After about ten months, I went up for trial in Winchester Crown Court. But the evidence was really shallow. You couldn't identify me in the photographs. If I'd known that, I would not have pleaded guilty to even being at Blackheath. But they spun every relation of mine, every friend, every home, every business. I think one man's nose got broken when he didn't open the door wide enough, and he tried to sue the police for it. He was a straight man as well.

A very kind judge called Bristow gave me a two-year suspended sentence. He thought I'd suffered enough.

Scatty Eddy was sentenced to twenty-five years for shooting the customs officer. After twelve years of imprisonment, they found him dead in his cell. He'd OD'd. He'd had enough. He couldn't face another twelve years, I suppose, and he took his own life.

That's why guns are dangerous. If you haven't got 'em, you can't use them.

4

When Cops Are Bent and the Judge Is Plastered . . . The Wrong Arm of the Law!

Conversation in Fred's sitting room, 14 December 1999

THEY COULD BEND THE RIGHT WAY

Fred The Premier club used to be in Little Newport Street. I still walk past it. If you come out of Stringfellows and walk round to the Hippodrome, you pass it on the right. The doorway's there, but it looks all closed up.

That was the 'in' place many years ago. If ever you had to do a deal with the Old Bill, you know, to part with a bit of readies and get out of trouble, that was the club you went to. You got the introduction and you'd go over in a corner and sort your business out. It was like a policemen's canteen. Full of coppers in there.

Going back to the Fifties, I had a lock-up garage round the back of Herne Hill. I think they're still there, them garages.

Tony Everyone had a lock-up then.

Fred Yeah. Anyway, this guy who Charlie Kray introduced me to was a buyer. He had a little firm that worked for him, and they used to go all over London picking up loads of crooked gear and taking it back to Walthamstow way. He was the only one who used to come over to the lock-up and my brother George's shop, Larkhall Stores in Larkhall Lane, Clapham. We used to call it, 'All down to Larkin'!'

Tony *(Laughing)* Having a lark.

Fred My George had a good thing going. This was a wholesale shop that sold everything, pots and pans to blooming petrol for the old oil stoves, sets of Prestige knives, stuff like that.

We used to have a right load-up out of Hardings hardware store. It was a warehouse in a converted prison in the Borough. The night watchman used to leave a door open for us, and we used to go in there. We used to load up the cars and vans and drive off, and George used to sell it all down in his shop.

All of a sudden, George's shop and my lock-up got raided by the same copper on the same day. And we can only put it down to him, this buyer, cos he was the only one who used to come over. So I had to straighten it out.

And where did I have to go? The Premier club. And the coppers was all right. I came up in court, they backed me up, we had a nice drink, and they got their money. That's how it was done. It was all very amicable. It was only a bit of crooked gear anyway.

My George, unfortunately, got some bird over his part in it, cos it was a different scenario. I'd claimed I'd been renting out the lock-up, but George couldn't put it down to no one – it was his shop, his gear.

But that's how they played, the coppers. They had to like you. The introduction had to be good, and you had to be nice and spend money over the bar. They used to buy you drinks as well. I mean, they was all right.

Tony The best one, I always found, was when you didn't want a certain conviction read out in court.

Fred They could cut them out.

Tony That helped. I was up at the Old Bailey in January 1965 for attempted armed robbery at the Wimpy Bar at Dalston Junction, and having an offensive weapon. The copper that nicked me was a horrible bastard, but he was all right for a bit of business.

The ID was the newspaper-stand man. He recognized me. So I couldn't win in there, but I wanted a previous conviction taken out of it. I had a meeting with the copper down at Dalston police station, and they dropped the conviction. That's all I wanted. I got a thirty-month sentence.

At the other extreme, I was always getting nicked for silly things. There was this copper out of Old Street, and he was always pulling me for driving offences. It was my first car, a Zephyr, the two-tone, rounded one, blue and beige, with the shade over the top. What was the advice in them days, Fred, with your licence? Keep a five-pound note in there.

Fred Oh yeah.

Tony And if they took it out and give you the licence back, you was OK. If they didn't, you were nicked. This copper kept doing it and doing it, and he was always pretending to take care of things. And one day I saw him in Kingsland Road by the old baths there. I thought, I'll run the fucker over. He come up to me and he went, 'Why should you be driving a Zephyr while I'm riding a bike?' That's what irritated him.

   Another copper I remember was a bit more helpful. Do you remember the section houses, Fred?

Fred Yeah, for the young trainee coppers. You'd go in court and see about twenty or thirty coppers come in. They'd all sit at the back, listening to the cases, getting their education.

Tony They was a bit of back-up in case you done a runner! Anyway, he lived at a section house in east London, this police cadet. He used to hang around with us, Fred, and give us information. If we was doing a bit of villainy round there, he actually used to mind us. He'd look out for us. Course, he'd get his bit.

Fred Oh, it was good for us in those days. If we could negotiate and have a little deal, all the better for us, wasn't it? I can't imagine coppers doing that these days, can you?

Tony No, it's a different ball game now.

Fred The introduction of women police officers made it very difficult for 'em to carry on doing it. Because the women police keep it a straight business. The male coppers can't do the villainy in front of a woman. She has a conscience, and worries. She won't stand for the brutality or the injustice of something.

Tony Clever move, what they done. Very clever.

Fred It was. I mean, you can still probably do your moves if you can get a good contact, but I don't know any police officers who are corrupt. I don't know any at all.

Tony There are no more clubs where you can go and make a deal. Oh, no.

Fred The boys did come unstuck from time to time. My pal Joe Carter used to run a street bookmaking pitch round the corner from Drury Lane, on the borders of Covent Garden market. It was a fruit and vegetable market then, and all the traders used to come and place bets with Joe. And he got nicked a few times. He'd been a boxer, a title contender, but he'd retired, and that's how he finished up going on ramraiding – what we used to call smash and grabs.

They knew him in Bow Street [police station], and he used to say, 'Can you get me on [in court] before they break for lunch?' Or, 'Get me on this afternoon.' And he'd give one of the sergeants a fiver. Managed to straighten it all out.

Well, I was in Wandsworth at one time doing a nine months. It was the last day before the Christmas holiday, and Joe comes in. The court was closing for the holiday. Joe's gone into the station, and he's given the sergeant a fiver and said, 'Get me on early, eleven o'clock,' otherwise they've gotta put it over till after Christmas.

So he goes in front of the beak, he's got his fine all ready, the usual thing – fifteen or twenty quid. And the magistrate said, 'You deliberately flouted the law.'

Tony (*Laughter*)

Fred He said, 'I'm sending you to prison for three months.' He fucking nearly fell over, Joe. Next thing he knows, he's down the cells in Wandsworth and he's going fucking mad.

You could never guarantee how things were gonna turn out. Where he expected to pay a fine, he finished up in prison. He was gonna appeal, but I said, 'You're wasting your time. It'll cost you money. Just do your three months and you're out.' Cor, he hated it.

And then, after Christmas, Tommy McGovern came in. He was a British lightweight champion. He got nicked for receiving some gear and he got six months.

So I wound up with two fighters in the cell with me, always talking about boxing. Joe couldn't keep still, and he was jumping about, shadow-boxing, and Tommy was a very quiet, laid-back man, smoking his cigarettes. He really didn't like his bird at all.

Tony (*Laughter*)

Fred This is the first time he'd ever fucking got caught for anything. They took a liberty with him. And, course, they talked to me so much about boxing, when I came out the nick, you've got to give it a try. Cos I was a fit young fella. I'd had, like, forty amateur fights, you know. But this is when I had a go at professional boxing. Which didn't last long, cos I had the one fight and I got fucking nicked again.

Tony   (*Laughter*)

Fred   I was on the bottom of the bill. I knocked this guy out in the third round and the bell saved him. Then he came out and fucking done me in the later rounds and I got beat on points. It was a hard fight and a crowd-pleaser. It was the end of my boxing days.

THEY COULD BEND THE WRONG WAY

Fred   We didn't have it all our own way, did we? They used to do deals with the grasses as well, the Bertie Smallses.

They often used to be the first ones over the counter in the bank. They had a licence to do it, cos they was already on the payroll of the coppers. They knew all the dates and figures and cut-ups, all the addresses. They was ready to go when it came to being arrested. They was gonna shop everybody and walk away from it.

And another thing we had to contend with was the coppers who would fit you up. When I had the 211 Club, one copper, who was a DI, had the right hump because I put on an amateur boxing show.

It was full up, the place, and Charlie Kray and the twins came over. The DI came up ranting and raving – 'What are they doing on my patch?' And the two guys who was with him, they was half on the firm, they were sweet as a nut, and they were looking at me as much as to say, 'What can we do?' They were making all sorts of faces, and he was yelling his fucking head off – 'I don't want them people on my patch and I'm gonna close you down.'

I said, 'We sell tickets to anybody who wants to buy them. They bought tickets to come and see a couple of east London fighters on the bill.'

He says, 'You've invited them over here, it's your fault, and I'm gonna object to your licence, I'm gonna object to everything.'

He even tried to fit me up. One of the coppers said, 'He's gonna try to put a shotgun in the fucking boot of your car.' They tried, apparently, but couldn't get into the car.

I was living in Dulwich at the time and my young neighbour next door, Barry, used to do quite a bit of work for me. He helped me build different places down in Gillingham. He was a nice kid.

One day he had to go and get some materials and he borrowed my car. As he drove down through the village, these squad cars got him into the kerb and front-and-backed him. They've jumped out, dragged him out of the car, got the keys out, thrown him across the bonnet and they were putting something in the boot of the car, making out they've just found it in the boot. Gelignite or something like that.

Then the head copper's come running across the road, calling them everything – 'You silly bastards, that's not him!' It was the kid next door. Once they did that they blew it completely.

Tony They fitted me up with a knife, put a blade on me. Fred, what they did was cunning. Being seventeen, eighteen – what do you know at that age? This copper in the police station handed me a knife and he went, 'You ever seen that before?' And I've picked it up.

Fred Now your dabs are on it. Oh, they do that to kids. They tried to do that to me once. I know.

Tony I fell for it. I had no way out of it. I'd fractured my leg badly falling off a lorry in an accident at work, and the day I was arrested, I'd just been to physiotherapy at the hospital. It was about three in the afternoon. I was standing in an amusement arcade at Dalston Junction by the jukebox, with my crutches, when these two dirty-mac detectives came in. They said, 'We'd like to see you down at Dalston Lane police station.' And they fitted me up with having the knife. To this day, I haven't got a clue why. There wasn't even a pocket inside my jacket. But they charged me with having an offensive weapon. I was found guilty and I got a conditional discharge.

Another copper who nicked me was done for corruption – Harry Challenor. He nicked me for shopbreaking in Ilminster in Somerset in 1961.

We were doing Co-ops round the country, me and a friend called Phil Keeling. We specialized in blowing the safes, that was our game then. Challenor was the detective sergeant who came down to Somerset to nick us. He brought us back to London and then back to Ilminster Magistrates Court. I got three years' probation.

In 1964, there was a big scandal. Challenor was in the dock with three other detectives. He was accused of planting and fabricating evidence, but he was found mentally unfit to stand trial. The three coppers got eleven years between them for conspiring to pervert the course of justice.

One big scam the coppers had in them days was insurance money. The insurance companies pay out a reward when somebody gets done for stolen property. It's meant to go to the person who helped get the conviction. The police used to recover a load of stolen property and put it back in, then they claimed the insurance money on it under other people's names.

Fred The coppers had a trade with me one time. We had a deal. A gang of robbers had been nicked, and I went to the police as an intermediary to get two of them out of the charge. I gave the coppers £5,000 to see that the men got a straight ID and they took the money. The men did get out of the case on the IDs. But the police knew four robbers were involved, and they thought they was being short-changed with the five grand.

Some time after that, Tony Block, a solicitor we knew in Camberwell, invited me to a Christmas party at his office. I went with my George and a couple of other faces. There was all these fucking Robbery Squad coppers in there. We was surrounded by them. One was a big, fat geezer with a moustache, about eighteen, twenty stone, and his guvnor, a detective inspector, was with him. They were pointing their fingers at me, saying, 'You know who the other robbers were. We should've got more money.'

I said, 'I don't know who the rest of them were and even if I did, I wouldn't tell you.' I said, 'Why are you digging me out? I've come here to have a drink with Tony, not to have a row with you. Come outside. I'll beat seven bells of shit out of you, you big, fucking lump.'

Tony Block did take sides with me, give him his due. He said, 'Fred's come here as my guest. I've invited him here for a Christmas drink.' Anyway, they swallowed it. The sack of shit wouldn't come outside with me. And just as well he never, because about a month later, he dropped dead with a heart attack. If I'd battered him . . .

Tony   He might've died.

Fred   And I'd have been up for fucking murder.

A QUESTION OF RESPECT

Fred   Oh, it was always there, a little bit of respect, yeah, between the coppers and the major criminals.

Tony   More so then than now. Some of the old coppers wanna have a drink with us these days.

Fred   Yeah, old adversaries. It's like fighters when they get in the ring. They're fucking gonna kill each other, but after the fight's over, they shake hands and they're cuddling and kissing each other. Not that I've ever kissed a copper!

Tony   It's that scenario.

Fred   I mean, look at Slipper [Chief Superintendent Jack, 'Slipper of the Yard', who tried unsuccessfully to bring the fugitive Ronnie Biggs back from Brazil]. He made a good friend of Biggsy. He writes to him, phones him – 'Hope you're all right, Ron.' He was bitter at the time, but he speaks up for him now. 'Why aren't they letting the man come back and finish his days out here?'

Tony   I bet today's coppers wish crime was a bit more like it was then.

Fred   Oh, I'm sure they do. (*Laughing*) I mean, who wants to be involved in what's going on in the streets of London today? I wouldn't wanna be a copper today in any shape or form.

THE PUBLIC AND THE POLICE

Tony   There was a police officer called Geoff. He lived in Belford House, Queensbridge Road, which our family moved into when we was kids. And he got engaged to a bird called Tilley who lived on the third floor. I'm going back, now, to 1950. In them days, you had anything to do with the law, you were fucking ostracized, Fred, weren't you? And the father-in-law, Ted Tilley, wouldn't talk to the copper. And he couldn't understand it, Fred. Nearly cracked up over it.

Fred My mother's brother, Ted, he lived up in the north of England in Huddersfield, somewhere like that, and went into the police force. He wound up being a uniformed inspector. And when he was ever down in London, he used to pop round to see us. This was when I was a little kid.

And if he knocked at the door, my old man used to get his coat and his cap and out he'd walk, straight down the pub. He wouldn't acknowledge him. It was really rude. But that's the way they were brought up. You never spoke to the police. He was good as gold, Ted. He used to treat my mum when he came down, but she used to get terribly embarrassed by the way my old man kept walking out. Then he'd come back when Ted had gone.

THE JUDGE IN THE PUB

Fred There was an old fella out of the Elephant. I know he nicked a television and they gave him twelve fucking years for it.

Tony Who was the most famous judge for giving those sentences out, Fred? Seaton.

Fred Oh, yeah. Justice Seaton. He was the Recorder for the London Sessions.

Tony He was the man. They were going up and getting fourteen years for a bottle of milk.

Fred You know what – he was drinking in my pub! He was coming in and out for about two years, towards the end of the time I was there.

He always used to be on his own, and he used to come along late, cos he'd get fucking slung out of one pub and come to another. And he'd walk past about five or six pubs that'd barred him to get to me.

Tony (*Laughing*) The service was very good.

Fred He was in a stupor when he came in. He sat there drinking Scotches and brandies. He wouldn't talk to no one. He was in his own world. He used to just drink himself into fucking oblivion, you know. He didn't know whose pub it was and he didn't care. If I'd gone up in front of him in court, he probably fucking wouldn't have recognized me. He wouldn't have known the bar staff or anybody else.

Tony He was a right old boozer, then, Fred.

Fred Oh, he was a fucking drunkard. We used to have to carry him out into the street and get him cabs. We had a terrible job getting him out of the pub at closing time. He kept wanting to fucking order more drinks, and that was why I objected to him. He wouldn't go home.

If he came in before time, I couldn't refuse him, same as I couldn't refuse anybody. And, I mean, he was dishing out bird during the day, and there he is getting pissed, and I didn't want him in the pub. He was a problem.

Sometimes after we were closed, I used to have a little drink with my pals. None of them used to take liberties with me, cos they didn't want to jeopardize my livelihood. They'd drink during opening hours, and if I had the right company, then I'd take them upstairs afterwards to my living room, I'd get my booze out and we'd have a nice drink. It didn't cost no one nothing.

Loads of times, just after I'd closed up and before we went upstairs, we'd hear *tap, tap* on the door, and we'd say, 'It's that fucking judge again! Turn the lights down. Lock the door. Leave him out there.' He'd be rattling the fucking handles of the door.

His clerk was all right. He didn't come into the pub, he didn't socialize, but you could speak to him. He couldn't influence the sentencing or give you any help, but he could tell you when Seaton was on and when he was off, and you could go up in front of a different judge. The clerk would fit you in on the right days. Or if you was on bail and you wanted to give yourself a bit more time, he'd set it back for you, so that you could get yourself a few quid before you go up and face the music. He was helpful like that.

Tony You know judges, when they were on a trial, all their food used to be supplied and delivered by Harrods. I don't know if it still is. But in them days, they called it the Harrods hamper. Have you heard about it, Fred?

Fred Yeah.

Tony I remember some local thieves nicking the London Sessions van with all the hampers on it. You know the yard, as you're pulling round the back there, Fred, where the cells are? The driver's jumped out and they've had his van, haven't they, with all the Harrods hampers in it. And there was bottles of port in each one of them, there was bottles of Scotch, there was caviar.

Fred All the best of everything. You could see it in their fucking red, bloated faces after they came back into court from lunch.

5

Police and Thieves

Conversation in Fred's kitchen, 1 March 2000

GOING FOR GOLD

Fred Gold! You could see how people fall in love with that stuff
– get hold of it, give it a cuddle . . . you don't want to let it go
(*laughing*). I wish I'd put down a bar or two.

Janice (*Popping in for a glass of wine*) Yeah, I keep asking him, 'Are
you sure you didn't bury one?'

Tony (*Laughter*)

Fred I'd love to have one today.

Tony Give him a memory pill, Jan!

Janice I'll give him a box of them . . .

Fred I heard about a gold robbery in 1962, the year before the
[Great] Train Robbery. There was only five involved, they had half
a ton of gold ingots and it came to half a million pounds, so they
had a nice cut-up. No one ever got nicked on that robbery. It was
at a bullion dealer's in the City.

It was put up by Ronnie Kray. The twins couldn't handle it.
They hadn't got a clue how to go to work, but they called this firm
round. The twins had a geezer who knew all about what was going
on there. To look at that building, you wouldn't suss out at all that
they're gold bullion dealers. But Ronnie introduced the firm to a
man who knew the routine there, so he put the work up and he
got his whack.

The man told them that the staff all leave and go to lunch at a
certain time and only a few people are left on duty. They had to
wait for the gold to be delivered late. If it came too early, or on
time, then all the staff was in the building. It was alive. But if they
got there a few minutes late, when the workforce had left and gone

to lunch, then it was the right time to go, cos you only had a few in the back of the office and the man in the front. He would open the gates, and they would back their security van in and throw all the bullion off the back.

They had to go there about four or five times before it was a goer. Once they saw the staff all going to their lunch before the van arrived, they knew that they was on. That was the time to pounce.

As soon as they saw the van, it was all systems go. One man went under the front of the van while they was unloading it at the back. It was flush with the street, the van, when it was backed in.

Tony It was jammed in.

Fred You could squeeze down the sides of it, but he dived under the bonnet, on the ground and up the side. Then he slipped behind the gates that were open, got through a side door and was inside. And he let two of the firm in. There was only three of them and the driver, and then they had a whack for the guy who gave Ronnie the information, so it was cut five ways, plus what they gave to Ronnie for the introduction.

They waited in the well of the staircase in the passageway. When the van pulls out, the bullion has been unloaded and left on the bay, and then the guard comes up and shuts the gates. But they're inside, aren't they, so they just came out and copped for him. No guns – they weren't necessary then. They wrapped him up, put some rope round him.

He was an old ex-copper, so he put up a bit of a struggle, but they told him they were just tying him up and they left him in the office. Then they opened the gates, brought their own van in and loaded it up with gold bars.

Tony Must have been some weight in there.

Fred Half a ton of gold. Which was nice. They were big bars, long ones. It was soft gold, pure, twenty-four carat. The sort you could put your thumbnail in it and mark it. That's how soft it was.

Tony I have a very good friend whose brother's a bullion dealer down at Tilbury. On one occasion, they were moving the bullion from Stratford to Tilbury. And I was there one lunchtime, there was hardly no one there, and it was all lying about on the floor, ingots of it, all over the place. I mean, they take some shifting. The weight of them!

Fred Well, when I first saw it, I was a kid, working on the Southern Railway. They used to lay 'em in fives, because the weight is so dense that if you put them in a small area in an ordinary van they'd go straight through the floor.

So they put two bars one way, two bars another way, and one on the top so you can get your fingers underneath them. Cos if it's laying on the floor and it's just stacked up, you can't get your fingers under it. You're gonna want something to stick under it, a screwdriver, to prise it up and then get your hand and fingers under it.

I mean, I see 'em on television when they throw these bars about. Fucking hell, they've got a big box of gold and they're picking it up with one hand and throwing it around like it's nothing . . .

Anyway, the gold from that job finished up in Switzerland. One of the firm wanted some money right away and couldn't wait, so he sold off a couple of his bars. But when you've got 250 grand's worth of fucking gold around you, you want to sell it at the right price, which they did by going over to Switzerland.

THE GREAT TRAIN ROBBERY

One of Britain's most famous crimes took place on 8 August 1963. Robbers stopped a Royal Mail train travelling from Glasgow to London at Bridego Bridge, near Linslade, Buckinghamshire, and stole £2.5 million. They hid out in a farmhouse hired by posh solicitor John Wheater and solicitor's clerk Brian Field.

The team were Buster Edwards, Gordon Goody, Bruce Reynolds, Ronnie Biggs, Charlie Wilson, Jimmy White, Bob Welch, Tommy Wisbey, Roger Cordrey, Jimmy Hussey, Roy 'The Weasel' James, Bill Boal, John Wheater, Brian Field and Leonard Field.

The Aylesbury judge handed out sentences of twenty years plus, with the major players receiving thirty years each.

Ronnie Biggs escaped from Wandsworth Prison in July 1965.

Tony I'll always remember that night. I was going down to Bognor and I picked up a newspaper, and they had a little bit about a train being stopped in Buckinghamshire and there being a robbery. No one took a lot of notice. But the night after, all hell broke loose. There wasn't a place in London the police didn't turn over. Everyone was shitting themselves for weeks.

They didn't have the regionals in, they had the Flying Squad and local police, so the coordination wasn't there. And, my God, did they learn about that. But I think it changed crime in general. People were then starting to look for big prizes.

Fred Well, there were plenty of big robberies before the Great Train Robbery. The first big one, that was the Post Office robbery in the Fifties. Quarter of a million on board. They all got away with that. Billy Hill [top villain of the time] set it up, although he didn't take part in it. But I knew people who did and are still alive today. That was the Eastcastle Street mail-van robbery.

Tony There had always been major robberies, but not on the scale of the Great Train Robbery. It was such a massive thing. We'd never had nothing like it in this country. It's become a Sixties legend.

I didn't know it was gonna happen. But, afterwards, one or two names came up. You've gotta remember, two and a half million pounds in 1963 is like twenty million today, and everybody in the underworld had their ears to the ground.

And the repercussions of it . . . what hit everybody after the trial, especially in the prison system, was the sentences. No one could believe they gave them thirty years.

Fred The train robbers were not armed, but at the time, the authorities was trying to wipe out the armed robber. They thought, We've gotta stop this. It was very prevalent at the time.

Tony *Cor!*

Fred I mean, you only had to pick the newspaper up. Every week there was a snatch somewhere, and it was only five or six firms doing it all in London. It was a guessing-out thing, who had what, you know, when it was going off. But we was all in the major league at the finish, going for the big prizes.

I was in Ireland the first time I ever heard of the Train Robbery, probably about a year before it happened. I'd been in Mountjoy Prison and the lawyers came over to get me bail and get me out of trouble. I was walking around Dublin one night with a solicitor's clerk who worked for Brian Field, and he said, 'I know he'd like to have a meet with you, Brian Field.' And that was the first I ever heard about this bit of work.

But I fancied it had been bandied about quite a bit beforehand, and I thought there was too many people who knew about the work, so I never went to discuss it.

Tony Rumour always had it you was on the Train Robbery, Fred.

Fred I know that. Well, they all thought I was because the people who was on it were my friends who I grew up with. People like Bruce and Charlie Wilson and Buster.

Tony And Gordon.

Fred And Tommy Wisbey was my best man at my wedding and his wife Renee was the maid of honour. We had the wedding party at her sister Janie's house in Walworth Road.

Back around '56, '58, there was me, Tommy Wisbey, Buster and another fella, little Billy Hart. We were just four-handed, and we used to go out with the twelves [keys] unlocking all these lock-up stores and shops in main shopping centres.

Tony So it was all that that put you in the frame there.

Fred That's what put me there. Anyway, after Ireland, I never thought no more about it. And then Gordon, Buster and I think it was Bruce, came down my local pub, The Spanish Patriot in The Cut, where I had my Sunday morning drink. I was standing in there with Patsy O'Mara and Tommy Sullivan, an old pal of mine, and they walked in. We all end up drinking together, and I was approached then about going on the bit of work.

I didn't want to know anything about it. You don't want to be in possession of the knowledge in case something goes wrong.

They fancied that the gold robbery in the City might have been my bit of work, so when I knocked back the Train Robbery, they sort of laughed. I said, 'We're having a little rest at the moment.' But we've got money in the bank. We don't have to go out and risk our liberty on anything. So I said that I didn't want to be in the Great Train Robbery.

When I heard it had gone off, naturally, you're rooting for 'em – 'Good luck to 'em, please God they get away with it!' – but there was such a hue and cry at the time. I mean, they [the police] was tipping up everywhere and everybody, wasn't they?

Tony   People were getting pulled in because the Train Robbery gave the police an excuse to go into every criminal circle there was, because they were looking. It gave them a licence to bust anybody who came their way.

Fred   But they knew everybody who took part in that robbery. They scooped up all the right people, which made me think that there was someone involved who must've fucking opened his mouth. They always say nobody opened up on that robbery and it was kept clean, but not everybody knew everyone else. They was all different people from all over London, and an informer wouldn't be able to put them together. But the police seemed to link everybody. It must've come from someone who was actually at the farm and knew all the people that were there, who took part.

Tony   That's right. It makes sense.

Fred   I mean, people was arrested that I'd never fucking heard of. I'd never heard of Roger Cordrey or Bill Boal. I didn't know Jimmy White. And Roy James, The Weasel, I'd never met him. When they all got arrested, I thought, Who the fuck's this lot? But once Bruce's name's come up, and Charlie's, I thought, Oh yeah, it's the old firm again, with Gordon.

Tony   Who was it that they caught first, Fred?

Fred   Roger got caught first, with the garage and the car – a Ford Prefect, I think.

Tony   Oh yeah, that's right.

Fred   He was renting a lock-up garage, and the woman he was renting it from got suspicious because he paid a big advance in cash. He'd also paid cash for the car. She notified the police. They ended up arresting him, but they never noticed him put the car key up his arse – cos he had his whack, a big lump of dough, in the car.

Tony   Eighty grand, weren't it, Fred?

Fred   Something like that. And he couldn't stand the key up his arse any longer, so he had to tell the police about it. 'You've gotta get a doctor ... I've gotta get this removed.' He was in pain, I suppose. It was only a little key. I should imagine most people could've sweated that out, couldn't they? Must've had a sharp edge to it.

Tony　Yeah, yeah.

Fred　I'd never heard of Biggsy before he got arrested. But I helped him after he escaped from Wandsworth. We had a mutual friend, [armed robber] Eric Flowers. I did a couple of bits of business with him and his brother, Robert. They was game bastards, weren't they?

Tony　He was thin as anything, very quiet, Eric.

Fred　To look at them, you wouldn't think they was at the heavy game.

Tony　You would never know in a million years.

Fred　Well, he came over the wall with Biggs. That's how I got to meet Biggs. I wouldn't have known or met him, other than that. But he was a nice enough guy. I kept him and Eric for six months in a flat I had in this fourteen-storey block in Kennington. No one knew they was there. My sister-in-law used to go up there and cook and clean and do their laundry.

I was living over the top of my pub at the time, but I'd kept that flat on as a safe little house, paid the rent. Everybody thought I'd got rid of it.

Biggsy had a big suitcase of fucking money behind the settee. I mean, if we was bad people, we'd have fucking put one in him and nicked all his money. A hundred and fifty grand in the Sixties was a fucking lot.

Then I moved them down to the coast cos Biggsy wanted to meet his wife – what's her name?

Tony　Charmaine.

Fred　What I had lined up for 'em was to take them out to Germany and get their faces changed with plastic surgery. I put them on a boat at London Bridge. I stood at the bridge and watched it go out and it sailed over to Antwerp in Belgium. They went down in the hold with the captain and the first mate, who were straightened out.

Then, when they got to Antwerp, my pal – I can't mention his name – picked them up at the dock gate. They went on from there. They went into a clinic and had their faces done by a German plastic surgeon. Biggsy, they made him more handsome than he was, really.

It was horrible, painful. They was brutal, and it was early days then. They didn't have the techniques they've got today.

I did the same thing with Buster when he went on his toes after the robbery. I put him through the same route. I know he was looking through his eyelids when he was having his face done. He was conscious all the time and he could see under and over his eyelids when they was fucking cutting him about. And the surgeon was whistling German tunes all the time.

Tony   (*Laughter*)

Fred   Fucking Hitler's marches. Anyway, getting back to him, Biggsy, he needed another passport. The one he'd gone out to Germany on, which I'd got him in the first place, was a bit hot. He went all the way to Australia with it, but he needed another with his 'new' face on it. I got that done for him, and he used the two passports until he went to Brazil, when he had to get out of Australia. For the first time ever, the faces of wanted people were put on satellite TV, and it was beamed across to Australia that Ronnie Biggs was a wanted man.

SECURITY EXPRESS

In April 1990, seven years after the robbery, Fred was cleared of taking part but found guilty of handling money from the proceeds and sentenced to nine years.

Fred   I never knew nothing about the Brink's-Mat robbery, though we was accused of it in Spain when they were trying to get us back for questioning about the Security Express. That was to put the heat on, to say we was wanted for both robberies.

Brink's-Mat was the biggest robbery in British history. They got away with millions of pounds' worth of gold bullion from Heathrow in November 1983. Security Express was the biggest-ever cash robbery. Seven million in used notes.

It was in April 1983, the Easter holiday. The Security Express

HOW TO TURN A GOLD BAR INTO CASH

Fred   Well, it's a long and involved process.

Tony   It's very complicated, yeah.

Fred   A bar weighed twenty-eight pounds, and it was worth about five grand in them days.

Tony   Oh, I thought it was much steeper than that.

Fred   Don't forget you could buy a house for five grand then. Anyway, you cut the gold up into small pieces with a metal saw, the sort plumbers use, and put it in a smelting furnace, which a lot of gold dealers and jewellers have got. You can buy 'em yourself now – you can have 'em in your house.

You'd just mix it up with bits of other precious metals, silver and stuff like that, platinum, from old jewellery or bundles of scrap that you could buy in the junk market and stalls, and make it into balls so it's unrecognizable. You could have anything mixed in with it. And then it goes into Johnson Matthey, the gold assayers' office in Hatton Garden. They can assay it, separate it and tell you exactly what the content is. So it's been laundered.

Tony   Cleaned up.

Fred   It comes back pure. But most people didn't go to that trouble. They got it straight out to Switzerland.

headquarters in Shoreditch was called Fort Knox. There'd been a furniture exhibition at Olympia and a lot of the money came from their takings.

Tony   Lot of money, Fred.

Fred   That's why there was that amount of cash in the vaults at the time. And it went off without a hitch, the whole robbery, from start to finish. There was no evidence left behind, nothing traceable, no fingerprints and no identifications. There was about eight guards tied up. None of 'em was hurt. They was all looked after with cups of tea and cigarettes in their mouths. They was uncomfortable, but they were treated humanely. It was one of the best bits of work that ever happened.

After six months without any arrests, people are thinking, Oh, well, it's all right, and after nine months, Oh, well, it's definitely all right now. And that's when a certain person, John Horsley, got nicked in his garage.

He had nothing to do with the robbery. I personally didn't know him. He was, apparently, looking after some money for somebody who handled part of the proceeds.

And on this day, the Drug Squad raided him, thinking there was a speed factory in his garage. He said, 'Oh, I've been expecting you to come, it's been worrying me,' and he fucking spilt the beans. The coppers looked at each other and couldn't believe what they was hearing.

He took 'em round to his father-in-law's flat and there was like 360 grand in the cupboard from the robbery. None of it was marked, it was clean, but he told them it was from the robbery. On the inside of the cupboard door, there was all the figures of what had been there to start with and how much had been deducted, so whoever had the money in there knew what was left. At my trial they even produced the cupboard door as evidence, which had no bearing on my case at all.

Then this guy Horsley said he was on the robbery, and he wasn't. That's a fact. He wasn't on it. But he had to change his story cos he made statements – then he got himself ten years.

Tony Ho, ho, ho!

Fred Why he did that, I don't know. There was only five people involved in the robbery. And they have all been sentenced and done their bird. There was no one else involved and that's a fact! Now, the police was trying to make out that the 360 grand they found in the cupboard was a robber's share out of seven mill.

Well, if that was a robber's share, that meant there was twenty people climbed over that wall that night, which is a complete load of bollocks. You understand?

Tony Yeah.

Fred And that's where it started. I was already in Spain. I was only there to invest a little bit of money and buy a home.

I still had a place on the Bonhomie Estate in Bermondsey. I had my house out in Pennsylvania, in America, with a swimming pool, and a vending business running out there. I was going backwards and forwards between the States and Spain and London from 1978 to 1984.

And all of a sudden in the newspaper headlines – bang! They've nicked Johnny Knight, Ronnie Knight's brother, and a couple of other people I didn't know, who were friends of his. The crap hit the fan. And I thought, The best place for me is back out in sunny Spain. That's the time to go, Fred. So I just slipped out the country and took Maureen with me, and we thought, Well, we gotta stay here until we see how the cookie crumbles. And, course, arrest followed arrest then.

My daughter, Danielle, carried on living in the Bonhomie, got herself a little dog, and my son Jamie, who had come back to London from America, lived there as well. Whenever I came back, we used it as our home. We didn't go round spending. I had the same cars, never showed any wealth at all. Me and Teddy Dennis was still grafting the pool tables.

We had about sixty pool-table sites, and I was still going out collecting the money and stuff. I'd be off for a couple of weeks and come back and I'd go out on the rounds again. They were like money boxes everywhere, and we just kept emptying them. It was great. And I was still flitting about everywhere.

Now when the police came out to Spain, they're looking round to see who's out there and put people together. There's plenty of fucking criminals on their toes there – obviously not all involved in the same crimes. And that's another story . . .

THE ROBIN HOOD THEORY

Fred   There was some sort of respectability about our sort of crime. And when someone had it off, the general public used to say, 'They're game bastards, good luck to 'em,' especially if nobody was injured and it was against the establishment. You was robbing the people who had money, and the money you earned would circulate in your own environment. We used to knock it out either in the West End pubs and clubs or in the betting shops. We didn't fucking hoard it or send it out the country.

As soon as we had a touch, we'd go and treat all the kids and buy, like, £600 worth of toys from Hamleys. You'd treat your family and friends to holidays down the caravans. Everyone benefited. You never spent it only on yourself.

It's not a myth, the Robin Hood thing. You see, you find that the average thief in those days was very generous when he had a touch. It was like they say, easy come, easy go.

He might go out a dozen times and not fucking get any money at all, and then he'd have a good touch and he used to whoop it up and everyone around him got treated. It's like when the old lion feeds, then along come the jackals and then the vultures, the birds and then the insects until there's nothing left, and this is the way life is. Everyone shared in your good fortune.

That's all you did it for, for all the good pleasures in life. Buy yourself a new television or a radiogram. I mean, you had to be sensible, but you didn't have to watch the pounds, shillings and pence.

My brother-in-law, old Fred, we had a touch when he was carrying the wages one day and I had the payroll off. I said to him, 'Now, be careful, Fred,' cos he was going to get married. 'Don't go rushing into it straight away, cos they might spin back on you in a few months' time.' And he hid the money away. It's a good job he did. About two or three months later, a knock on the door. In they come. 'Oh, that's a nice new radiogram you got there, Fred. Where did you get that from?' 'Oh, I got it on the book, I'm paying on the never-never.' Thank God, he was. But forewarned, forearmed. That's the way it used to be.

All most of us wanted to do was become respectable, you know. You think there will come a time when you don't have to do it any more if you've got good businesses going. All the money I fucking got, I got out on the pavement risking my liberty. I put it into straight businesses so that one day I would be able to be a straight businessman and not have to do the things that I did. That was the objective.

I didn't go round fucking twisting people's arms, or wanting to be put into their businesses, or taking over businesses or strong-arming people.

But, unfortunately, legitimate businesses never seem to produce the same profit as you're used to, and you're keeping twenty, thirty people employed. You're struggling to pay their wages every week, they're ripping you off or the business is not making a profit, and you're reverting to going back out on the pavement. It's a vicious circle of crime and trying to be straight. You'd just as well put the money in the bank and let it breed and just live off of it, rather than investing in business.

Tony There's not many major criminals who have gone on and made money out of straight business. I know that.

Fred That's why I won't get involved in business any more. Cos I've done so much money in straight businesses – casinos, betting shops, pubs, clubs, drinking, dining, restaurants – I've had all those things and at the end of the day, I've spent good money after bad.

A SLIP-UP HERE AND THERE

Fred All the big crimes have been committed in London mostly. You don't hear of many major crimes going off in other cities. Up in Scotland they've had a couple of big tickles, and Birmingham a few good touches, but sometimes it's London firms going up there to do 'em anyway. I had a couple of touches up in places like Manchester. Couple of banks up there.

Tony I met a man called Tommy, who done a vault in Liverpool, and when they nicked him, he gave his brief a gold watch, lighter and ring to get him out of it. In the court, the solicitor would be playing with the watch and the ring, and the copper recognized them.

Both (*Laughter*)

Fred Back in '57, '58, I went on my toes for a while after a job in Southampton with Tommy Wisbey and Buster Edwards. We'd done a few things down there, emptied out warehouses and electrical shops. We used keys to just go up and bang the door open, early in the morning before they opened. I would have a white coat on and a pencil behind my ear to look like the manager – 'Take this, take that, load up!' – and if the coppers walked by, which they did sometimes, we took no notice, just carried on loading up and then we just drove off.

You couldn't walk around with gloves on, because it would

look suspicious to a copper or anybody walking by. So whatever you took out, you left your prints on.

Anyway, one day Tommy Wisbey left a radiogram behind inside the doorway. We get down the road and he's realized what's happened, so Buster and I went back to get it while Tommy drove the goods back to London.

When we arrived, there's a newspaper stand opened right outside the fucking shop and there's a geezer cleaning the windows. We pick up the radiogram, open the boot, stick it in, shut the boot and drive off. But the paper seller and the window cleaner's got a good look at me.

We got home all right and everything was sweet as a nut. Tommy used to work with his father, he was a bookmaker, and he's borrowed my van, a brand-new little Ford. He finished up having some of the gear in the back of this van. He says, 'Can I borrow it, Fred, and run a bit of gear about?'

So he's got it parked up on the pitch where he's taking the bets. All of a sudden, he gets nicked for street bookmaking. They swooped on him. Cos they used to come disguised as old ladies, and milkmen and fucking postmen, they'd come along in a horse and cart, and then they'd all spring out and pounce on the guy taking bets on the corner of the street.

They turn the van over and find these crooked fucking televisions and radiograms and records and stuff like that. So now, they trace it back to Southampton. They take Tommy down to Southampton and put him up on ID at the local nick. The paper guy and the window cleaner are up on the ID and they can't recognize him but, course, they can recognize me if I go down there. That's who they're looking for.

I had a house in Herne Hill at the time. Beautiful it was, in nice, tree-lined streets, but now I've gotta leg it. So I go over to the East End. You've just got that bit of river separating you but you've got different cozzers – and they didn't know me over there. That's what I call fate because it was to involve me much more with Charlie Kray and the twins.

6

Murder!

Conversations in Fred's kitchen, 11 and 16 January 2000

THE CRIME OF PASSION: TOMMY 'GINGER' MARKS

Fred This guy, Jimmy Evans, shot my brother George, not knowing what the repercussions would be, because we were so low-profile, laid-back and getting on with our work that this guy didn't know nothing about the strength of us.

He was in his own world with his own little fucking mob round him, going out doing jewellers and stuff like that. He wanted to get some revenge because his wife, Pat, and George had fallen in love. And they're still together to this day.

He didn't realize that George had a brother – Fred – until it was too late. And the same for Ginger Marks. None of them really knew me, did they? I mean, the twins' firm knew . . .

Tony Quite a few others did as well.

Fred All the people around me, and people all over London who was in the same business as me, but they never spoke about it. Jimmy Evans and these guys were third-division criminals. They think they're the fucking tops in their little area. You move them any further out and they're out of their depth.

But, course, when they did that offence on my George, they had to go. Someone had to fucking pay for it, and it was unfortunate that both of them didn't pay instead of just the one.

Ginger Marks knocked on my brother's door not long before Christmas 1964, and when George opened the door, he asked for another address, a number. But George recognized him and he shut the door and he thought to himself, I fucking know that geezer, I know his face.

The door knocked again. George opened it, expecting to see the same fella, but it was Jimmy Evans, and the next thing you know,

George is blasted with a shotgun and he's hitting the back wall of the passage. He wound up nearly dead in St Thomas's Hospital.

Tony And that justifies what you did. Cos, after all, they shot your brother.

Fred People knew that the guy had to get punished. I had to put it back.

Tony That's right, yeah.

Fred Unfortunately, Jimmy Evans escaped with his life. The night I spun 'em, Evans used Marks as a shield when the action started. Marks was stopping the bullets, and Evans was hiding behind him. One bullet just got by and went through Evans's coat before he legged it and disappeared.

The police had their suspicions about who did it, because of what happened to my George, but they couldn't prove it. It took 'em twelve years to get a case together.

Evans finally rolled over when he stabbed to death some poor fucking Scotchman, a carpenter, over nothing, a bit of road rage over his wife's driving. If I'd got Evans when I wanted to that night, the Scotchman would still be alive today. I would have saved a young man's life.

But that's when Evans struck the deal with the police. He got seven years – he was out in three – and part of his agreement was that he had to be a Crown witness against me. That was the reason that I got charged with the Marks murder, along with my pals Alfie Gerrard, Jerry Callaghan and Ronnie Everett – although only Alfie and myself were involved.

But the case against us fell to pieces at the Old Bailey at the end of 1975 because of unsafe evidence from Evans and other witnesses for the prosecution. Ronnie was discharged first, and the rest of us walked out when the jury told the judge that they'd heard enough. The trial was stopped.

This was the second attempt to convict us. The first Marks trial was also stopped, but not until all the evidence had been heard, when a juror suddenly pops up and admits to knowing one of the defendants. So the prosecution had a full rehearsal.

THE ASSASSINATION: FRANK 'THE MAD AXEMAN' MITCHELL

The following conversation refers, in part, to Carlton's two-part pro-gramme The Krays, *which had just been screened on ITV. The documentary centred on the disappearance of Frank Mitchell, and featured major contributions from Fred and from former Kray firm member Albert Donoghue, who spilled the beans to the police.*

Mitchell escaped from Dartmoor Prison in December 1966 – allegedly with the help of the Kray twins – and was taken to a safe house arranged by them. On Christmas Eve, Albert Donoghue, one of the people guarding Mitchell, lured him out of the flat, telling him he was being taken to a new hide-out. He climbed into a van parked around the corner and was shot to death.

Reggie and Ronnie Kray and Fred stood trial for the murder in 1969 and were found not guilty.

Tony He was a simple man, Frank, a bit retarded. About thirty-two, thirty-three, he was. A massive, dark-haired fella. Very powerful. You couldn't miss him.

Fred Yeah. He was six feet fucking two, wasn't he? He was a big lump. But, I mean, his future was zero. He was a fucking villain who'd been certified.

Tony Oh, capable of killing. *Cor!* He would've done it sooner or later. I didn't really know him though. I bumped into him in Wandsworth a couple of times. It was a nodding acquaintance. I wasn't involved with the escape. I'd just come out of my sentence on the Wimpy Bar.

The first time I saw him, he'd come up on a visit from Dartmoor on a coach. And, of course, the screws are waiting for him.

Fred Yeah.

Tony There was two Mitchells on the coach. The other Mitchell was this weedy little geezer, and he got off the coach first. The screws gave him a bit of stick, didn't they – 'You're the Mitchell . . . right, then.' And all of a sudden, a big hand came out – '*I am* the Mitchell. What do you want?'

Fred (*Laughter*) He used to pick the screws up and walk round with them, didn't he? There's so many stories about him.

Tony He carried a blade openly in the nick. If he got up in the morning with the hump, or someone upset him, he'd get the blade out and start sharpening it on the step. He was always down the block.

Fred He was, yeah. He'd get nicked for the slightest little thing. And that was his buzz for the day, getting nicked, wasn't it? If he found out anyone had been in his cell, he'd kick right off.

Tony Oh, murders.

Fred But it was the twins who got him to be a good boy. Then he started really behaving, cos he wanted a release date. He was a good boy for four years – a feat. And that's when the authorities at Dartmoor started trusting him to go out on the moor on the work party. They had a little shed where they used to make their tea and have a cook-up, get out of the wind and the bad weather.

Tony The screws used to saddle the pony up for him. It'd be waiting outside the gate. It was common knowledge.

Fred (*Laughing*) I know that when he got across the moors, he got on board and had a ride around, but the ponies were fucking wild, and where would the screws be keeping a saddle? I can't imagine them saddling up at the gate for him anyway.

Tony They did, Fred. The horse was waiting.

Fred (*Still laughing*) The groom waiting with the fucking horse till he comes out ... I'm not having that! That's got to be a load of bollocks!

Tony What was going on? I mean, he goes down to Plymouth in a cab to get a budgie!

Fred That was true. Don't forget, he was on his own, fixing the fences, and he didn't have to get back to the meet with the others and the screw until four o'clock. Then they all got picked up in the prison van, and back to the nick. And he was getting a drink in a pub in the middle of nowhere. I mean, if I was doing a life and I had that sort of freedom, I'd make the most of it.

Tony Oh, what? Rubbing your hands. Yeah!

Fred You'd be down the pub, you'd bring your friends down, bring the wife down, and you'd have a room upstairs in the pub, wouldn't you?

Tony Course you would, yeah.

Fred Get him straightened, the old publican. I mean, Frank wasn't short of cash. He could've gone upstairs, cos he behaved himself there – the publican said so. He spent a lot of money there. He was treating everyone in the bar, all the locals.

Tony (*Laughing*) Well, it says it all, don't it?

Fred He knew Ronnie Kray from Wandsworth, when Ronnie was doing that three-stretch over the fight with the dockers. I'm sure they knew each other from the East End anyway. Frank was from Bow.

Tony The twins did look after him in the nick.

Fred They did more to help him and keep him happy than all the governors and authorities during his last four years in prison.

It was useful for them to have an ally like Frank inside. You've gotta have power inside the nick as well as out so that if you want something done, you can just send in a message on a visit. You can say, 'So and so is in here, he did this or that, see that he gets served up.' And then whoever does it, they get a nice joey sent in to 'em. So Frank would have done that for the twins.

Tony He did do it!

Fred He'd say, 'I'm doing this for the twins.' Doesn't matter if he goes down the block. He's the same, Charlie Bronson, now. If I was to say, 'So and so's in your nick, serve him up for me,' I've no doubt that Charlie would do it, if it were possible. I would never put a man in that position, but some people would!

So it suited the twins for Frank to stay there. They never, ever intended springing him from the nick. They wanted to get him a [release] date, legally, through their connections with Lord Boothby and the MPs Tom Driberg and Manny Shinwell. There were loads of influential people they could get a bit of help from in those days.

And the twins wanted to move through the proper channels to get Frank out. Think of the prestige, the kudos, they'd have had out of that.

Tony   *Cor!* Not much!

Fred   'They've got Big Frank out the nick.' I mean, it's a terrific result.

Tony   Let's put it this way. Good intentions went wrong, Fred.

Fred   It was all good intentions.

Tony   They meant well. They never told him to escape.

Fred   The best use they could make of him at that time was inside, not outside, the nick.

The Governor had rewarded his good behaviour by letting him go out on that work party. Frank was going out every day and having a drink in the pub. But, course, that was the fucking big mistake, because he got the idea of escaping.

The twins were writing him letters saying, 'We're helping you to get a date. Be a good boy. Don't do nothing wrong.' They're not saying, 'Escape.' They was trying to put it *out* of his head to escape, to be patient and wait. But he'd waited for four years, he'd been working the system, and there was no sign of him getting a result. All he wanted was a date of release.

Tony   But he couldn't wait.

Fred   What topped it was when [Home Secretary] Roy Jenkins said, 'Life means life,' when the law isn't even passed. And all them lifers in the nick are all looking for a date, and that's gonna knock 'em really hard. Can you imagine the effect it must've had on them? What a stupid thing to say. So one day Frank just phoned up and said, 'I'm escaping. Send someone down to pick me up.'

Tony   It was stuck on the twins.

Fred   It wasn't planned at all.

Tony   [Albert] Donoghue said in a statement, 'We got him out of there to counteract ['Mad' Frankie] Fraser.'

Fred That's bollocks. Who did they think Frankie Fraser was? King Kong? *Please!* Anyway, the Richardson firm were all locked up in the nick at that time, including Frankie Fraser. And even if they hadn't been, what could the twins do with Frank Mitchell? Would they say, 'Come on, we'll take you over south London and parade you up and down and show the Richardson gang who we've got on our side'? With every copper in London out looking for him? That's complete bollocks.

Anyway, by escaping, Frank's lost his credibility, he's lost the trust he's built up over four years and he's put the Governor in a fucking position, cos when you're on a work party, you're on your honour. So now he's upset the whole fucking party. No works parties after that. He never looked at the damage he would be doing to other prisoners. And now he's absconded, he can't negotiate with the government for a release date. Too much damage was done.

So Albert went down there with Teddy Smith to pick him up. Teddy Smith was in the phone box where they'd arranged the meet. Frank come up and he thought he was a stranger. He pulled out a fucking blade and he was gonna do Teddy Smith. He was all charged up.

Tony And no one would like the idea of that knife being on him, Fred.

Fred Well, they threw the knife out the window but he soon got himself another one when he got back to the safe house in London.

Tony Prison security at that time . . . I mean, they drove him off the moor without a stop.

Fred They never missed him. They was driving up Bow, apparently, when the scream went up on the radio. They was home and dry.

Tony Had they stopped him, he was well capable of taking three men out.

Fred They were stopping cars and lorries in the moors weeks later, still thinking he was holed up there. They thought he'd got in a house and kidnapped an old couple or something, like he did before. They didn't realize he was back in London.

Tony They worked on a pattern – 'Oh, he's gone to ground. We'll find him in a barn somewhere.'

Fred Some isolated house. It wouldn't have surprised me if they'd captured him in a fucking farmhouse or in some haystack or something, but when they never, I knew that he'd been got away. But I never knew what had happened until later. We just used to guess and surmise.

Tony Two and two together, yeah.

Fred We knew he must have had help because he couldn't have survived that long on his own.

First thing he did when he got to the safe house in Barking, he got the carving knife. He thinks he's going to club it and go round all the pubs, and have birds and booze.

Tony (*Laughter*)

Fred But as Nipper Read said, he just swapped one prison for another. So then, he wanted to creep out of a night and go round to the twins' house. He said he would go walking with a velvet fucking mask on. And a blade. The mask was so no one would recognize him, and he did have a thing about masks, too. He had a mask on when he escaped before.

Tony It shows you how backward he really was. Everything he was doing was a danger signal.

Fred He was always on about arm-wrestling. Cos he's gotta win every arm-wrestling contest.

Tony And the members of the firm who was looking after him in there, they had to let him win. Well, no one could beat him anyway.

Fred It's like a kid, innit?

Tony Oh, you're dealing with a child in a man's body. Frightened of him? *Cor!*

Fred They was fucking terrified. [Scotch] Jack Dickson, he woke up with Frank looking over him with the carving knife. Bet he crapped himself. He said, 'I'm not going back there,' and he didn't, after that episode.

Tony They sent [Billy] Exley round there. He's shitting himself. He said, 'Frank's gonna wind up killing one of us.' Now you've got a big problem. You've got a man stuck in the flat. There was Albert Donoghue, Connie Whitehead . . . it's like they were his warders. He was better off down the Moor.

Fred They kept interchanging because they had to stay with him twenty-four hours a day.

Tony I remember Connie Whitehead saying to me, 'I'm not fucking going back. Fuck him. You can't control him!' And they got that bird Lisa in to try to keep Frank entertained, and he fell madly in love with her.

Fred Yeah. She was a hooker in a club. They paid her money. I know they gave her a few hundred quid. She got about a monkey.

Tony And it's always said that she was kept a prisoner in there, that the twins held her hostage. She *weren't* held hostage.

Fred She was free to go. Oh, it was such a fuck-up.

Tony She went to a party with Donoghue the night Frank left, and he went to bed with her.

Fred He told people, as well. It was to sweeten her up. But getting back to Frank, one of the things that was driving him crazy in the flat was the fact that the only Kray brother who had come to see him was Reggie, and that was just once. Ronnie was on his toes at the time, hiding.

Tony He was on 'missing'.

Fred Cos they wanted him to give evidence against the police, didn't they? And he wouldn't give evidence against anybody. That's the way he was. So Reggie and Charlie obviously couldn't see Ronnie, and they couldn't go visiting Frank in case they were tailed by coppers looking for Ronnie.

Now Frank was making a threat – 'They ain't come to see me. Who do they think they are? I'll go round there.' Now what do you do? The twins was worried out of their minds.

Tony Course they was. Shitting themselves.

SO YOU'VE GOT A BODY ON YOUR HANDS –
NOW WHAT?

Fred   There was a right smuggling operation going on in the late
Fifties and early Sixties. There was Alfie Gerrard, Paddy O'Nione,
who we called Paddy Onions, and a few others.

They used to go out from Newhaven in a converted fishing
boat, built for the rough seas in the Channel, and they were bringing
back Swiss wrist watches from Belgium. They was buying houses
with it. They was earning, like, forty grand on a trip, which was a lot
of money in them days. They had the old fishermen there helping
them.

But it came on top with the customs and there was a tear-up.
They came out – 'Good morning, gentlemen, we're customs officers.' The next thing you knew, there's a fucking Jag tearing at
them, trying to run them down and that, and they was jumping over
the bonnet for their lives, you know. A load of watches went in a
ditch. Then the farmer decided to fucking start digging his ditches.
He found these big holdalls full of watches and he reported them to
the police. The firm went back there to get them and they was
gone.

Tony   (*Hearty laughter*)

Fred   There was this fisherman who used to go out with them,
the captain of the boat, and they said they won the pools. They used
to give him all these different stories about fishing, and he used to
ask questions. They'd say, 'Cock a doodle doo, it's nothing to do
with you.' And that's what he gave as evidence in the Old Bailey
when they was nicked later on.

Tony   (*More laughter*)

Fred   Paddy got five years. Alf got nine months, cos they managed
to get him a retrial. There was a bit of bird dished out. You know,
Paddy finished up getting shot later on in the old gang wars.

Anyway, it was convenient. They still had the facilities down
there at Newhaven after the Old Bailey trial ... to wrap 'em up.

Bodies. They'd get chicken wire and put a few weights in it and tip 'em overboard.

Tony Chicken wire, yeah. It's the best way, isn't it?

Fred If anything sort of breaks up, it don't come to the surface. If the arm broke off, or the head, that would surface and it would wash up on the beach. You've gotta make sure that doesn't happen.

Tony So you roll 'em up. But in certain parts of the Channel, there's only about four foot of water. You can walk in it, so you've gotta know what you're doing.

Fred You've gotta know where the shipping lanes are too. It's a burial at sea, you know. So I suppose you'd have to wrap it up, the person's body, in a bit of sacking. In any case I imagine that would make it look better if you were dealing with it. It's not a thing you'd want to do, is it, unless you hate the person that much.

Then you'd put some weights, some bits of scrap iron, inside the twist of wires that you'd seal it up with.

Tony And the eels get through it, and the fish and all that.

Fred They eat everything, all the deep-sea dwellers. All the fish feed up.

But they say the best way is to put 'em in a fucking furnace, cremate 'em, if you know someone with a crematorium. Ah well, you can't talk about things like that. It's all in the past, anyway. Everything must change with time.

Fred Ronnie was definitely worried sick about him [Frank]. He was worried about his mother. Loved his mum, didn't he? Well, we all loved Violet.

Tony Frank made that threat, Fred. Now, Reggie didn't particularly like Frank to start with. Reggie never really knew him.

Fred Reggie didn't know fuck all about him. Or Charlie. It was all down to Ronnie. He was the only one I had a discussion with about what to do with Frank. Reg and Charlie had nothing to do with the arrangements.

Tony Reg was worried sick about the whole situation. He was a real worrier. *Cor!* Not much.

Fred Oh, yes. So when Frank threatened to go round the house to their mother, well, that was it, you know what I mean?

Tony I don't think he'd have done any harm to Violet Kray intentionally.

Fred He'd have done the old hostage bit, I suppose.

Tony Yeah. I mean, that's how he got his nickname. He broke into a house and he held them hostage, didn't he? Didn't the old man get a clump?

Fred He got a whack, yeah.

Tony If I remember it right, didn't Frank sit there with the old girl, stroking her hands and apologizing to her? He had funny turns, Frank.

Fred He had the axe on his lap. I mean, you sit in anyone's house with a fucking big axe on your lap, I don't think they'd be very happy, would they?

Tony So had Frank gone round there . . . well, it shows you how serious the twins took it. They had to do something quick.

Fred Frank knew he'd fucked up. He was sending out letters to the newspapers, offering to give himself up in return for a release date. But he knew that the authorities could promise him anything, and once he'd surrendered, bosh! He'd be right back into Broadmoor or somewhere.

Tony They would never have controlled him.

Fred He was threatening to take six fucking cozzers with him, rather than go back to prison.

Tony What you gonna do with him now?

Fred You couldn't contain him. If the authorities couldn't contain him, how could the twins contain him, especially since they couldn't even come to see him?

Tony They couldn't phone the law up and tell them where he is.

Fred Nah. It's not in the criminal code, is it? Also, they had to think about what would happen if the police tumbled where he was. He'd kill a couple of coppers and then you're all up on murder charges. If you're in the room and he kills a copper, you're an accessory. So it was a matter of eliminating him, really, from the scene.

Ronnie sent a message to me, and I went and met him secretly, through Albert. Ronnie had decided that there was only one way out of it. Could I do the business for him?

Tony It was stuck on you.

Fred 'Hold up, Ron,' I said. 'This ain't a thing you can do overnight. This is serious fucking bollocks, here.' I said, 'It's all right just doing someone and walk away and leaving them on the fucking kitchen floor – that's the easy part – but you think of the jeopardy you're putting other people into. They've gotta pick him up and take him away and lose him for ever. There's a lot of risk involved.'

But it was the best, most merciful thing for Frank Mitchell. It was like euthanasia, really. His life would have been like slowly dying, in Broadmoor or somewhere.

Tony Yes, I agree with that. One hundred per cent.

Fred They would've been giving him the liquid cosh until he was a fucking cabbage. His big, strong, healthy body would have been wrecked by drugs. The family would have spent all their lives visiting him. They'd still be visiting now if he survived the nuthouse treatment, which I doubt very much.

Tony I've no doubt about that.

Fred The way he performed . . . he was a sick boy. Medically, he needed help. Maybe in years to come he might've been all right, but I doubted it very much. And so it was more humane to get it over with and do it . . .

Ronnie had done me some good favours, and it was like a debt of honour to pay back.

Tony What a debt. *What a debt.* You needed that at Christmas, didn't you? *Cor!*

Fred I wanna be home with my wife and kids on Christmas Eve, having a fucking party. Instead they want me out putting somebody down . . . I mean, that's nice, isn't it? I had a business to run and better things to do.

I didn't fucking relish it. Course I would have been happier if I hadn't got involved. I wouldn't have stood on murder trials and had all the family worrying whether I was gonna go away for life or not.

Tony It's a terrible thing.

Fred I didn't want to be in that position with Frank, but I got involved for Ronnie. Not for Reggie or Charlie. Just Ronnie. Cos Ronnie was true to his word, he was a genuine man and he helped me when I needed help.

You know, when they're putting Reggie and Charlie in the frame here for conspiracy, they wasn't conspiring with fuck all. Nothing. And Reggie was up on the murder charge with me and Ronnie! I made it clear for the documentary, but it was edited out, that when I discussed what was to happen with Frank Mitchell, I spoke only to Ronnie Kray.

He was in hiding, so how could Reggie and Charlie be there? Even Albert [Donaghue] was outside the room. I wouldn't talk in front of him. It was Ronnie Kray and myself. Nobody else.

The only people who knew anything were the people involved. My Maureen never knew nothing. She'd have been worried sick, wouldn't she, if she'd known what was happening?

It was dark and miserable, the night it happened. Albert brought Frank out the flat and round the corner into Ladysmith Avenue, where we were waiting in the van.

Tony (*Laughing*) And a copper walked past Frank without recognizing him! I bet he got the sack. And Frank went for the driver, didn't he, as soon as he got in the vehicle?

Fred Yeah. He half-suspected something was amiss. Cos, I mean, we ain't making polite conversation.

Tony So he was prepared to put up violence there.

Fred Then he was all over the place. And he's a big fucking man, locked in the back of a little van. But he was dead within a minute or so of getting in that van. I mean, he didn't know what had hit him. But I don't like talking about it. I don't glorify it. It's not nice, is it? All I can say is that he didn't suffer. It [the shooting] was over in a few seconds.

Tony A couple of people phoned me after the programme went out. One was a well-known boxer, and do you know what he said to me? He said, 'No matter what Fred says, I know the SP. I know what happened to Frank's body.'

Fred Oh, he knows the SP, does he?

Tony Whatever you say, Fred, the public don't want to believe that. They want to believe he's under a motorway.

Fred They're never gonna believe what you tell 'em. If he's holding up a motorway or a flyover, don't matter . . .
But a lot of people ask to be buried at sea. They put it in their wills. They can have their ashes scattered across the water, and their families throw wreaths out. Not a bad way to go. A lot of good men finished down there during the war years. Anyway, it was after that [the Mitchell murder] that Ronnie showed me his list.

Tony Ho, ho, ho! That was a famous list.

Fred 'I'm gonna fucking do this one and do that one.'

Tony Let's put it this way – it was very easy to get on it and very hard to get off it.

Fred Most of the people who were on it have survived because I'd paid my debt to Ronnie. He knew I wasn't gonna get involved in any more, and he would have had no one to clear up the mess.

Tony He would have carried them all out if he'd had you as a support to it.

Fred And after I'd had all that aggravation with him on the Christmas! I said, 'I can't do no more. I'm not a fucking undertaker, Ron.'
They was all assigned to different members of the firm. He didn't assign no one to me, but, I mean, I wasn't part of their firm. I was with my own people.

Tony Going back to the documentary, ain't he aged, Fred? Ain't Albert aged?

Fred Oh, yeah. He's had a bad time all these years, looking over his shoulder.

Tony Bad, bad time.

Fred It's only through his own doing – he should've used his brains at the beginning. All he had to say was that he took Frank round the corner and saw a van waiting in Ladysmith Avenue with the engine running and the lights on. His instructions were to put Frank in the back. He opened the back door of the van, Frank climbed in, Albert shut the door and the van drove off. He didn't see a face. He didn't see anybody.

Tony Yeah, lovely. Everything fits.

Fred He could've admitted that he heard the gunshots go off.

Tony Yeah, but he didn't see no one.

Fred And he walked back to the flat, cos he *was* back there inside a few minutes. That's all he had to say to get himself out of trouble.

Tony I could never understand why he didn't.

Fred Then he wouldn't have had to say, 'I saw Freddie Foreman and Alfie Gerrard.' And on the programme, he mentioned Jerry Callaghan as the driver. He had no need to say that.

  And he said that he got out of the van as soon as he could cos he thought he was gonna get one in the nut. He got out at the first bus stop, didn't he? He couldn't get out quick enough – 'Here, drop me off here!' But I don't think he really believed he was gonna get one.

  He was a witness to a fucking murder, the only one who could implicate the three of us [Fred, Alfie Gerrard, Jerry Callaghan]. He's gotta keep his fucking mouth shut.

Tony Yeah, yeah.

Fred Really, when you think of it, I should've fucking give him one. I would have if I'd known that he was gonna roll over!

Tony (*Laughing*) I knew you'd say that.

Fred I trusted Albert, you know.

Tony He's never really slagged you off.

Fred Well, he don't wanna fucking ask for more trouble, does he?

Tony I know where he lives.

Fred Yeah. Oh, yeah. But, look here, if I wanted to pay back Albert, it would have been done long ago. I feel sorry for him. He ruined his life, and that's punishment enough.

Tony I know where Scotch Jack Dickson lives [he gave prosecution evidence in the Mitchell and George Cornell murder trials]. He's seventy now.

Fred People like him and Albert, they're still worried, to this day.

Tony It's best to leave them alone, let them live with what they did.

Fred Yeah. I didn't know Albert had been shot by Reggie in the past. Well, Albert wasn't gonna tell me, was he?

Tony I told you that in Brixton.

Fred But that's after the event. If I'd known that then, I'd never have felt the same way about him, you know.

Tony I think what frightened him in the first place was when the twins said to him, 'You take the Mitchell.' That's when he rolled over.

Fred Yeah, they wanted him to take the blame for the murder. You can't put a man in a position like that.

Tony He tries to justify what he did. If you read his book, *The Krays' Lieutenant* [published by Smith Gryphon in 1995], there's a message in there for you, Fred. It's an apology.

Fred I know. I read between the lines. He's saying, 'I had no choice.' And I'm sympathetic in a little way. I mean, he tried to life me off. I was on my own, weren't I, Tone? I was facing the murder charge with the twins. But, at the same time, Albert gave his evidence grudgingly, because he wasn't happy about what he was doing. I'd really liked him.

Now, being put in that position has completely ruined his life. Somebody fucking battered him the other week. But that's gonna happen. And he's getting to be an old man now, and these young guys are coming up and bashing him, for old times' sake. He's gotta expect that.

Tony I have no sympathy. He went down that road like we all did, but some of us didn't turn off. We went down it, we stayed there.

THE MURDER SUSPECT

Tony You know, I got accused of a murder that I knew nothing about. A man called Jewell, Fred, remember him? He shot Tony Maffia.

Fred I was in the next cell to him in Brixton.

Tony Yeah, and I was in the next cell to you.

Fred That was in the hospital.

Tony Me and you, Jewell . . .

Fred He was a fucking coalman from Manchester. I got on all right with him. I knew Tony Maffia too.

Tony They questioned me. I was there the night Reggie went to cut Tony Maffia, and Buller Ward got it instead because he tried to protect Maffia.

Fred Oh, did he?

Tony Anyway, when they done Maffia's safety deposit box, what did they find there, Fred?

Fred A bar of fucking gold. That was off the gold robbery – remember I told you one of them took his whack cos he couldn't wait for his money? He sold it to Tony Maffia! And when he got murdered in 1967, the police opened his box, and there's the bar of gold.

Tony They questioned me and my [brother] Nicky about Tony Maffia. They had the murder down to us for a while. We had nothing to do with it.

Fred We know it was Jewell who killed him. He wound up doing a life for it.

Tony My [brother] Chris and I were questioned about [Glasgow hardman] Jack Buggy as well. He floated up to the surface of the sea at Brighton, bound up in chicken wire, in 1967. Two coppers were off duty, fishing, and they pulled him out of there.

Fred (*Laughing*) And what's the odds on two coppers going out fishing and finding a body floating in the sea?

Tony Incredible. Well, one day in Gartree Prison, [Great Train Robber] Roy James said to me, 'Why did you and your brother do Jack Buggy?' I went, 'What are you on about?' By all accounts, Jack Buggy had control of Roy James's money, Fred, from the train.

Fred Oh, did he? I never knew Roy James, although people whose word I respect spoke very highly of him. He was nicknamed 'The Weasel'.

Tony See, what bothered him . . . did Jack Buggy get murdered over Roy James's money? I think it played on his mind.

Fred Oh, I see, yeah.

Tony That was what the problem was. He seemed very relieved when I told him we didn't have anything to do with the murder.

Fred Let me tell you something. Bobby Welch [another Great Train Robber] told me about this. Roy James shot his father-in-law, and he got twelve years.

Tony That's right, yeah.

Fred His father-in-law was nicking his money, because Roy had split from his wife and he couldn't see his kids. Then Roy had a heart attack or something and he went in hospital. He appreciated what they did for him so much. Then they asked him if he would come back and try a new treatment and medication for future patients who were suffering from this particular heart complaint. It was experimental. He felt obligated to them because they'd saved his life. He felt duty bound to go in and repay them.

Well, they gave him some treatment and OD'd him. Bobby Welch goes up to the hospital, and he's talking to him at the bedside. Roy said, 'They've fucking killed me, Bob. I'm dying.'

Bobby Welch went home and, shortly afterwards, he got a phone call from the hospital to say that Roy James was dead.

Tony Sad.

Fred And he was trying to pay back a favour, as we do in life.

7

Reggie and Ronnie:
A Personal View

Conversation in Fred's sitting room, 25 August 1998

Tony See, the twins . . . I mean, let me explain about the twins. They didn't like no one going over to see you, Fred.

Fred Nah. They were so jealous, possessive, weren't they?

Tony You was their man, and they wanted people in the East End to know that without coming to you, drinking in your pub. They discouraged that at all costs.

Fred Mmm.

Tony As you've said, you'd ask for someone like Albert Donoghue to come over if there was a bit of business or a meet. But people just didn't pay you social calls. We never went there.

Fred Only if *they* were there.

Tony Yeah, on a social evening, but you never encouraged it, either. Very rarely did we see you over in the East End, Fred.

Fred No, I never went over there much.

Tony Couple of times in the Carpenter's Arms . . .

Fred I went only when it was necessary.

Tony But I always got the impression they didn't want you to know too much of the other side of it, cos perhaps you would have frowned on it, see.

Fred I would've frowned on it. I never knew for a long time that Ronnie was gay and was, like, playing around with boys. I would've lost a lot of respect for him if I'd known the things he was getting up to.

It come as a fucking shock when I found out, quite late on. I thought he was a strange one when I went to one of their parties, in Commercial Road, and saw all these priests dancing around in their cassocks . . . Catholic priests, weren't they?

Tony Yeah, yeah.

Fred They were novices and they used the cassocks like skirts. And I thought, What's going on here? And, I mean, [Lord] Boothby, I saw him there.

Tony (*Laughter*)

Fred And, oh, I knew he was an old poof, and I figure, 'They'll only just use him. But I didn't realize that Ronnie was doing the things he was doing. And Charlie [Kray] would never say a word about 'em. He was their elder brother and he was covering up for 'em all the time.

It took so long for me to realize what Ronnie was doing. I suppose it must've been around '67 or '68. He come out the closet and told people that he was gay.

Tony They kept a lot from you, Fred.

Fred (*Sighing*) Yeah, they didn't want me to know.

Tony But if you had an upset over on your side, they would take care of that. They wouldn't be happy if it had been caused by anybody they knew.

Fred That was respect. When [Kray associate Jack 'The Hat'] McVitie performed up my casino . . .

Tony Woh, ho ho . . .

Fred . . . it caused murders.

Tony It caused murders. They weren't having that.

Fred I have to give 'em credit for the way they thought of me and looked after me. I had a business relationship with them but, at the same time, I knew 'em when they was young. I met them when they was about sixteen, and Charlie always spoke of 'em, and I knew them being round the house with their mother. Didn't old man Kray look like Reggie?

Tony Ringer. I went over there once not long before he died, and Charlie had had a row with him. I went upstairs to see the old man, and he was dying, and he went, 'Is that bastard down there?'

Fred Who was he talking about?

Tony Charlie!

Fred (*Laughter*) Anyway, the twins put bits of work my way, and they got the money, their whack out of it.

Tony See, a lot of firms would never do what you done. Even if someone on your firm wasn't on a certain bit of work, well, they was entitled to some payment.

Fred Yeah, they got their money. I mean, if people got nicked, I'd put them in their whack even though they wasn't there.

Tony Not many would do that. I mean, I got the impression from the twins – it was always put around, and I think they were very good at doing it – that their men would always be looked after. See, your people were looked after.

Fred Yeah.

Tony And the twins let it be known that if something happened, then they'd take that off of their people. But it didn't exactly work.

Fred It didn't work that way.

Tony You was expecting that if you happened to get nicked, you had 100 per cent backing off them. I think probably Charlie put it to them, 'Do it the way Fred does it.' But would they listen?

I mean, I never actually went to work for the twins. We had strong connections with them. My [brother] Chris and I, we had our own thing in Manchester and places like that. We used to go around the country taking money off of clubs, and it was important for us to be able to use the twins' name.

The motorways had just started to open up then, and it gave you an in to everywhere, so we were into heavier stuff as well. Robberies then were carrying, eight, ten years – a long time out of your life when you're young. So you're weighing up the odds all the time. It's like looking at the FTSE index – 'That's the going rate for that . . .' But being youngsters, we were game for anything. There weren't many places safe from us lot.

Talking about it today, I mean, twenty years is not uncommon. You go and rob a bank today, you're looking at fifteen to eighteen years. That's the going rate.

But the biggest-earning robberies we ever did were in London with the Scammells. In the early Sixties, they used to have these Scammell trucks about then, three-wheelers, handling parcel post. They was linked to the railways, and they would do runs round the City. At that particular time, all the money from the Mint, paper money, was moved in brown paper parcels – just wrapped up, put on Scammells and distributed round for wages, that type of stuff.

One accidentally fell off one of the Scammells one day in the City and it burst open. It was full of £5 notes, £10 notes. So the idea was to drive round the City, wait for one to pull up and as soon as he turns his back, get a few parcels off . . . They lost fortunes with it. Fortunes. We used to get forty grands, thirty grands, twenty grands.

So I had my own criminal career that was nothing to do with the twins' firm, though I saw a lot of them when I was in London.

I used to use 'The Dungeon'. Remember that Dungeon, the flat they had that they put John Pearson [author of *The Profession of Violence*] in?

Fred   Cos he was writing the book. Oh, that was round the back of Vallance Road [where the Kray family home was, in Bethnal Green].

Tony   That's right. Stuck him down this Dungeon. He lives in Greece now. He was very successful. The rights of that book were sold for the film, *The Krays*.

And we used to have parties down there. They used to go on all night long, and they had Pearson stuck in there. There were always booze-ups around the twins, and there were times that they'd turn violent.

I saw Ronnie cut a geezer one night – Johnny Wakefield. His nickname was Johnny Guitar. This happened in the Old Horns – Teddy Berry's pub in Bethnal Green. You remember, Fred, it was the HQ for a while?

Fred   Yeah, oh yeah.

Tony   And he was standing there, that Pearson, and his eyes nearly fell out of his head. Ronnie just walked up to Johnny Guitar and done him. He cut the geezer down the face with a glass for looking at him the wrong way.

Fred Is that all it was? For looking at him? There must've been more to it than that.

Tony No. It was just for looking at him. Then there was the night Ronnie done Johnny Cardew in a club in the West End. He was from a family of brothers, a boxing family, and he sent over some drinks for our company, 'including the fat one', which referred to Ronnie. He said to Cardew, 'I wanna see you in the toilet,' and left half his face on the floor.

Another one involved the Webb brothers.

Fred They was enemies, the Webbs and the Krays, weren't they? Going back a long time to when they was teenagers.

Tony Yeah, and Ronnie cut Billy Webb. Do you know what brought it out on top? They were in the Old Horns that night, and Billy Webb made a comment to Ronnie about him being 'nutted off' and being in a 'nuthouse'. Well, that's the wrong thing to say.

Fred Is that what he said?

Tony Yeah. I was there, Fred, when he said it.

Fred Oh, that's enough to get one down the boat.

Tony And Ronnie Kray and another member of the firm set about him. They cut him to pieces. I dragged him out the pub. Opposite the Old Horns there used to be an alley, and as I'm pulling him out, who walked in? Jimmy Nash.

They didn't half do Webb, Fred. He was standing at the bar and Ronnie just hit him with a glass – bang, straight in the face. And he was on him like he was a dog with a piece of meat. He went on the floor and there were people standing there in shock. Ronnie just went into one. Cos when he lost his temper, Fred . . .

Fred He had no control.

Tony You couldn't control him, and no one really tried to interfere with what was going on there. There was nothing you could do anyway. Billy Webb said the wrong thing at the wrong time.

Fred Well, it wasn't very tactful was it? Certain things you say to people, you press the wrong button, don't you?

Tony At that time, Ronnie was very hyped up . . . I mean, there was countless parties that we used to go to, but you could never really relax with Ronnie around (*laughing*).

He used to sit there with his brown ales! We was at a party in a flat one night, a crowd of us. And Ronnie put on 'Land of Hope and Glory', and there was all these birds trying to dance. Not the easiest song to boogie to! Ronnie was insisting, 'Leave it on!' and everybody ended up standing about, you know. The atmosphere, Fred . . .

Fred (*Laughing*) I'd say it's very stirring, that tune. Gets you up and running. It gets my blood up – I'll fight anyone. It's, 'Fix bayonets and over the top, boys!' Great music!

Tony Charlie and Reggie had a straightener that night, and Charlie wound up with a black eye. Remember they had the fight?

Fred No, I don't remember. They never used to tell me these things. They knew that I wouldn't like the idea of them fighting each other. It wasn't the right thing to do. It's not the right image to put out.

Tony Exactly.

Fred You want to keep solid and strong together, as a family, as any family. If people think you're fighting with each other, it shows weakness, doesn't it?

Tony That's right. But, I mean, they used to have some good parties. The crowds used to come in. There was a stage and a piano in the Old Horns. This woman used to be playing the piano – and she ended up being called to the Old Bailey to give evidence in our defence. One night, they had this poor bird knocking out East End tunes on this piano, and the more gins they gave her, Fred, the quicker the piano went.

Fred (*Laughing heartily*) Well, he was patriotic, you see. They didn't want the twins in the army, but he was British, Ronnie!

Tony And he liked his friends in the British establishment! During our trial, Kenneth Jones QC said, 'Let's talk about your underworld friends.' So Ronnie Kray went, 'No, we'll talk about my well-known friends,' and he brought up Boothby. What did Boothby do, Fred? The week before, he flew out to the Bahamas and married a young girl, didn't he?

Fred Oh, yes.

Tony It was a little kick, a delight, for Ronnie, having Boothby as a friend. But if them people wanna get around Ronnie Kray, then that's their problem. I don't think there was a great relationship there, Fred, do you?

Fred Nah.

Tony All we heard around the firm about Boothby was that he was an old queen. That was about it. But the firm were calling the twins Gert and Daisy. Never said it to their faces, though. *Cor!* (*Laughing*)

Fred Ronnie Kray kept Boothby right quiet. I'll say that for him.

Tony Right secret, yeah. He never expanded on it. He saw it as his private life, end of the matter.

Fred They had all sorts of friends in high places, like the MPs Tom Driberg and Manny Shinwell ... It was his son, Ernest Shinwell, who introduced the twins to members of the Nigerian government. They were looking for investors for a big building project, and they were promising a right return on the money.

Tony (*Laughing*) Nigeria, yeah.

Fred Ronnie went over there. They've got the mayor and the local dignitaries, and there's Ronnie, the big white hero coming in to invest money, build houses for the poor and all that ... he was taken on a tour of the fucking prison!

Tony True, that.

Fred He was going round looking at all the conditions. Charlie finished up in there afterwards.

Tony (*Laughing*) I remember it, cos Ronnie always spoke about it, and I recently seen a photo of him in Nigeria in the compound. They're not prisons like we got 'em. It's a military nick.

Fred   Yeah. Then Ronnie came back. Charlie and [the Krays' financial adviser] Leslie Payne went over there. One day Ronnie came over to my pub and said, 'They're in the nick.'

Tony   (*Still laughing*) Poor Charlie.

Fred   They was nicked for fraud, something to do with some money they bounced. Well, you can imagine with Payne [who later turned on the twins to become, arguably, 'the first genuine super-grass'], there was cheques bouncing every-fucking-where.

So now the twins have gotta raise thousands to get Charlie out. I forget how much it was. They had so much money and I said, 'I'll make up the rest of the balance,' which was about £5,000. Anyway, it did the trick and got them out the nick.

Tony   You know something? I used to meet Payne during the Seventies when they brought me down from Gartree to the control unit in Wormwood Scrubs.

Fred   I was in the visiting room one day and he was sitting down the end of the room. Next thing I know, there was about four screws came in, got hold of him, and escorted him out.

Tony   Straight out. He was the first one to crack on the Kray cases.

Fred   He was the first one to make a statement. He kicked it off.

Tony   You know, Fred, with Nigeria, I think the twins really wanted to be respected as businessmen and dignitaries, and that's why they kept all these MPs and lords around them, especially Ronnie.

It came up around that time about George Brown being friendly with Ronnie Kray. You know who George Brown was, don't you? He was the Foreign Secretary in 1968 in the Harold Wilson government. Then there was Reginald Maudling. The scandal about him was that he lost his office because of links to American money in New York, with the Mafia.

Fred   As it happens, Reggie Maudling was all right. Cos he was approached on my behalf. He was very sympathetic that they'd kept me on Cat A for nearly eight years.

Tony Well, I never knew that.

Fred But he couldn't do anything for me because I had just jumped on another prisoner named Johnny Barry who gave evidence against us in the trial.

Tony He was known as Caviar Reginald, wasn't he?

Fred Oh, yeah.

Tony He loved lunch at the Hilton Hotel in Park Lane. But he got linked up with the Mafia and he resigned over laundered money in New York. Of course, the twins were friendly with one or two from the Mafia.

Fred Well, Ronnie went to New York and met a few faces out there, and we met them when they came over to the Colony Club and the Pigalle. They were moving into these clubs, and they expected to pay their dues like they do in America. If you move into someone's patch, like they say in the books, they've gotta dip their beak.

Tony (*Laughing*) Dip their beak!

Fred They expected the same thing to happen here when they came over, but they didn't have to pay anybody anything, really. There was some money put up with them with bonds and that, a couple of touches, but I don't think there was a lot.

These clubs were not American-owned. Their interest was in the gambling. The twins were drawing the money out of them, and they cut the money up with me. The Americans run it, but we just drew out of it for the protection of the club. We didn't really do anything for the Mafia in that sense. Nothing at all. As long as the trouble-makers knew you was connected with the Krays, they kept away.

The Americans wanted no aggravation. It's worth X number of pounds a month to keep the wrong people out of the clubs. If there were people down there giving them trouble, you could go and say, 'You're not welcome, keep out,' and that's all they wanted off of you – to run a good, orderly place. They didn't want you there to do any villainy, they just wanted you to be a sort of protection, because Americans don't know who's who when they come here. It was just like paying a security firm.

Tony I met a few of the Mafia geezers. They were very nice, very respectable. We'd bring 'em to the East End, into the pubs. They've got nothing like this, have they?

Fred They love London. Frank Sinatra's minder was here, Eddie Pucci. I never met Sinatra personally.

Tony I once met his son when he was over here. He was a pianist. I didn't even know who he was, Fred.

Fred When I came out of doing that ten for McVitie, I saw Sinatra's show at the Palladium, and I was invited to go backstage to be introduced to him by my pal Alex Steene. He was a fight promoter and a ticket agent, and he was a well-connected man. I regret that I never went. I didn't want to be in that sort of environment. I didn't want crowds of people round me in the dressing room. You know when you come out the nick, you can't handle big crowds of people?

Tony Yeah.

Fred He was connected to the Mafia, Sinatra. Of course he was, although he had to deny it when he was alive.

Tony His whole history is linked to it, isn't it?

Fred I mean, we got introduced to all these famous entertainers and personalities, the twins especially. It's incredible, really. I wonder where the interest was in the twins, why they would be courted by people like Judy Garland? I think it was all a part of show business. As I always say, we all hit the headlines sometime or another. There's a very thin line between us and show business. But to have people from the Mafia wanting our help, that was a very big thing.

And the reputation of the Mafia is as massive today as it always was. That's because Hollywood's got a living for donkey's years out of this gangster thing, haven't they? And they're still churning it out.

Tony It'll still be going on and on when we're gone, Fred.

Fred When we're dead and buried.

Tony You've had a heavy day today.

Fred All-day session. But I've only had a little drop of brandy tonight.

Tony I noticed that. You've had a little bit of brandy there.

Fred That's all.

8

The Last Taboo:
The 'C' Word

Conversation in Fred's kitchen, 8 March 2000

Fred I did actually smack a woman once. She was in a pub in Bermondsey.

Tony Well, someone told me about that. She was out of turn, weren't she, Fred?

Fred Her husband was a friend of mine who did some building for me. And she was driving him fucking mad mentally, cos she was half alcoholic. She was a spitfire type of woman.

I took him and her to a party at the Dorchester in the Seventies. Barbara Windsor was there with her husband Ronnie Knight, and she was so rude to Barbara. Maureen was there, it was all family, we was having this nice evening, and this woman was drunk and abusive and insulting to everybody on the table. And I said to my pal, her old man, 'Just do me a favour. Take her home, for God's sake. She's drunk.'

Some time later, she drove her Mercedes car up Albany Road. Right outside where my niece Barbie lived, there was roadworks, and she's drove down the wrong side of the road, drunk again, where they'd been laying the tar down. She can't get out of it. She's fucking stuck down.

My Barbie and her husband ran out and tried to help her get the car out. She told them to mind their own business, slagged them off and was violent with it. They said, 'Well, fuck you, you get on with it,' and they went back indoors.

Well, of course, they're looking out the window. She's revving up the car, buried in all this tar and trying to get out of it.

The police arrive. Well, she's had a fight and she's broke a policewoman's wrist. She got nicked for that.

Next time I see her, I'm having a drink in the pub down in

Bermondsey. There's loads of people there, all the young crowd, all nice people, all out having a nice, sociable drink, and she's in the company with a dykey bird. She's driving everyone nutty, as usual.

I'm standing at the bar talking to the guvnor of the pub, Billy Tarrant. She comes over and she calls him a cunt.

Tony Bad word. Terrible word.

Fred For a woman to keep coming out with it . . . I said, 'Do you mind going and leaving us alone? We're having a conversation here.' I was really polite with her. She went away and then she come back again and she said, 'Not only is he a cunt, you're a cunt as well. You fucking cunt, who do you think you are?' and all this business. She said it a torrent of times. And before I knew it, I've give her a fucking backhander. I must admit to that. I'm not proud of it.

Tony She was totally, bang out of order.

Fred She got up off the floor and she come at me again and the dyke wants to fucking fight me, so what you gonna do?

Tony You're gonna have a row with them.

Fred They had glasses in their hands. They were gonna start aiming glasses. So I clipped her.

Tony That's enough.

Fred I've seen a drunken woman take a guy's eye out. And an old pal of mine, years ago, was stabbed in the back and died. His old woman done him through the back of a chair, through the wood and right into his back. She didn't mean to kill him but she had a wicked temper when drunk. You've got to treat them like a man when they cross the line and behave in that way.

Anyway, I said to her husband, 'Don't ever bring her in my company again, John, cos she's fucking trouble, and I don't want that, and what happened? The police came. So she screamed to the police. The witnesses in the pub told the coppers she fell off the stool, drunk, and hit her jaw on the foot rail.

Tony Backed you up.

Fred John came round to see me the next day. He said, 'What can I do with her?' Well, it wasn't my problem, it was his. I told him, 'You've gotta keep your fucking missus in order. If she's gonna carry on like that, she's gonna get hurt, badly.'

Tony   I've slapped a woman a couple of times for crossing that line.

Fred   It's not a nice thing to do.

Tony   It's a distasteful thing to do, but when someone calls you that word, even as a joke . . .

Fred   You can do it in fun – 'You're a cunt, you are.' That's different.

Tony   Yeah, but even in fun, I wouldn't do it, Fred.

Fred   People do get away with talking like that.

Tony   Well, it's not a nice thing to do.

Fred   It's a degrading word.

Tony   You know, I seen Reggie Kray go to cut a man one night in Bethnal Green. We was at a party. Reggie, Ronnie and their father was there, and Ray, their cousin. Remember their young cousin, Ray? Old Charlie's [their dad's] brother's son.

Fred   Oh, I don't remember.

Tony   Quite a few people were about, and in a corner, this geezer went, 'You're a cunt, Reg.' Now, Ronnie was standing there, Fred. This was what was dodgy about it. Had Ronnie not been there, possibly nothing would have been said.

Fred   He might have let it go.

Tony   But it was the word that got him. Next thing, Reggie's got hold of him and he's got the blade out and he's got it to his face. And something Micky Regan said to me a long, long time ago in prison – 'Never take a living off a man. Never do him on the face, cos it takes his living away,' which is true.

Reggie was gonna cut this guy. He was only about twenty. It took us about ten minutes to talk Reggie out of it. I think it was Harry Jewboy came over and he went, 'He's only a boy, Reggie (*very softly*).' You know how you had to talk to Reggie at that time, Fred. He'd just lost [his wife] Frances. Very touchy time for Reggie.

Fred Yeah.

Tony I'm just glad he never done it.

9

Jack The Hat:
Why He Had to Go

Conversation in Fred's kitchen, 4 August 1998

Tony You know that film *The Krays* – no way. *No way*. I was shocked when I saw it.

Fred It was a joke. The characters never came to life.

Tony I know five or six films loosely based on the twins. I've seen plays. Comedians make a living out of it – look at Hale and Pace.

Fred Sixty-odd books have been written and they've mentioned us in 'em one way or the other.

Tony Why? What was it so great that we did?

Fred Well, it's a bit of folklore, innit, now? It still sells.

Tony Big.

Fred It makes money and it fills the cinema and that's what the people like to see.

Tony There's a film on TV that I rate one of the best I ever saw on the underworld, *Goodfellas*. It's on tonight.

Fred It's on tonight, is it? What time?

Tony Ten o'clock.

Fred I like the *Goodfellas*.

Tony Everything about it was right.

Fred And *Casino* was very good, wasn't it?

Tony Yeah. It was a very good film. But, you see, people watching films like *The Krays* really believe we're like that.

Fred   The only one who played a good part was Tom Bell, who was Jack The Hat, but it was nothing like Jack, the real person. He's a good actor, Tom Bell, and he played the part to his best ability. This is how he perceived the character, but they've got it all wrong. He [Jack] wasn't that character at all. He was completely different to that.

Tony   Cos, you know, when I see that film, I see this pathetic, thin man. Jack was nothing like that. He was an 'andful. He was six foot two.

Fred   (*Laughing*) Six foot two, yeah.

Tony   He weighed about sixteen stone.

Fred   He could walk around on his hands, couldn't he? He'd do a handstand and he could walk from here out the passage, right out into the front room on his hands.

Tony   So when you see *The Krays* and you've got this little skinny man . . . it was geared that way to make you feel sorry for him.

Fred   He was a frightening bastard.

Tony   He was. Make no mistake. I saw him one night shoot a pub out. I was with Pa Flanagan, and Jack walked in this pub in Balls Pond Road, the Mildmay Tavern. The pubs then used to shut at half past ten, and it must have been about that time. He walked in and when the guvnor refused to serve him a drink, he pulled out this surplus revolver and he blew the bar out. It was a big service revolver, a big .45.

Fred   Army revolver.

Tony   He just pulled it out of his belt like that – 'You ain't gonna serve me a drink in here?' Bang! And two bullets went. One went through the bar and the other went in the ceiling. And Pa Flanagan turned round – 'Is he potty?' The five Flanagan brothers were very well known in the pub. Pa married Maureen Flanagan, who was the first Page Three girl.

Fred   The twins got Jack going to different places, doing things for them, and he was taking money off of them and he was letting them down. This all happened after he'd caused trouble in my place, the 211 Club. He was shooting up the Regency [club in Stoke

Newington], wasn't he? He had a shoot-out with Tommy Flanagan
– a different Flanagan, not one of the five brothers. He was a
Scotchman who later got nicked with Freddie Sewell when he shot
a copper. And him and Jack, they were shooting each other down
the bar like the OK Corral. You were there that night.

Tony   I was there. It was a Friday night. There was me, Reggie,
Albert Donoghue was there, Scotch Jack Dickson . . . They'd had
an argument, Tommy and Jack The Hat, and it stemmed back from
the days of the Moor [Dartmoor Prison]. Every time they saw each
other, there was a row. They started shouting and screaming, and
Jack pulled out this revolver in the Regency, Fred. They were
shooting up and down the stairwell. I dived out of the way. Right
out of the way. People were coming in and out of there, going
through the restaurant, diving for cover, and there's him, Jack, on
the stairwell. It was chaos. Then he ran out of bullets, I presume,
and they threw him out the club. Nobody got hurt that night.

But the facts of the matter was that he'd gone too far. When
he'd had a drink, Jack, he was capable of anything. I mean, he'd be
in a club, he'd pick up a phone and pretend to be talking to
somebody about the twins. He'd be saying, 'Who do those two
mugs think they are?' He wasn't actually talking to anybody. It was
his way of having a dig at the twins. And, of course, that got back.

One night at the Regency, he came in and he'd had a row with
some Greeks in north London. His hand was cut to pieces, and as
he walked in, there was me, Reggie was there, my Nicky was there,
Johnny Nash, One-Armed Lou – remember One-Armed Lou, Fred?

Fred   Yeah. I was going to rip his one arm off and hit him over
the head with it at Waterloo Station one day. He was waiting there
to go to the races and he was having a go at all the girls in the tea
bar.

Tony   So the lot of us were there in the Regency. It was on a
Tuesday night, and Jack came in there in a grey suit with a brown
trilby and the blood was going everywhere. And Johnny Nash and
Reggie said, 'You wanna go to hospital with that hand.' It was cut
badly. And there was women there. You know what it was like, it
was a well-known place, the Regency club at the time, and
everything was very easy-going. And I think Reggie always felt
sorry for Jack. I must say that. I don't know why.

And that was the end of that. Jack disappeared. The next time I see him was on the night he died.

Look, you see, I'm not gonna condemn Jack McVitie, cos he wasn't a grass, and as long as he played by that rule, that was fair enough for me.

If he was confronted with a problem, Jack was all sorry. He was all, 'I didn't mean it.'

Fred   He was a soldier sort of thing. If there was a row, he would play his part, wouldn't he?

Tony   He did. He did. But, I mean, I'd been in his company on two or three occasions where he'd misbehaved.

Once in the Tempo club in Holloway in north London. What a lovely place it was, Fred, a snooker hall, down in the Holloway Road, you know where it is?

Fred   Yeah, yeah.

Tony   It was well known. Friday night, the chaps used to be out, that was their night out, and there was a lot of firms used to use it. We'd go out there for a laugh.

I went in there one night with a few of the boys, and who's performing on the stage is Dorothy Squires. Sitting to the right of her is her husband Roger Moore, who was famous around that time for *Ivanhoe* and *The Saint*, the TV series.

Freddie Bird, an ex-docker who was looking after the Tempo, came over to me and he went, 'Look, I had to go and have a talk with Jack, told him to quieten down, cos he was getting a bit loud.'

There was Jack, he'd got himself in a state, he gets on the floor and there's Dorothy singing and he drops his trousers and starts the moving. And he always had this habit of wearing these candy-coloured shorts . . . Fred, when I look at them shorts you've got on tonight (*laughing*), it brings it back to me. It was a regular thing with him, once he had a drink and a pill.

Fred   He was on Dexedrines.

Tony   Oh, he loved pills. He loved them.

Fred   He had a little scam going with some fucking chemist or pharmacy where he had these 5,000 pills in a carton, in a can, you know, and he'd be popping them like sweets. It made him an aggressive bastard. I mean, that was doing his brain in, wasn't it, and he was on them all the time.

Tony   All the time.

Fred   It's just speed, isn't it?

Tony   And all of a sudden, Dorothy Squires started burbling. She was legless. She always had a bottle of Scotch, and she was swigging from it. She really went into one over nothing at all.

Fred   She can verbal.

Tony   And she can. I'll tell you what, the language (*laughing*). If I told you what she was coming out with.

Fred   She knew how to swear.

Tony   She knew. Anyway, he shouted some obscenity over to her, Jack. And he's dropped 'em and Freddie Bird wants to have a fight with him.

Now I said, 'Fred, do me a favour. Supposing he's got a shooter on him,' cos that's the way he was. He was with Jimmy Briggs and Patsy Murphy, and Patsy came up to me and he went, 'Look, he's had a drink tonight, you know what he's like.' I went, 'Never mind what he's like, it's nothing to do with me, really.' I'm middled up here, now. I'm right middled up. Because Freddie Bird weren't a bad geezer.

All the firms were sitting there, and there was a couple of Scotch boys come down from Scotland with suits on, bow-ties and that.

Fred   (*Laughing*) If they've got bow-ties on, you've gotta watch them, you know.

Tony   In the end, there was a bit of a scuffle on the floor with Jack and Freddie Bird, but Jack didn't have to be thrown out. He was told to go, and he just faded off the scene.

You know, Fred, it was well known he'd upset you at the 211 Club. He'd gone up there and caused trouble, and he was told to behave himself. 'Don't do it over there.' You know, 'Leave it well out.'

Fred   Yeah, the 211. That was in Balham High Road. It's the Polish Embassy now.

Tony   (*Hearty laughter*)

Fred   It was Lady Hamilton's house, you know, and when I first went in there, the handrail was all carved like a ship's rope, going up the big staircase. It was a lovely place. Great big ballroom, which served as the main club area, and then three drinking bars. I had a big pool room at the back with six tables in it, French windows and a bowling green out at the back. We put a suspended stage over the French windows, and a spiral staircase. The band used to sit up on this high-rise stage.

I put a boxing ring in and I had, like, two or three thousand people in there. It was a massive place, with a big forecourt in front. And I had a casino upstairs which was totally legal. It used to be mobbed up there. There was a crap table and American and French roulette, blackjack tables and the full works. It was very well laid out.

George Raft, the film star, came and opened it for us.

What happened was, I was downstairs in the bar when someone comes and says, 'Some people are performing on the crap table up there, Fred. A fella's just pulled a knife on the croupier.' So I said, 'Oh, all right, I'll be up.'

I went up straight away and I looked, and it's busy in there. Bobby Neill, who was British lightweight champion, was sitting with his wife at a table, and as I walked in, he went, 'Fred, some guy's just thrown this under our table.' It was a big knife. So I said, 'All right, keep it there, Bob, keep hold of it.'

I looked round the tables. A pal of mine, Terry, was up there, and also Mungo Jerry – Jerry Swain – with a few others, and who else? Jack The Hat. The table was packed.

I said, 'Who's causing the trouble?' The croupiers said, 'Him, there, throwing the dice now. He pulled a knife on one of us.' So I go up behind Jack and he knows I'm there. I said, 'Hello, you misbehaving again, Jack? You're always causing fucking trouble.'

I said, 'Listen, come outside, I wanna have a talk with you.'

So he said, 'What, and get a fucking bullet in the head?'

I said, 'Never mind about all that. I'll tell you what I'll do. I'm going downstairs and I'm gonna have a drink and I'll give you five minutes. And when I come up I wanna see you fucking gone.'

Apparently there was a couple of faces there with him who said,

'Oh, we'll back you, Jack, we'll make one with you, we'll mind your back.'

Terry knew the strength of me and he said to Jack, 'If I were you, I'd head straight for that fucking door and get out of here fast.'

Tony Get out of it, yeah. I mean, the thought of him going against you was bad news.

Fred I went downstairs, had a drink and when I came back, he'd gone. They'd all gone. If they hadn't, I'd have fucking served him up there and then. I'd have come up a few-handed, two or three people on the firm. I'd have took him out forcibly into the car park and then we would have really served him up. He would have been raspberried up. He would have been a permanent hospital case. He wouldn't have just been walking away.

Cos I'd already done it with other people up there. I told you about that night when the geezers smashed the girl's jaw.

Tony Not many East Enders went over to your place. The twins always said it – 'Don't go over and misbehave, because you'll have a problem. It's Fred's manor.'

Fred They were welcome if they behaved themselves. We were there to take money and serve people.

Tony There were certain rules.

Fred If they behaved, they got looked after. So, anyway, I said to Ronnie Kray, 'That fucking Jack's been over here, performing.'

Tony Which caused a lot of bad feeling towards Jack.

Fred And I said, 'When you see him, tell him not to come over here again or he'll get served up and that's the end of it.' So he never came near me no more. That was it. That's my bad experience of him. And that was months and months before anything happened to Jack.

Tony Jack had took a liberty with you in your club. They took it upon themselves to put that wrong right, in a way . . . or several wrongs.

Fred Several, yeah. It wasn't just down to me, was it?

Tony No, no. But they saw it as an insult to you.

Fred I mean, he was up there in the Regency shooting at people and cutting people up there and everything, wasn't he? And there was so many things that he was doing wrong he was embarrassing them, cos he wouldn't take no notice of what they said. I mean, they've got to have a bit of respect. The man's got to do as he's told. But he disregarded everything they said. He was undermining them, he was making them a fucking laughing stock, so they had to act, and the only way to hold credibility was to fucking do him.

He came up to me once, months before the 211 incident, when I was down the Stork club and he said, 'We're six-handed, we're gonna go and do the twins with a machine-gun. We've all got machine-guns and we're fucking gonna run 'em over when they come out of the house [in Vallance Road].' I said, 'What are you telling me things like that for?' But this is the way he was going on, so I told the twins.

I said, 'You've gotta watch that Jack. What's going on in his head? He's got a can of worms in his head. He wants to bloody well iron you out and he's talking about shooting you and God knows what.'

Later someone tried to run Ronnie over on the pavement outside their house. So they had to strengthen their security.

Tony Hence we called their house Fort Vallance.

Fred He had a few people around him, Jack, didn't he? He had his own little firm.

Tony Yeah, he had his own crew.

Fred I don't know why the twins didn't do something about it then. They went, 'Oh, he talks like that in drink.' They took no notice.

Tony The ironic thing about it is, on the Friday, the night before Reggie killed him, me, Reggie, Albert Donoghue and Chris sat down and had a meal with Jack The Hat in the Regency, a Chinese meal, and as true as I sit here, Reggie gave him fifty quid.

Fred Fifty quid then was quite a bit of money. A couple of hundred quid by today's standards.

Tony   We left him that night, Jack, and everything was sweet as a nut. I think he was pleased – he thought he'd straightened it out.

Fred   What made Reggie do it, then?

Tony   I can go back to that night, Fred . . .

10

Dead and Buried

Conversation in Fred's kitchen, 7 February 2000

Jack 'The Hat' McVitie was knifed to death at a party in Stoke Newington by Reggie Kray, who had earlier made an abortive attempt to shoot him. McVitie was taken to the party at 'Blonde Carol' Skinner's basement flat in Evering Road by Tony and Chris Lambrianou.

The Lambrianous and Ronnie Bender drove the body to south London and dumped it by a church, where it was recovered by Freddie Foreman.

There were no immediate arrests but a police team led by Chief Superintendent Leonard 'Nipper' Read was doggedly investigating the Kray firm over the suspected murders of McVitie and Frank Mitchell, whose bodies were never found, and that of George Cornell, a killing which did not involve either Tony Lambrianou or Freddie Foreman.

Nipper finally brought the cases to court by persuading various witnesses and firm members to give evidence for the prosecution. The Cornell and McVitie trials were held together. Some defendants were not involved in both, although they remained in the dock throughout. The Mitchell case was heard afterwards.

At the Old Bailey on 5 March 1969, Tony and Chris Lambrianou were sentenced to life imprisonment, with a recommendation that they serve at least fifteen years, for the murder of Jack 'The Hat' McVitie. Reggie Kray got life with a thirty-year recommendation for the murder, as did Ronnie, who was also found guilty of killing George Cornell. Reggie received a concurrent ten years for being an accessory to the Cornell murder.

Ronnie Bender and Ian Barrie got life and a twenty-year recommendation for McVitie and Cornell respectively. Freddie Foreman and Charlie Kray received ten-year sentences for being accessories to the McVitie murder. Connie Whitehead got off more lightly, with seven years for the same offence, and Albert Donoghue, the only man to plead guilty, was sent down for two years as an accessory to the murder of McVitie. Tony Barry was found not guilty of the McVitie murder and discharged.

28 OCTOBER 1967: COUNTDOWN TO A KILLING

Tony You see, it came about this way. Chris and I went to a pub called the White Bear in Aldgate to meet the Mills brothers out of west London. They had a very good name at the time. I'd met Alan Mills in Bristol Prison and my brother knew Ray Mills. They wanted to see the twins, cos Ray Mills was very pally with Roy ['Pretty Boy'] Shaw – you know, he was doing a fifteen then in Broadmoor, over that robbery in Kent. And Roy had some business with the twins.

We took the Mills brothers to see Ronnie and Reggie in [their own Bethnal Green pub] the Carpenter's Arms. They had their family round them, and a lot of the firm were there too. When we left, the twins were as sweet as a nut. Reggie was with a girlfriend called Carol Thompson, and Ronnie was going home. As far as I was concerned, that was the last we'd see of them that night.

We took the Mills brothers on to the Regency, where we met up with my Nicky, my young brother. And who walked in? Jack The Hat. His usual, boisterous self. About a half hour later, Tony Barry [who ran the club with his brother, Johnny] walked out of the office and he says to me, 'Reggie's here.' I was surprised because I'd just left him, and he hadn't told me he was coming. I go into the office and Reggie said, 'Who's downstairs?' He wanted to have a go at Jack in the Regency club, but he changed his mind when I told him there were women there.

Then he asked me to bring Jack The Hat to a party at Blonde Carol's. I knew there was a chance that Reggie might give Jack a right-hander, but I never thought it was too serious, Fred, because you don't do anything heavy in front of a load of people, do you? So I never even mentioned it to Chris or the Mills brothers. I just told them there was a party at Blonde Carol's and we were taking Jack.

Fred I don't suppose you knew that Tony Barry gave Reggie a gun to shoot Jack?

Tony I never knew who gave him the gun. Now, the whole crux of the case against me and Chris was that we knew there was going to be a murder. But, I mean, if we know that, do we take the Mills brothers – two witnesses?

Fred   To see Jack get fucking murdered? Nah.

Tony   You don't do that. I'm sorry, it doesn't wash. Albert Donoghue says in his book [*The Krays' Lieutenant*], and I'm reading from it here, that Jack The Hat would never have gone to the party 'if they had sent a member of the firm to get him ... the Lambrianous could not foresee what was coming because they had no idea then of the twins' manipulative mentality. Chrissy and Tony were gofers, boys. They were sent to the Regency because they weren't on the firm. They were just the right level, well enough connected to invite someone to the party, but not senior enough to frighten him . . .'

Fred   Now, that's important.

Tony   Well, yes. We were used.

Fred   You took Jack along not knowing what the end result would be, so you're not involved in premeditated murder. Well, if Donoghue had said that at the trial, that would've dug you out of a hole.

Tony   Thank you very much.

Fred   But he wasn't giving evidence in this trial. He wasn't called, cos he'd put his hands up for two years as an accessory to the McVitie murder, and he couldn't sit in the dock with us cos he's giving evidence [for the prosecution] in the trial after that, which is the [Frank] Mitchell case. Which nobody knows about cos they haven't issued any papers on that. They haven't charged anyone yet.
   The other thing is that if Reggie said in front of you in the Regency club that he was 'gonna do Jack', that doesn't mean he was gonna kill the man.

Tony   He never said that, Fred.

Fred   Well, this is in evidence. It's what they reported that he said.

Tony   He never said it.

Fred   Reggie's supposed to have said he was gonna do Jack 'because he's a cunt'. Well, he might have said it to somebody. But if you say you're gonna do a person, it can mean you're gonna hurt him or beat him up. Maybe it'll be a serious injury, but it doesn't necessarily mean that you're gonna fucking murder someone, does it? Cos they'd already shot a few people in the legs and, you know, hurt them in different ways.

They did Nobby Clarke. He was a pal of mine, and I didn't like the idea of him getting shot – I don't know what he did to deserve that. He was a loyal member of their firm. But, see, that was a shooting in the leg. So if he did give Reggie the gun, Tony Barry, he probably thought he was just going to wound Jack.

Tony Reggie shot Donoghue in the leg, which is a very important fact, because he was one of the ones who rolled over. I wanna say it – if I shot someone in the leg, I am never gonna trust that man again in my life.

But he does make some fair points in his book. He says, 'The only thing Jack really did wrong was to go to the party, as he knew just how kill-crazy Reggie was . . . He knew what the twins were capable of. He also knew it could happen any time.' Reggie was in a terrible state.

Fred He had a bit of a death wish in those days because of what had happened to his wife, but how can you call him 'Kill-crazy' when he hadn't killed anyone at that point?

Tony He become extremely dangerous to himself.

Fred He did, yeah.

Tony Cos he was never sure, Reggie. He had that way of biting his lip. Wherever he went, people were frightened. You must know what was going on.

Fred I know about it, yeah.

Tony It had got to that state of affairs.

KILLING JACK

Fred Who was in the room when it happened?

Tony The first person we see is Ronnie Kray. He's got a drink in his hand, and a fag, as usual. Reggie's there too, and Ronnie Hart [distant cousin of the Krays], and there was these two young boys, Terry and Trevor, dancing. They were friends of Ronnie's. Ronnie

Bender and Connie Whitehead were both around later, but I didn't see either of them when we arrived – Jack The Hat, me, Chris and the Mills brothers. As we walked in the room, Ronnie looked up, picked up a glass, walked over to Jack McVitie and with a quick one . . .

Fred   Smashed him.

Tony   Cut him underneath the eye.

Fred   It says in reports that it was his lip.

Tony   No, it was under the eye, Fred. I'll never forget it. Then Ronnie went, 'Now, fuck off, you cunt,' and turned away.

Fred   And then, I've heard, he takes his jacket off, Jack, and he's shaping up to them to have a fight.

Tony   That's right. That's when he walked over and punched the window out. He went, 'Who the fucking hell do they think they are?' and he went to walk out. There was nothing stopping him. And if he had've left, end of game.

Fred   The killing wouldn't have happened. If he'd have been in his right mind, he'd have fucked off when he had the chance.

Tony   But he came back in, and next thing, Reggie's got a gun out. They all start whacking into Jack, including the young fellas, and then Reggie jumped up, put the gun to Jack's head and pulled the trigger.

Fred   And nothing happened.

Tony   I jumped back, waiting for the explosion. And it went *click*. Then he sat down on the sofa, Jack, and he started moaning about it – 'What have I done?' Then Reggie jumped back with the gun and it went *click* again. Reggie went to Hart, 'He gave me a duff 'un.' And I'm convinced there were no bullets in it.

Now, Ronnie's supposed to have been winding Reg up – 'I've done mine, you do yours!' That was never said.

Fred   Course not. Can you imagine Ronnie saying that? It's ridiculous.

Tony   So Chris has gone out and he's sitting on the stairs. It's been said that he was crying. He wasn't crying, he was just, 'What the fuck's Jack done?' We didn't know what was going on. We had an argument between ourselves. Reggie came out and Chris told him he thought it was a fucking liberty bringing him over into this.

Really, logically, the twins don't have to do a thing now. They could've walked out the flat, because *we've* gotta fucking do Jack. We set him up, even though we didn't know that's what we was doing. Help me out, Fred, you know what I'm saying here?

Fred If the twins are not gonna kill him, if they let Jack go, he's gonna come after you.

Tony Of course he is. We're the guilty parties.

Fred So that's what Chris is worried about, cos Jack's a right nut-nut.

Tony Jack's a nut-nut, thank you.

Fred And he's capable of anything.

Tony So I said to Chris, 'Go and get one of ours [guns].' To finish him off. We can't let him go, Fred. And Chris was capable of shooting him.

Chris and Connie Whitehead had gone to get the shooter when the knife appears on the scene. Someone brought Reggie a knife out of the kitchen. I've heard it was Hart, although I didn't see what was happening in the kitchen. I saw the first one go in, and then I looked away.

By the time Chris comes back with the gun, Reggie's stabbed Jack to death and the twins and Hart had gone. I mean, the whole thing was a cock-up, Fred.

Fred I wouldn't have allowed it to happen if I'd been there. I would've said, 'Now, look, this is ridiculous. You're going to get fucking nicked here.' You can't kill someone in front of all them people, can you?

They didn't do it like a proper business transaction, where you go, 'Well, we're gonna do this,' no witnesses around, and they find him in the fucking alleyway or on a bomb site with one in the nut. They've gotta do it in a fucking party with a roomful of people. How can you expect to get away with it? You can't.

Tony Well, they did, Fred.

Fred They did for two years. The only reason was because I fucking cleaned it up.

They didn't really intend doing him that night, did they? It was a fuck-up, weren't it? It wasn't premeditated.

Tony Never in a million years.

Fred It was a party and a row that went wrong. How long was they arguing?

Tony The glass, the window, the gun, the arguments in the room and on the stairs, the screaming and shouting . . . it went on for fifteen, twenty minutes.

Fred They [the books] are making it look that it all happened in a matter of seconds. So that's even more proof that it wasn't premeditated. You don't sit down arguing with someone if you're going to kill them.

CLEANING UP AND CLEARING OUT

Tony I mean, they've done him, and the next thing was, 'Fucking get rid of that.'

Fred And they [the twins] just walked out and left it.

Tony Walked out the fucking door, Fred. And I'm standing there, implicated up to my bollocks, excuse the language. There I am, me and my brother and Bender, stuck with a body. What are you supposed to do, Fred?

Fred You gotta clean up the fucking flat.

Tony Clean up the flat and get Jack out. No one wanted to get involved in it because it wasn't a very nice sight, let's be fair. I was gonna go and get a gallon of petrol and just burn the lot down. That was my intention. A fire. All over. You know, just pick the pieces out of that. It would've been the logical thing to do.

Fred To leave him in there. And they wouldn't have found the stab wounds or anything, you know.

Tony But I looked up the stairs, Fred, and I saw two young kids looking down at me, and they were crying.

Fred No, you can't. You can't burn it down with two little kids in there. No. And there was other people in the house.

Tony I wasn't aware of that until the trial. I never saw Carol Skinner or whatsisname, the geezer who was with her, Georgie Plummer. She said, and I have no reason to disbelieve it, that she saw my brother with a pair of socks on his hands, which is correct.

Fred Yeah.

Tony She saw Ronnie Bender moving about. That's true.

Fred They were carrying bowls of water.

Tony Bowls of water, up and down the stairs, clearing up the flat, the mess. So we're stood in the passage with a body there. We're talking about half past twelve on a Saturday night, while people are still around, there were people in a bakery across the road, and we gotta carry him out.

Fred And put him in his car.

Tony We get him upstairs, wrapped in a candlewick bedspread.

Fred Cleaning tabs on it and everything, so if they find it, it's back on the address in a matter of days.

Tony This is this so-called premeditated, gangland fucking murder we're talking about . . . this load of crap here. I mean, it was easy for them to say, 'Oh, just get rid of him.' They'd gone. They was away.

Fred And he'd cut his hand, hadn't he, Reggie?

Tony Where he grabbed the blade. Now, I think Ronnie might've said something about a train, to throw Jack under a train or something.

Fred He's supposed to have said that you should throw him over the wall at the railway in Cazenove Road.

Tony I don't think he mentioned Cazenove Road. But, anyway, I tried to get Jack in the boot first. Couldn't get him in the boot.

Fred Because the fucking boot was full up with rubbish.

Tony So in the end, I had to sort of try to jam him in between the front and back seats on the floor and throw the candlewick over him.

Fred I couldn't make that out. I thought to myself, Why have they got him in the back when they've got a nice big boot on a Zephyr?

Tony A Mark II Zephyr, two-tone.

Fred With one headlamp smashed to fuck, no wipers, rear light fucking missing.

Tony No indicators . . . So we pull the car round and none of us wants to drive it away, Fred. There's an argument now. My brother wouldn't want to do it. Bender ain't gonna do it.

Fred So you drove it. You're taking all the chances.

Tony Yeah.

Fred Are you on your own?

Tony I'm on my own with him [Jack] in the motor, and my brother and Ronnie Bender are following me up in Chris's blue Corsair. But Chris had a shooter on him, and if he gets a stop or I get a stop, it's gotta make a difference.

Fred Well, you've gotta explain that away.

Tony And I said to Chris, 'If we get a stop, you'll have to do 'em.' So I come out of Evering Road, there was hardly any juice in the motor, I haven't got a clue where I'm going. It's panic stations now.

Fred Of course.

Tony And I end up at the Blackwall Tunnel.

Fred Rotherhithe Tunnel.

Tony Blackwall, Fred.

Fred Rotherhithe. It was just up from Rotherhithe Tunnel.

Tony No, Blackwall, cos I'll tell you what – as you come out the tunnel, I came round the roundabout and I happened to see a church on the right-hand side of the road. There's been a wedding that day; there was confetti all over the ground. I parked it down the side of the church.

Fred Well, that's Rotherhithe. Not Blackwall. Another East End face gets his tunnels mixed up! I wouldn't have found it if it was at Blackwall Tunnel.

I wouldn't have even fucking bothered. You'll find it's the Rotherhithe. You will.

Tony Is it? You're right, yeah.

Fred So it *was* the Rotherhithe Tunnel; we got that straight.

Tony A police car happened to be coming along the other side, in the tunnel, about two thirds down. Well, he's looked at me coming through that tunnel.

Fred What time of the morning's this?

Tony Two o'clock.

Fred And you've got one light not working..

Tony They couldn't stop there, I suppose. I put my foot down and got out of it. But it panicked me a little bit, seeing the law coming towards me.

Fred (*Laughing*) With a stiff in the back, it would panic you, wouldn't it, to see that coming towards you. I wasn't too happy driving it myself, I'll tell you. But why fucking drive it all the way through the tunnel to south London when you could take it up the road and dump it round the back of an alleyway? What the fucking hell did you drop it over south London for, right on my fucking doorstep?

Tony I don't know why. That was never the intention.

Fred You took a terrible liberty driving all that way.

Tony I know, thinking now. You don't think of that at the time. Ask me a million questions about it, I couldn't answer.

Fred You went a long way off the manor (*laughing*), far enough from fucking Hackney.

Tony I mean, you saw it – it was a complete fuck-up, the motor. All I wanted to do was get rid of it. I pulled away from my brother and Ronnie Bender after passing the police car.

Fred So they wasn't with you? They was a lot of help to you if they didn't keep on your fucking tail.

Tony I put my foot down and went, rather than hang about. I just wanted to get out of that motor.

Fred Of course, now that explains why you dumped the motor so quick near the tunnel. If you go past the Old Bill, you wanna get out of it quick. Where did Chris and Bender pick you up after you dumped the car?

Tony I walked back up to the roundabout and they were driving round looking for me.

Fred So you locked it up and left it. I don't know what you done with the keys – did you throw them or something?

Tony Threw them in the Regent's Canal, yeah.

Fred What happened next?

Tony So we dropped Ronnie Bender down at Hackney Road and we go home to Queensbridge Road. And I remember sitting there with Chris that night, Fred, and I said to him, 'What the fucking hell happened?' We don't know what it's about, but we're up our to necks in it, whether we like it or not.

Fred Yeah. And you don't even know the reasons why.

Tony Not a reason, up to this day. Now, we know it to be true that after we dropped Ronnie Bender off, he went to Harry Hopwood's flat round the back of Hackney Road, where he found the twins and Ronnie Hart. Hopwood was washing the cut on Reggie's hand, apparently. And Ronnie Bender bounces in there and he says, 'I've got rid of that.' He did not at any time say that me and Chris was with him when he dumped the body.

Fred He's taken the credit for it.

Tony And Ronnie Kray went, 'Oh yeah, where?' Bender says, 'Over south London by the tunnel,' and then Ronnie hit the roof.

Fred Ronnie screams, 'I gotta tell Fred!' (*Laughing*) But why tell me? I'm in fucking bed, why do I wanna know what's happening? I don't want him [Jack]. He might be on my doorstep down the road, but why the fucking hell do I need to know that?

Tony Cos Ronnie thinks in his mind that you're gonna get the blame for it.

Fred If they find it, ain't got to be down to me, has it?

Tony It's nothing to do with you. And if Ronnie Bender had not gone to Hopwood's flat, you wouldn't have been involved in it.

Fred I wouldn't have been involved. Jack would've been found within a few hours. You could see him laying by the fucking back seat.

Tony So from Hopwood's flat, they sent Ronnie Bender round to Charlie Kray's.

Fred Charlie was out late that night, and Bender told Dolly [Charlie's first wife] all about it, which he shouldn't have done. I mean, you wouldn't want to go and tell someone's wife what's fucking happened, would you?

Tony I never told my [first] wife, Pat. Not a word.

Fred Maureen never knew about anything. Why worry them, why put them through it? My wife never knew anything of what went on. She guessed a lot.

Tony They can guess what they want . . .

Fred As long as they don't hear you say it. So anyway, Dolly calls in Tommy Cowley for help and when Charlie gets back, he and Tommy send Bender away and talk it over. Charlie went to Hopwood's flat, and he bollocked the life out of the twins for being so stupid, killing somebody in front of a roomful of witnesses – 'I'm finished with you, I don't want nothing to do with you' – and fucked off home to bed. And that's what happened, didn't it? And he got ten years for that.

Tony Meanwhile I go home to Pat, and Chris had to go down to Euston and pick up a bird of his who come down from Stoke. She was nicknamed 'The Squirrel'.

Fred He met her at the station, didn't he?

Tony She was waiting there.

Fred So now it's four o'clock in the morning.

Tony Yeah, yeah. She'd been phoning up and no one's there. He gets her and they go back to Blonde Carol's cos Chris wanted to have a look at what was going on. The Squirrel stayed outside while Chris went in. Carol was there, and so were Georgie Plummer, Hart's bird, Blonde Vicky, and Connie Whitehead. They were still cleaning and scrubbing.

Next day, I believe, Ronnie Bender took out the carpet and had it burnt by a scrapyard dealer he knew in Poplar.

Fred Listen, was Albert Donoghue involved in it?

Tony Apparently he came over the next day as well to redecorate the flat.

Fred So what happened with Chris's car, then?

Tony The Corsair? It disappeared. We got rid of it, me and Chris. It was cubed.

Fred Oh, you did it yourselves.

Tony Fred, let me ask you something. Did you ever know we was involved?

Fred No. I didn't know who'd brought Jack over. They said he'd been left there, but nobody mentioned any names.

Tony Did you know we were there at all that night? Did the twins ever tell you?

Fred They said a couple of the firm were in the room. I was told it was a party. I thought, Well, if there's only a couple of the firm in the room who know about this, then it can be contained. They won't incriminate themselves. They're not gonna put themselves in it by talking about it unless they want to go up for fucking murder. So, I thought, It's safe. But if I'd have known that there was two young kids in the room dancing, there were women and children on the stairs or that they'd moved the whole party across the road . . .

Tony I never knew that!

Fred Kitty Collins had a party, so they moved Carol's party across the road to there so the twins could have her flat for their own party. They emptied the flat out. So they must have all being saying, 'What the fuck? Why did that happen?'

Tony What did I know about all this? I knew nothing. The first time I knew anything about you being involved was when I saw you in the dock at Bow Street. I've got to say this in the twins' defence – never once did they mention your name.

Fred That was kept very quiet. They didn't know much themselves. All they know is that it [the body] is not there any more.

Tony I knew nothing of what happened in that flat, with Hopwood and Bender and Hart and what happened in between. I pick up the papers the next day expecting to see a body found, but, Monday, nothing on the news, Tuesday, again, nothing. I don't know what's happened. 'Fucking hell, he's disappeared!'

Fred Now you feel better, don't you?

Tony Feel better, Fred? I'm clicking my heels, thank you very much. I'm thinking to myself, Fucking hell, did it happen?

Fred 'Was it a bad dream?'

Tony My brother's going to me, 'Shall we go and have a look?' Then rumours started going about that he [Jack] been killed in a car smash, that he'd been done or whatever.

Fred But after a year, you've gotta feel a lot easier then, safe as houses.

Tony Yeah, I did, but you're still wondering . . . certainly I was worried about it. I'm still up to my neck in it.
    The twins went away somewhere for a week. They called a meet on the following Monday night. I didn't want to go, but if we hadn't turned up, we would've been making ourselves look guilty of something, which we weren't. Chris was in Birmingham by then, and he came down for this meet in the Carpenter's Arms.
    Ray and Alan Mills were there, cos the twins had to straighten

it out with them. And I think Chris said, 'What was it about [Jack]? Was he a grass, was he a fucking wrong 'un?'

Reggie said, 'He was just a fucking nuisance.'

Fred According to Chris, Reggie also said that 'it was just unfortunate that it happened like that'. Well, that says it again, doesn't it, that it wasn't premeditated. But Jack *was* a nuisance.

Tony Well, we know that.

Fred He was a hair's breadth away from killing some poor bastard.

ENTER FRED

Fred Now I've got this little ginger bastard, Tommy Cowley, ringing my doorbell, getting me out of bed at fucking three o'clock in the morning to tell me about Jack The Hat.

There was two cars brought over. One was Ronnie Bender's Mini, which they left behind. They needed the other car to go back in.

It was bloodstained, the Mini. The twins and Hart left the murder scene in it, and Reggie's hand was cut, so it was bleeding in the Mini. The reason they brought it to my pub was to have it washed and cleaned. Why can't they wash a fucking Mini out themselves? Why bring it over and dump it outside my pub? Anyway, it was Reggie's own blood in it. It wasn't gonna be anybody else's, Jack's, you know. It was perfectly all right. It was out on the road, driving, about two days later.

Tony Yes, that's right, it was.

Fred But I don't know who was driving the second car. I didn't see anybody other than Cowley. So, now, I ain't gonna go out at three in the morning and start looking round for fucking bodies. I waited till early morning when it's still dark, just before breaking daylight. About six o'clock, I start to move. It's pissing down, and I thought, Well, that's handy, it's raining.

Cowley told me it had been left outside a church. My old pal Alf [Gerrard] was tailing me up. It took me a while, cos there's plenty of churches in the area. But I reckoned they'd want to dump it as quick as possible after they come through the tunnel, and I just drove around until I found it. I can't remember the name of the street. You're right about the wedding – there was all confetti on the floor. Anyway, I looked in and Jack was just laying there, all curled up, in a candlewick bedspread. You can see it's a body by the shape of it, and I thought, Oh, that's fucking nice.

Tony If you hadn't have turned up when you did, it gets found.

Fred Oh, yeah, because there's people moving about, walking down the road.

Tony Going to church and that. It was a Sunday morning.

Fred Luckily, they had their heads down cos it was raining. Anyway, I tried to get in the car and it's locked. They had a little side window in those days. Just one screwdriver, put it in, lift the catch up and you're in, ain't you? It was easy. And I had a set of twelves with me. So I just went through the keys and found the right one. It didn't take long. Then I started it up with a little bit of difficulty.

Tony It was a wreck, wasn't it?

Fred Oh, it was a wreck of a motor. So anyway, I got it started, and the windscreen wipers wouldn't work.

Tony They would not.

Fred The lights come on, so I think they're OK. I put it in gear and I just drive away. Now as soon as proper daylight breaks, someone's gonna look in the back and spot it, so I've gotta take it away. I drove up to Camberwell from there, to a row of lock-up garages that we had. As we were driving along, Alf pulls in. He said, 'Your rear light's not working.' I said, 'Nothing's fucking working.' He's saying, 'You're taking a right chance in that, the state it's in.' I mean, it's a pull-in job.

But I got to Camberwell unchallenged and put it away in the garage. Then it had to be transferred into a van and driven down into the country to a scrap metal yard. The body finished up going out to sea, from Newhaven.

Tony   See, I could never tell anybody about this part of it until you decided to talk about it, Fred. But every time I told the story of Jack The Hat, I had to come up with an ending. So I said he was buried in a graveyard.

(*Laughing*) I had the *News of the World* looking at tombs in Gravesend. I'll always remember this photographer. He couldn't stop laughing. I mean, they *knew*.

Fred   That's harmless enough. What was a lot more damaging was what Ronnie Hart's said at the trial. He turned Queen's Evidence in the McVitie case, and he told some terrible lies to make sure that we were put away.

Tony   He told the police he only did what he did because Ronnie Kray told him to. He never even got charged with anything. It's the first time I know of that the police did a deal for murder. They made him marry Blonde Vicky because we were gonna call her as a defence witness. She was the main player as far as he was concerned, the one person who could really implicate him. Once they were married, she couldn't be called to give evidence against her husband.

Fred   He told his whole story to Nipper Read in the library in Wandsworth Prison at twelve o'clock at night. But being that he never actually took part in that particular thing, he fucked it up because he never knew the details. He said that he brought Charlie Kray over to my pub that night to tell me where the body was. Well, that didn't happen at all. Charlie never came near the pub, and Hart wasn't there. That's a guarantee. I proved it in court.

Tony   That hurt me, with Charlie. He done nothing wrong. With you, you know that Hart said, 'If you want me to give evidence, Freddie Foreman has to be out of harm's way. You have to nick him.' It got a bit shaky, Fred, when you got bail.

Fred   That's the only thing I've got the hump with Nipper Read for. Because he blanked my bail application right over the Christmas period. Took 'em two weeks to fucking get me out and when they did, it was for four days, I think. I should've had my Christmas and New Year at home with my family.

But, getting back to the trial – Hopwood, listen, he was a prosecution witness, and he says that after the murder, Ronnie Hart came into his flat with Reggie and Ronnie, and that Hart's laid on the couch and crashed right out for the night. All the witnesses proved that he was still there in the morning, when I cross-examined them. So he can't be in two places at the same fucking time. If he's on Hopwood's settee, he's not at my pub knocking on my door with Charlie Kray, is he? Ronnie Hart was an accessory to the fact of murder. Yet, the jury take his word against another prosecution witness, Hopwood, who has nothing to do with the murder. They've just gone to his house afterwards and he can't refuse to let them in.

Tony   It couldn't have happened the way Hart said it did.

Fred   In his evidence, he said he sat in a car and watched Charlie go over and knock on my door. He definitely saw him knock. Well, I presented photographs of my door. There's no fucking knocker on it. There was only a bell, right up the top, high, on the jamb and the only way you can get any answer is by reaching up and ringing the bell.

Then he heard a window open, and I put my head out and said I'd be down. Well, the window he pointed at was the fucking broom cupboard. I'm in bed, don't forget, and the bedroom's on the top floor of the pub. If I want to put my head out, I'll put it out the bedroom window. I'm not gonna come down two flights of stairs, go into a broom cupboard where the window's jammed anyway and try and put my head out, am I?

But after he said I put my head out this window, he changed his mind and suddenly he ain't seen me!

He's supposed to have parked up round the corner while Charlie went in. Well, he couldn't see the door if he was parked where he said he was. He cannot possibly see round corners. So he wouldn't have been able to 'see' Charlie at the door, or me putting my head out the window either.

Another part of his evidence was that he overheard me say that the body had a film over it, as though Jack been sweating from where they'd been fighting. When challenged, he can't remember where or when he heard this. But it was never fucking said. I wouldn't have said anything like that in his presence.

COMING TO COURT

Fred The day we got weighed off, the atmosphere in the court . . .

Tony *Cor!* It was like the old hang, draw and quarter 'em days.

Fred It was packed solid up in the public gallery. All the celebs there, everyone who took part in the trial came back, and the jury's got their ties on. It was like a hanging. And that case was fucking nothing. I mean, it was uncorroborated evidence. They had no case.

Tony Terrible, terrible.

Fred But we went down, the lot of us, because we all stuck to the one story: it didn't happen. But it did happen. I mean, there's too many witnesses, and all the fucking people who were grassing and rolling over, to say it didn't happen. And where is Jack then? He's disappeared and he's fucking left his family?

Tony You was with a different firm of solicitors. And looking back on it, it was a sensible thing to have done. We should have listened to you. We were stupid, Fred. You weren't having it. They wanted you to join the rest of us with Sampsons Ralph Haeems and Manny Frede and them.

Fred Nah! I'm not gonna say and do what the twins want me to – I'm fighting my own defence. We all should've had different solicitors, because then each man fights the case the way he sees it. Somebody's gotta win somewhere, providing you don't put other people down.

Tony Yeah, it's stupid. Unfortunately, we fell into it.

Fred Other solicitors would have got together, looked at it and said, 'You can't say it didn't happen. You've got to play this as a party that went dramatically wrong, what with all the booze and the pills. It turned into a fucking row and a man got killed.' That would've been a manslaughter charge. Maximum, you'd have got a twelve-year sentence, which you do probably eight of. It would not have been a premeditated murder, and it would not have involved anybody else.

Tony   I remember they was talking about a deal. I go on a visit one day to Brixton [Prison] and the twins and [firm member] Ian Barrie and Ralph Haeems are standing there, and that other young clerk that used to be with him, the one that committed suicide.

Reggie went, 'Look, there might be a deal on,' and what the twins wanted was life imprisonment with no recommendations. This was all that was ever said about it, and I jumped in and I said, 'Well, to get the others out of it, I'll take the accessory after the fact.' That's ten years, Fred. I'll come out in six or seven. That won't fucking hurt me, will it? But it gets my brother and Bender out of it as accessories.

Fred   They wanted to do a deal, yeah, the twins. I'm not so sure about Reggie, but Ronnie's felt guilty for all of you going down. He wanted to admit to everything. He said, 'I'm gonna take Cornell and Reggie'll take McVitie,' and he wanted Donoghue to take Mitchell. And Donoghue just went, 'Fuck that for a game of soldiers, I never killed no one,' and that's when he rolled over. But Ronnie wanted them to take the blame, the three of them, then there's no big show trial and all the rest of us get off.

Oh, it was just a crooked trial. Everybody involved in the case was fucking corrupt. The prosecution, the defence, none of them wanted to do a deal and get the hands-up situation. They wanted a show trial where they're all getting thousands of pounds in fees. It's lasted six months.

And the McVitie and Cornell trials should've been separate, because you, me and Charlie sat in the dock with several others and our names wasn't mentioned once all the way through the Cornell trial. And then we had the McVitie trial after that.

That jury's been looking at us all that time, thinking, What are they doing in the dock if it's not serious? It was unfair.

Then you had Donoghue deciding to plead guilty, so he was taken out.

'Oh, don't worry about him,' said the judge, 'he's already pleaded guilty.' That is a miscarriage of justice. There's one of the defendants pleading guilty to what we're saying never happened, and the judge is telling the jury that he's pleaded guilty and he'll be sentenced at the end of the trial. That should've been a retrial.

The whole thing was a travesty of justice. It would never have gone through the courts today.

Tony Then you've got Tony Barry sitting at the back of the dock with us, screaming all through the trial. His line of defence is pure duress. He did have different representation, so everything we're saying, his guy is saying, 'My client takes no part in this.'

They got a witness for our defence, a pianist from the Old Horns, and she even started to go against us (*laughing*).

Fred Who was that?

Tony The old bird – do you remember her, Fred? Every time they questioned her about her playing the piano in this pub, she'd talk about a fight or a gun being pulled. 'Fucking hell, get her out of the witness box!'

Fred (*Laughter*) It must've been her piano playing that caused the trouble. She should've been in the dock with us!

Tony Oh well, this is what we was up against. But I will say something now about Bender, cos I never was aware until this weekend that he tried to do a deal, to join the bandwagon, before and during the trial.

Fred It's in here. [Fred is referring to Martin Fido's *The Krays: Unfinished Business*, which suggests that Bender had wanted to change his legal representation and give evidence which did not insist that 'nothing happened'. It further proposes that he stayed in line after pressure from the twins, through Ralph Haeems.]

Tony He's not a great friend of mine, Ronnie Bender – I've only seen him once since I've been out of prison. But I always tried to keep him out of it. I'm disappointed now. It's shocked me, that.

11

Sunny Spain

Conversation in Fred's kitchen, 16 November 1999

THE GOOD LIFE

Fred I was seven years in Spain. I went out there in '82, before the Security Express. I fancied staying there. Course, when I had the bit of money, the touch, that was all the more reason to go. But, in the beginning, I wasn't going to live in Spain full time. I was going to be travelling backwards and forwards between Spain and London and America. I still had my house and my business in America, from when I was on my toes after the drugs bust and the customs officer. I had a home and businesses in London too. Spain was going to be a holiday home at first.

When the Security Express went off, then I moved out to Spain and started buying up a few bits after nine months. I thought, Well, I'll retire now and I'll just invest locally and make a living that way.

Tony The first time I went out there, I travelled with a mate of mine, Bill. Came from out of the mountains in Scotland, he did. Worked on the boats all his life.

Fred He was a big bear.

Tony Used to always be with me. Money-lender, he was. This was when I lived in the Borough. He used to live round the New Kent Road there.

He used to sweat like a pig because he was on speed. And all the way over on the plane, I'm on the inside by the window and he's beside me, and it was literally pouring off him. I don't want to be sitting there, Fred. Anyway, I was invited out there by Dan. Do you remember him?

Fred Oh yeah, Dan.

Tony I always thought he was well-named. He looked like Desperate Dan, the way he walked with his toes tucked in. He had a plumbing business over in Ilford. I know he's got a few quid. He had this place in Spain and he bought our tickets.

Fred He lived up at the back of San Pedro in a villa owned by – who's the fairground people?

Tony Chipperfields.

Fred I think it was Chipperfields. And inside the villa, the decor made it look like a big top as you went in. It was in two sections, and in the middle was a swimming pool. He rented it.

Tony He told me he owned it.

Fred No, he didn't own it.

Tony That's where we stayed, me and Bill. It was a lovely place, Fred. Gotta be '87.

Fred Dan was down my place in Marbella, the Eagles Country Club, all the time. I rented the premises. It was up the back of Puerto Banus, behind the bullring.

Tony Yeah, that's it, the Eagles. And when we go over there, the first place we go to is the Eagles to see you. Remember that day I walked in, Fred? We get out at Málaga Airport at eleven and by half past twelve, we were talking to you.

Fred Oh, I was surprised to see you. I hadn't seen you since . . .

Tony Wormwood Scrubs.

Fred The Scrubs.

Tony That was '75.

Fred That's twelve years later, then.

Tony You looked well. I was very gaunt then.

Fred I thought you looked fine.

Tony It was a nice place you had there.

Fred It was drinking, live entertainment, a full-size Olympic pool. I used to have the Swiss synchronized swimming team come and do all their rehearsals there. And I used to organize beauty contests round the pool. Then there was all the kiddies doing their swimming races and relays.

It used to create a right afternoon there in the season, especially August. There used to be rock bands on the beach on a Sunday. Then they all came off the beach bars to my club in the evenings to eat.

Remember, it backed on to a golf course? You had a watering hole there where they could come over, ring the bell on the eighteenth hole and get a drink from the bar.

People used to sit outside my club in the gardens. It was a real meeting place. And if you wanted to see anyone from London, you only had to go there. They used to travel from Mijas, where [club-owner, West End entrepreneur and ex-husband of Barbara Windsor] Ronnie Knight lived, and from places like San Pedro. They used to come from all along the coast. A lot of people were on their toes from London, and they all had plenty of money out there then. I made a lot of new relationships with lovely people; Spanish and English, different nationalities.

Tony   Yeah, plenty of dough.

Fred   If it wasn't from the Brink's-Mat robbery, it was from gold or fraud . . . It was full of thieves and crooks and rascals.

Tony   (*Laughter*) I never spoke to a Spaniard all the time I was there, and I never met a straight person, Fred.

Fred   There were a lot of crooked people out there who we know. It was a bolt-hole, wasn't it? Marbella was a lovely place, and there was no extradition until 1987. They brought it in because they had so many villains living over there, and there was pressure from the British government.

Tony   You know what your nickname was in Spain? The Benevolent Society!

Fred   That's right. It was. Always paying people money to get back home when they were skint.

Tony   If you was ever in trouble, 'Go to Fred.' Everyone come to you for money.

Fred   I used to put them up and they liked it so much, they wouldn't fucking go home. I had five apartments and I never got no money out of them until I sold them. I bought them at a reasonable price, I had one myself, and then I sold that and bought a bigger one for £450,000. It had palm trees out the fucking roof.

Tony   I'd like to know how many people ever paid you back, Fred.

Fred   I can't think of any.

Tony   You must have been out a fortune.

Fred   (*Laughing*) I didn't want it back. I used to go into the Greek taverna, the Red Pepper, in Puerto Banus. It was run by a bloke called Chrissy, and I always took people down there cos we had a nice meal in there. It's still there, but the food is not what it was.

Tony   (*Laughing*) You get to you through your belly.

Fred   He used to do me a favour, Chrissy, because I spent so much money in there. I used to change my pounds for pesetas with him at a decent rate, so I saved a few bob.

If I was short of money, and the banks were closed, I could just go in there and say, 'Give us a monkey,' and that would be the night's boozing.

I used to sit there and people would come over in the afternoon. It might get a bit chilly around half past seven, eight in the evening, and the women would feel it. I'd say, 'Oh, come on, come with me,' and I used to take them and buy them cashmere jumpers, nice little cardigans and things. I got a kick out of that. But I only did it because I didn't want them to take all the men home and spoil our drinks. It never got started down the port until one o'clock in the morning.

Tony   Oh yeah. And we had a drink and all that, you, me, Dan and Big Bill. A big lump Bill was, as well – an 'andful. He was a merchant seaman. In Jamaica, when he was travelling the seas, he threw one geezer over the ship. And they nicked him and he got a not guilty, just to get him out the country. Anyway, out in the West Indies somewhere, he done another geezer. And he got out of that, Fred. He was a man they wanted out the way. He always reminded me of . . . what was his name in *Popeye*?

Fred   Bluto.

Tony Yeah. But Dan is the one who wanted to be introduced to you. Now, I don't know he's used me as a way to approach you, but he was doing me a right favour. We was doing business out there, which we can't talk about, but down to you, he gave me twelve grand.

Fred We got a bit involved.

Tony Very wary of you, he was, Fred.

Fred Yeah, I was wary of him as well.

Tony I didn't know that he's wanted for murder. They were gonna hang him in Malaya or Thailand or one of them countries he'd been out to.

Fred He was a bit notorious.

Tony The IRA wanted him for something over in Ireland, and there was something he was doing in Spain which he wanted to use you on, but you weren't having none of it. And when I come back, I met him again at his place in Ilford and he was on the run again then. I haven't heard of him since.

THAT FLAMING CANADIAN

Fred On the other wing of the villa that Dan lived in was a Canadian, and he was up to a bit of mischief with drugs, cocaine and stuff like that. I went to a couple of parties at the villa when it was owned by another guy. But, well, I fell out with him, and he got busted up afterwards.

Lucky, very lucky, he was. He fucked people for their money. Business deals, you know. It caught up with him. He got sprung in his apartment and they nearly killed him, some gypsies out there. They really done him. Blood everywhere, climbing up the wall he was. People tried to blame me for it – but he owed everyone.

Anyway, Dan comes up to me one Sunday morning at Mel's beach bar. Mel was number-one entertainer down there, and he used to book bands, and he'd play the guitar and sing rhythm and blues.

Tony Oh, yeah.

Fred He comes over to have a drink, Dan, and I was with somebody else, having a little chat. He said, 'There's a couple of birds over here from London, couple of little office girls, you know, I'll introduce you to 'em. Is it all right if I pull 'em over, Fred?' I said, 'Yeah, it's all right.' So I'm having a laugh with the two girls and Dan and then they all went off somewhere else. I thought no more of it. But I did notice two guys at the end of the bar who looked out of place. And it turns out they was Guardia – you know, Spanish police. Well, the next day when I got up . . .

Tony You got a pull, didn't you, Fred?

Fred Yeah, they all came steaming round to the apartment – 'We want you up to the police station.' I thought, Oh, here we go, they're going to capture me, sling me out. Cos I was fighting extradition at the time and they had no case against me, but they'd taken me to Seville, Malaga, and I was up in Madrid now. Every province in Spain, the major town of that province brings an action against you in turn, so as one stops, another one starts, and that's how it kept going. The whole fucking country's objecting to you being there and wanting you out.

So these police come round, drag me to Marbella nick and they said, 'Do you know the villa?' and I said, 'Yeah, I've been there several times to parties.'

They asked, 'Do you know this man?' And I've looked at the photo. I did recognize him – it was the Canadian fella – but I said, 'No.' So they said, 'When was the last time you was up at the villa?' I said, 'Oh, fucking months ago, there was about a hundred people at a party up there. That's the last time I was there.'

Then they show me these other photos of a burnt-out car. This fucking Canadian geezer's slumped in it and someone's put a bullet in his head.

Tony *Cor!*

Fred And he's burnt to a fucking crisp. He's like a bit of roast pork (*laughing*). I said, 'Do you mind? My missus is cooking me a nice dinner today.' So they said, 'Well, you knew this man, you've been in the villa.' With my track record, you know, they've got all my history, so they're putting it down to me.

I didn't know fuck all about it. I knew the Canadian was in the car game. You could buy a nice Mercedes out there for four grand

– a fucking £60,000, brand-new motor with the paperwork and everything.

The Guardia said, 'We're burning open his safe. Do you know where the keys to the safe are?'

I didn't even know there was a safe in the villa. They did burn it open, and they found a couple of kilos of fucking charlie in there, cocaine in the safe. So now the plot thickened. Whatever he was up to, the Canadian, somebody had the hump with him and they done him up on the mountain and set light to the car.

They had Dan in as well. And that was the two cozzers who was in the bar. Talking to him, him bringing these couple of birds over – that's what put 'em on me. Otherwise they wouldn't have put us together.

Then they found another one on the beach, washed up with his head missing and his hands cut off. A torso. So they had me in there again, for that. I said, 'I'm fucking fed up with all this.' They kept finding bodies along the beach and they kept fucking coming round to me. I don't know if they were pulling anybody else like that. They may have done, but they always dug me out.

Tony   (*Laughter*)

TIE-ME-DOWN JANE

Fred   Remember Tie-Me-Down Jane?

Tony   (*Hearty laughter*)

Fred   There was a few naughty girls out there on the Costa Del Sol . . .

Tony   One night, we went to the Eagles and this bird's hanging about there, Tie-Me-Down Jane. She's coming on a little bit heavy to a mate of ours, Matt. So he thought, Might as well enjoy it.

Fred   She was the local bike. You could guarantee that Tie-Me-Down would look after you.

Tony   And we're laughing. We said, 'Oh, you'll be all right, you'll be tied up tonight.' He just took it as a laugh. So me, Bill, Matt and Tie-Me-Down Jane go back to the villa. Beautiful, all lit up it was, on the hill. We had to go along this highway in a little Fiat, Fred, right by the sea. They call it Death Highway.

Fred   Oh, yeah, yeah. That was the old road.

Tony   On the way back there, we saw three crashes. Over the cliff. It was known for it.

Anyway, Bill had found a .38 in the garage at this villa. And I ain't having him with a .38. He was out of his head on speed. He had bags of it, Fred. He didn't want cocaine and he didn't want puff. He wanted speed. He used to do incredible amounts of it. Cos nobody has that out there, do they? Nobody touches that stuff. Cannabis – it was everywhere you'd go. I mean, you'd sit on the beach and they'd approach, them Moroccans.

But Big Bill, he was so whizzy. I never seen a geezer take that amount of gear in my life. Packets of it.

Fred   Oh, you can't do it. It's gotta kill you.

Tony   It killed him in the end. He had a heart attack. I mean, bang. Gone. But it used to make him very aggressive, and he was always sweating buckets. He used to terrorize the Borough, Fred. (*Laughing*) When he died, he had all this money loaned out. They got him to Greenwich Hospital and they revived him for a while. 'Don't let the bastards have my money,' he said. He had bundles of it.

Fred   Did he have a little black book?

Tony   He had a book. I used to watch him go round collecting, all over the Borough.

Fred   (*Laughing*) So, did you collect it for him after he died?

Tony   No, I didn't get the book.

Fred   (*Still laughing*) You slipped up there, Tone.

Tony   I did slip up. But anyway, he found this gun at the villa, you know. I've actually got a photograph of him in a dressing gown with it, walking round the pool. And I couldn't think of him with that shooter on him, wondering what he was gonna do. I had to get it off him. So Matt's gone into a room with this Tie-Me-Down Jane, and I go to the garage and I find a big knuckleduster. Great big metal knuckleduster. The next day, I gave it to Bill in return for the gun, and he handed it over. I gave it to Dan, cos he was absolutely terrified of Bill. He had a thing about him killing someone.

But he was a funny man, Bill. As big and aggressive as he was, he was very romantic towards women. He'd sit and hold a girl's hand all night.

Fred   Yeah, talk all this nonsense about how much he loved them on the first date.

Tony   And yet he was into dirty magazines and all that. I used to find stacks of them everywhere.

Fred   (*Laughing*) I'm not surprised he died of a heart attack, Tone!

Tony   He was always chasing the housekeeper.

Fred   It wasn't the Filipino one, was it?

Tony   (*Laughing*) This old girl. And another thing, he used to fantasize. He said I nicked Wendy off him.

Fred   (*Laughter*)

Tony   Ridiculous! Ask Wendy about it. But anyway, I got the gun off him early in the morning after Tie-Me-Down Jane had left. That Matt hadn't hardly slept all night. He woke up handcuffed to the bed. And he was moaning about bite marks. God knows what she did that night! He was going on about the mirrors on the ceiling.

Fred   Did he have any whip marks?

Tony   I don't know! I tell you what, he couldn't remember much about it.

Fred   She'd make anyone lose their memory.

Tony   Gawd almighty!

THE COOK REPORT

Fred   I'm sitting on the settee in my apartment in Marbella, in [a development called] the Alcazaba. We was up on the fourth floor. Maureen, my wife, was out on the terrace reading a book, sunning herself, and I was relaxing, listening to a bit of classical music. I've got these earphones on and, all of a sudden, I see Maureen – she's wearing this bathing costume and she's on all fours, coming across the marble floor. I thought, What's the fucking matter with her, is she cracking up? She's crawled into the lounge and she's hiding behind the fucking table and chairs and pointing. And when I took the earphones off, I could hear all these engines roaring. I looked out and there was this fucking helicopter right level with my terrace. And there's Roger Cook (*laughing*) and a cameraman hanging out the helicopter, just outside these windows. Frightened the life out of Maureen, didn't it, cos one minute she's sunbathing, next minute there's this fucking helicopter. So then it pulled away and started circling the Alcazaba.

About twenty minutes later, there's someone banging on the fucking door (*laughing*) – 'Come out, Freddie Foreman, I know you're in there! What have you got to say about the Security Express £7 million robbery?' He's hollering through the door. I said, 'I'm gonna fucking batter him. . .'

Tony (*Hearty laughter*)

Fred And Maureen's hanging on my legs, and I'm dragging her along, sliding along the floor. 'Don't go, don't go,' she said. 'Get on to the security. They'll get rid of him.' So I go to the door and I look through the spyhole and I can see him standing well back. He's waiting for me to come tearing out, ain't he, and I can see this fucking big lens of the camera, right, waiting on the stairs for me. He's a bit of a masochist – he's had plenty of right-handers, so it don't make no difference – but that would be good footage for him, you know, to make me look bad.

Common sense come over me. I thought, I'm not gonna play his game.

So Maureen's ringing up security. They all knew me, cos I used to treat 'em well. At Christmas, I was the only one in the Alcazaba who used to take booze down for the Spanish cleaners and the security men, and I used to have a party with them, spend a day with them, a few days after Christmas was over.

They had a big, white Alsatian dog, a lovely dog which we used to make a fuss of, and they had guns and sticks. Course, they come charging over and they frightened the life out of Roger Cook. They escorted him and his cameraman off the Alcazaba.

Tony He was a big old lump, Fred, wasn't he?

Fred Sack of shit, yeah.

Tony I was talking to Roger Cook once in Birmingham at this TV show. There was me and [underworld friend] Les Long and Edwina Currie. I called him over. It was just after you was gonna oblige him, Fred.

I said, 'Why do you keep going out to Spain and making yourself busy?' And he looked at me and he went, 'I don't wanna talk about it,' and he ran away. He didn't wanna know. And I was standing there with Edwina Currie, the Minister of Health – the egg business, you remember? – and she went, 'Nasty man, nasty man.'

They asked her to be a prison minister, and she turned it down. She refused to have anything to do with it. She was telling me about that. 'Prison minister? That's not me. I'm an MP. Not there to do their bidding.' And, you know, Fred, she was up for a night out.

Fred (*Laughing*) Well, she's not a bad old sort, is she, Edwina?

FAME AND FORTUNA

Fred You could never guarantee getting hold of a lawyer. You could say, 'I want to speak to my lawyer.' The police would say they'd phone him up and they wouldn't. They'd pick you up, you'd be down in the fucking cells and nobody would know where you were. So you was at their mercy.

One day I got a pull and they took me to this room. They were typing and making loads of phone calls, and I thought, Something's fucking going on here, I don't like this. They've had me there too long, cos I always used to get out eventually.

I said, 'Is my solicitor [Mr Fortuna] coming over?' and they said, 'Yeah.' And they were gonna take me back down the cells again, and I said, 'Before I go, I must go out to the toilet.' I'm upstairs in the nick and I've got two floors to come down and long stairs, swarming with fucking Guardia, standing about there with the old shooters.

I got up and I went towards the toilet, walked down the stairs, and out the door. They had a little café outside, and the coppers are all stood outside the café with their cups of coffee, looking at me. I just sauntered past, and round the next corner, I broke out into a jog.

I went down to my solicitor. The receptionist's there, and there's a little waiting area with a glass window. I said, 'Where the fuck have you been? I've been in the nick. Didn't you get the phone call to come up and get me?'

'No, we didn't have that.'

I said, 'They'll be up here, them bastards. There's something going on there. I didn't like it so I've slipped out. I'm lucky to be here.'

She said, 'Mr Fortuna is in the office, but he's got a client with him. I'll put you in as soon as he's free.'

I said, 'Make it quick. I'll wait in there.' So I've got a magazine, sitting in the waiting room (*mimes nervous impatience*) and I heard the buzzer go. She releases the door lock from under her desk and I looked through the glass and I saw this arm come through. I could recognize it as a fucking copper's uniform, and I went, *zoomph*, I was on the fucking floor, flat. I'm picking up the conversation in Spanish. She's saying, 'No, no, no, we no see Señor Foreman.' And the voices was raised. The old coppers was angry.

So anyway, she got rid of them. They didn't realize anyone was in the waiting room, on the fucking floor under the seat.

She comes in going, 'Come, come, quick,' and she put me in a cupboard, a little fucking cubby hole (*laughing*). Oh, she was all flustered, but she was really good, the girl. She did know me. I'd been in and out of there so many fucking times over the last four, five years, cos I had him on the firm all the time, Fortuna.

And he was a count. He had a title. She got me in to him and he said, 'Ah, Señor Foreman. They've been on the telephone to me. You've got to go back to the police station.'

I said, 'I think I'd better head for the hills on the old donkey.'

He said, 'If I were you, I'd keep a low profile.' So I left. It was the summer of 1988. I got in touch with Janice, cos I was seeing Janice then, you see. We were going out. Janice got the keys to a villa up in the mountains and we holed up there. Once again, I was a prisoner, but I was her prisoner, her slave (*laughing*). I stayed up there for months and months till I fought the case. Then I lived in Madrid for a while before I went back to Marbella. My lawyer was in Madrid and they even took the case into the High Court in Spain, the highest court in the land, and proved that I'd not committed any offence and that there was no reason for them to extradite or expel me, and I won the case. It cost me a lot of money.

THE RONNIE KNIGHT CONNECTION

Fred My association with Ronnie Knight in Spain – that was what got me nicked on the Security Express. I should've settled somewhere else and then I wouldn't have been pulled in at all.

But they were investigating where Ronnie Knight was, after his brother was arrested on the robbery. Originally, Ronnie was forty miles away from me, up on the hill at Mijas, and he was safer there.

But he was travelling down to Puerto Banus and Marbella to drink and socialize, cos all they had up in Mijas was a little bar.

It was hairy driving up that mountain – a few finished up going over the side. The daytime's all right, but when you're fucking paralytic drunk in the pitch-black of night, you can't handle them roads so easy.

Ronnie Knight and [his wife] Sue drove up there pissed one night and went over the side. Only a tree stopped them fucking getting killed. The back wheels were on the road and the tree's stopped them from going down the mountain.

He saw where I was living, he thought it was lovely, and he thought it was a good idea to buy an apartment there to save him the journey home. He'd stay for a couple of days, and then poodle back to his villa afterwards when he'd sobered up.

So the police were looking through the register for Ronnie and they went, 'Fucking hell, look who else has got an apartment there.'

Tony Didn't do you no favours that, Fred, did it?

Fred Now I'm in the frame. Guilty by association. They could not prove a thing at all. There was no evidence, no forensic, no identifications.

The banks opened up to them [the British police] in Spain, told them everything. They helped all they could. Every transaction that was made, they knew about. But they couldn't say where the money came from, cos it was moved around.

All they found was £360,000, passed through my Allied Irish bank account. It was lodged in England, but it was in another name, an American address, and bits of paper were transferred out to Spain. And it went to different banks, all up and down the country. It was moved about five times, so you think you've 'lost' it. Now it's finished up in Marbella in three different bank accounts, and they've traced it. All my cash came from the sale of my house in Dulwich Village, my pool-table business and my house and business in the USA.

Tony It still didn't prove it came from the robbery, Fred.

Fred It didn't prove anything. Nobody could say to this day that it came from the robbery.

So, anyway, there was this team of coppers marching around Marbella with this big kitbag with all their evidence in. They took it on the beach with them. They never let go of it. We was looking at them. I would've loved to get hold of the evidence, you see. I bumped right into them at their hotel. I went to get in the lift and they was coming out of it. I was going up to find their room. But I never got the chance to nick the bag. It wouldn't have prevented anything – all it would have done was piss them off a lot. But they never left it in the hotel room. They carried it everywhere with them.

Back at the Old Bailey, they tried to find me guilty of the robbery, and they even brought over two Spanish coppers to say that I admitted to it – when they couldn't speak English and I couldn't speak Spanish!

Tony (*Laughter*)

Fred I'll tell you what really happened with these two coppers. I met them on neutral ground, in the bar of the foyer in the Don Pepe Hotel in Marbella.

Tony So you feel safe.

Fred I was drinking coffee. I wouldn't even have a beer. I bought them beers and we sat there talking. There was a nice, lady Spanish lawyer sitting between us, an interpreter for both parties, and all we were discussing was getting my *residencia* together. I'd been a resident of Spain for two years and they had two grand out of me in taxes. I'm trying to get them to sign a *residencia* to allow me to stay for another two years and thinking that they'd want a drink, some pesetas, you know. And I'm gonna fucking tell them I took part in the biggest cash robbery in England!

Tony   (*Laughter*)

Fred   That happened a year before they made their swoop and kidnapped me.

28 JULY 1989: A RELUCTANT DEPARTURE

Fred   They was trying to throw me out and I went into hiding up in the mountains with Janice, as I was saying.

Tony   And when you got back to Marbella, they dragged you out and they drugged you on the plane, and it becomes a totally illegal thing.

Fred   Course.

Tony   I remember waking up one morning and seeing it on the front of the papers. 'Foreman brought back.' With that famous photo of you – you wouldn't leave a country, willingly, dressed in a pair of shorts . . .

Fred   And a pair of slippers and a T-shirt.

Tony   What, did they just jump you, Fred?

Fred   I was going out to my car, I was putting the key in and they come out the bushes. I'm going to the hospital where Maureen was. She was having some treatment and they kept her in, over her liver. So I'm going to see her and to pay them some money. A monkey a week it was, there. They just overpowered me on the car.

Tony   What, got cuffs on you?

Fred   Yeah. All of a sudden, I'm cuffed up. I'm laying across the bonnet of the fucking car. They took me to the police station and banged me straight in.

Tony So you just thought it was a pull.

Fred Cos I've had loads of these.

Tony Yeah, yeah. I see what's happened. You've had a row with them, so what you think, they take you to the police station, you're gonna get it straightened out, and out you go.

Fred They've done it in front of witnesses. I'm right outside the reception of the Alcazaba. The gardeners and the security men have all seen what's gone down. And I tried to get the coppers to come back up to the apartment, so I've got more chance (*laughing*). I'd be out there and over the terrace and fucking gone, you know.

With Maureen not being there, no one knew in my flat, so I'm thinking, Nobody will get in touch with the lawyer.

Tony No one knows where you are.

Fred So when they get me to the nick, they throw me downstairs with all the Spanish fucking smackheads, you know, all half falling asleep. And there was one guy in there, he was an English guy and he knew me. He was a jeweller back here, he was on his toes. He done a runner from Hatton Garden or somewhere.

They sent over this guy who's an interpreter working for the police. It turned out that he was having it with an Englishwoman, and I'd sold him my first apartment in the Alcazaba. It was her money. He was like the Spanish gigolo who'd got on the firm with her. I'd bought this much bigger duplex apartment in the middle of the block, although I still had the four single ones over the other side. I used to rent them out to people, and put friends up.

The guy comes up to the cell and he's looking through the bars – 'Hello, Señor Foreman.' I said to him, 'Do me a favour – go over there to Fortuna's, he's only across the road. Tell him to get himself over here right away. Pronto.'

'Don't worry, I'll do that for you.' So he goes away. About ten minutes, fifteen minutes later, the screws come down to try and take me out. So I said, 'Is my solicitor there?' and they went, 'No, no solicitor.' I went, 'I'm not going.' I held the door shut and they're trying to open it, so I got the English guy, and I said, 'Hang on this door for me.' He's hanging on the door. I says, 'Amigos, amigos, give me some fucking help here,' so all the Spaniards are hanging on the door as well, going, 'Yeah!' I don't wanna come out of there cos I know if they get me out, they're gonna run me straight on a plane.

They was gonna do it before, that day when I walked out the nick. I sussed it out. So we're all hanging on as they're pulling the door.

Tony   It's like Keystone Cops, really.

Fred   Yeah, yeah. So anyway, the screws go off and about ten or fifteen minutes later, down comes this guy I've sold my flat to. I said, 'Is my lawyer up there?' '*Si, si.* Señor Fortuna upstairs.'

Tony   Just to get you up there.

Fred   Yeah. So I went, 'OK.' Cos I was on good terms with him and I fucking bought him drinks, the bastard.

Tony   (*Laughter*) You're good-hearted all the time, aren't you?

Fred   I am. And there I am, I let him open the door and I walk out and as soon as I get round into the passageway, bosh! It's on me. I said, 'You dirty bastard.' I've give it to him, ain't I? So now I've claimed the railings on the staircase (*laughing*). I've got a grip on them and I'm saying, 'I'm not moving until my fucking lawyer gets here.' They're prising my fingers off the railings, you know, and he's helping them, this bastard.

Tony   (*Hearty laughter*)

Fred   They've got me now. I'm on the fucking floor. So they run me up the stairs and out of the main entrance, straight over to the fucking motor.

Tony   Where?

Fred   In the back. One each side of me, two in the front.

Tony   Did you think you were going?

Fred   Yeah. I knew then. I knew.

Tony   So you just thought they'd sling you out the country?

Fred   Yeah. I said, 'Look, I'll pay you.' I said, 'Put me on a plane to Tangiers, Morocco.'

Tony Which wouldn't have been no skin off their nose, Fred, would it?

Fred No, no. Long as you're out. But they knew I was gonna be charged, and they're not gonna sling me anywhere but London.

First of all, they put us down as wanted for the Brink's-Mat, so we was wanted for two robberies to start with. Then it finished up with only the Security Express, but they're saying, like, 'Robbers of the Century'.

Tony But, getting back, you're on your way to the airport, Fred.

Fred Yeah, so in the car, as we went down the road, I've got the two of them, I'm in between, so I went over the top to get the driver. And the fucking car was going all over the road. I'm fighting all the way there, I'm trying to make him run off the road and crash the car and all that.

Tony Fighting in the back of it.

Fred I had my hands cuffed behind my back. I was trying to kick the windows and the doors open, but the doors are locked.

Tony (*Laughing*) They gave you a bit of stick as well, Fred.

Fred Oh, yeah. They're calling me everything in Spanish.

And then when we get to the airport, they don't come through immigration, they come through a gate straight on to the airfield, on the tarmac, straight up to the plane. The plane was there waiting.

When I see the plane, it's Air Iberia, innit, the Spanish flight, and I thought, Oh, all right. It's the Maroc planes that go over to Tangiers, so I know this one's going the other way. That's the ones you come back to London on. So as they open the car door, I'm off.

Tony (*Hearty laughter*) Legging it!

Fred My hands are still cuffed behind my back and I'm running round the wheels of the fucking plane. I could see the pilot looking out the window. He's going, 'What the fuck's going on out there?'

Tony (*Laughing*) It could only happen to you, Fred.

Fred I'm hoping that the pilot will go, 'Oh, I'm not taking him.'

Tony Yeah – 'Lunatic!'

Fred Because by law, they should not take anyone on board who's gonna endanger the flight. So, I mean, I'm showing out. This is for the pilot's benefit.

Tony Clever thinking.

Fred Then I went right through the swing doors, into the air-port, into the crowd of people with their luggage, all waiting to board. I come over the fucking rail, you know. I thought, I'll get lost, and I'm screaming out, 'They're kidnapping me, they're kidnapping me!' But they were right on my tail. I ain't got no chance.

Now they've got me at the foot of the steps going up to the plane. They were hitting me, punching me in the bollocks, all that, and they're trying to strangle me. There was one copper going to the others, 'No, no! Don't go too strong.'

Cos they was getting carried away and they was sweating like pigs. We go up the steps, and they've got hold of my legs. There were about six of them, all carrying me up there. And there's a little rail holding the handrail up every so many feet, and about half way up, as I've got to that thing, I've stuck my foot out quick and pushed myself backwards, and we've all gone down the stairs in a fucking pile, down to the bottom again. So now they're fucking raving.

Tony (*Laughter*)

Fred They're calling me everything they can. Anyway, they get me up there again. I'm fucking knackered myself, I'll tell you. We get into the plane and they dropped me face down on the floor with my hands behind my back.

Tony Was there any English law on there, Fred?

Fred No. The plane was empty. The passengers came on after-wards. I didn't see 'em.

Tony So they got you on first.

Fred They know what to do. It's all planned. I fucking hit the deck and they were kneeling on my back. They were all talking in Spanish and one of the male stewards came over. He was in his fifties, I suppose, and he's got a little plastic beaker. He looked down and he said, 'Señor Foreman, lift your head, I'll give you a drink,' you know, after the fighting and the running and the sweating. It was the end of July, when it's in the eighties and nineties, and I thought, Oh, bit of kindness here. I said, 'Thanks very much,' I turned my head round, he pours it into my mouth, I've gulped it down and that's it – bang.

They've got the knock-out drops, the old liquid cosh, for people who run amok on the plane. I said, 'You bastard!'

Well, the next thing I know, I'm being dragged around the plane, I'm fucking down on a seat and my balls were hanging out my shorts (*laughing*). The stewardesses were looking over at me and I said, 'Put my shorts down.'

Tony Who was sitting with you?

Fred The Spanish coppers. They are now delivering me to England. Meanwhile, my Jamie, his ex-partner Carol Harrison [famous for playing Tiffany's mum, Louise, in *EastEnders*], my Danielle and my son-in-law got the Spanish lawyer and drove to the airport at ninety miles an hour. As they're pulling in, my plane was taking off.

Tony Bad luck, weren't it?

Fred And then they're waking me up, and I can see these English coppers walking down the gangway. I'm in Heathrow. I'm fucking here.

Tony And the Spanish law are with you.

Fred Yeah, they're still with me.

Tony What did you do about it?

Fred Well, what could I do?

Tony So they carted you off. That's the famous photo.

Fred Yeah. There's all the press and the cameras.

Tony You've got a scowl on your face. Your eyes . . .

Fred I'd just fucking woke up, hadn't I? I'd crashed out.

Tony So they take you to Leman Street [police station].

Fred Yeah. I mean, I was still suffering with the old drug thing, you know, and they just flopped me down and I crashed right out. And the next thing I know, I'm being woken up again and it's Henry Milner, you know, the solicitor. He's come in to talk to me. And he said he's representing me.

Oh, and I went out to the toilet and there was all the top ones in the robbery squad standing there.

Tony All waiting.

Fred They was all talking and looking over and smiling, thinking, Oh, we got him. We got him. So then it's just a remand straight into Brixton.

Tony Didn't you ever do anything about it, Fred? Didn't you ever go into the legal side of it? They should have put you through immigration for a start.

Fred Well, I know that, yeah. I know what they're doing is a totally illegal thing, cos they should have let me see my lawyer and he's gotta say, 'Where's the signed affidavit?'

My QC jumped up in the Old Bailey and said, 'Before the trial starts, I'd like to put in the submission that the way my client has been brought into this country is totally illegal. He was arrested off the street without notifying his family or his solicitor, when he requested his solicitor he wasn't granted the request, he wasn't granted a phone call, he had no passport or means of identification on him when he was arrested, yet they took him to Malaga Airport by force, in handcuffs, and put him on a plane to England. He was really disturbed and upset, and they drugged him.'

But the reason that they did it this way was because my case had been heard in Madrid and I had won. The paperwork was on its way down to Marbella, but it takes a week to get there. So they know I've won the case.

Tony Yeah, course they do.

Fred The British police, the robbery squad, was behind it all the time. But I won all my Spanish cases against extradition because I entered the country legally, under my own name and my own passport. After the robbery, I went back and forward for a nine-month period, in and out of Spain, before the whistle went up. After that hit the fan, the next time I come out to England was when Ronnie Knight's brother, Johnny Knight, got arrested. I went back to Spain a few days after that, and I thought, Well, I'm going to fucking stay here until it all blows over. No reason for my name to come up.

So everything I had done was totally legal. And there was no reason for them to expel me. In Spanish law, the extradition wouldn't stand up. The British police were behind it, getting the Spanish to do it. They'd come over to talk to us, but we wouldn't speak.

The robbery squad in London, they've worked it out with the local police. They said, 'Do us a favour, you get him out and we'll invite you over for a nice fucking seminar to learn English. Have a holiday, down to us.'

Tony Lovely.

Fred Cos that's what happened afterwards. They brought the cozzers in the case to come over and give evidence for 'em at the Old Bailey. These are the two I was supposed to have 'confessed' to when I was trying to sort out my *residencia*.

I reckon the trial shouldn't have taken place because of the way I was brought back to this country. But [on 4 April 1990] well, I get weighed off, don't I? I get a nine-stretch on the Security Express, for handling.

They charged me with taking part. I've beat the robbery charge, but it shouldn't follow that I'm guilty of handling, cos they couldn't prove where the money came from. It could've come from a dozen different robberies, frauds or tax evasion. If I was in possession of two or three hundred grand somewhere, that doesn't mean to say that the money came from that robbery. They've got to prove it, which they never, ever did.

Tony Weak cases, ain't they?

Fred It still cost me a quarter of a million. I never received legal aid. So when I appealed, the judge took a three-month deferred judgement, then they dug up a precedent, this case of a fucking Chinaman who had actually been found guilty of robbery and handling, in Hong Kong, which is a British protectorate coming under British law. If you get Archibald's [book of historic legal rulings], you'll see my case in there.

(*Offering a bottle*) Are you drinking? Do you want a drop?

Tony   What is it, Fred?

Fred   Well, I'm gonna do a gin. Gin and Red Bull.

Tony   A small one, yeah, Fred. One'll do. You've gotta be so careful with drinking and driving. I don't want to lose the car.

THE
PRISON
YEARS

1

Sex: It Rears Its Head in Jail

Conversation in Fred's sitting room, 5 August 1998

Tony The nurses! I wish I'd had your cell at the Scrubs for the nurses. Them cells were in prize position, weren't they? They were.

Fred On the 'Four' landing, the top landing, they were worth money. That was a special pitch, that was. They'd pay fucking loads of snout to get a cell there, swap cells, cos the hospital's opposite, and the nurses' rooms.

Tony You know that Proudfoot that used to be there, Fred? You know David Proudfoot?

Fred Yeah.

Tony I used to go into his cell during association periods, cos that was the best view. Where you was wasn't such a good view, you know that.

Fred It wasn't, no, but my eyesight was a lot better in the Seventies.

Tony The best view was where Georgie Murray and all them was, on that side. That was the best part of D-Wing to see over the wall.

Fred I was a bit too far away, cos it sort of bent round, that block.

Tony I'll tell you something now. I used to watch shows there, and don't tell me it wasn't deliberate. Some of them girls used to close the curtains, but a lot didn't.

Fred Oh, yeah, some did. They used to come in and pull the curtains across straight away. But some used to walk in and put their leg up on the sink, start washing their . . . you know. We used to be up at the window and they'd give us a little show, over the wall. But only the top landing could see it, so they was like penthouse suites (*laughing*).

There was a few of the cons along there, they used to be up all night. They knew the rotas of all the girls, when they came off duty. And they used to say, 'Ginger's in Number Six,' and all that. You'd look six windows along, and the ginger nurse used to come in and she was washing her boobs and all that in the sink at the window. Really erotic when you hadn't seen a naked woman for five years or more.

Some of the cons used to string up hammocks across their windows and they was up there all night watching the nurses come off duty. Then they would fucking tap on the hot water pipe that runs from one end of the wing to the other, and you'd hear it, and that meant that there was some action, a nurse performing in the window.

Yeah, the nurses knew what they were doing. It was a fantasy, specially when you're locked up.

But after a while, you couldn't be bothered. I never used to take no fucking notice, especially if I was listening to *The Archers*. I couldn't even be bothered to get up at the window. Once you've seen it a few times, yeah, the novelty wears off. Nothing new, you've seen it all.

Tony It was notorious. I don't know if it still goes on there. One day I'm gonna drive past.

Fred And see if it's still the same. Are you sure?

Tony I must do that.

Fred What, and get nicked for a peeping Tom?! The cons used to smuggle in little spy glasses on visits. They used to get up to all sorts of things, just to have a better peep-up. They used to pass the glasses along. They'd pay a quarter ounce of snout, or a half ounce, and have it for a few days and pass it along.

Tony They'd all be found. The screws would have a turn-over – the burglars – and they'd find them. But they always got back. I don't know how.

Fred Those spot-searches – it was like coming home from work and finding your house burgled, because your cell was your home. And if you got captured with them spy glasses, you got nicked and you was on a nasty charge, like a peeping Tom. You'd lose a bit of remission, have to serve a few extra days, just over having a look at a girl over the wall, so it wasn't worth it. Not for me, anyway.

Tony Do you remember that Boysie Rust? He had a big mouth. They used to call him 'The Lorry Driver', didn't they, Fred? One day he shouted down to me, ''Ere! Have a look at this!' They was all up the cell fighting for position. And what had happened, this geezer was in the nurses' quarters.

Fred What, was he a worker, on the scaffolding?

Tony No. Must have been a boyfriend. She'd got him in there and the window was open, he's got her down over the bed, tackled up, and he's pumping away there, giving her one in the fucking room. We was all watching it.

And all of a sudden, the matron must've come round, and he was out the window, hanging on to the window ledge. And a big cheer went up from the cons, about a hundred voices went, 'Wuuuuuh, mate!' Well, he turned round and he nearly fell off. He couldn't believe it. Every pair of fucking eyes was on him. I mean, obviously he hadn't realized, but some of them girls used to play up to it, didn't they?

Fred Yeah.

Tony Do you know, when I came out of the nick, I could smell a woman, Fred, before I saw her?

Fred Uh?

Tony I'm telling you, I used to smell them before I saw 'em. I was very aware of women.

Fred Perfume, or a bit of a body smell . . .

Tony Oh, it's strong. It's so strong, the scent.

Fred It can't happen now because of the security cameras, but there used to be just one screw sitting up on a pedestal in the visiting room, behind a heavy wooden table, surveying the whole scene. And, obviously, the one thing that the prisoners and their wives and girlfriends miss in their relationships is the sex. So any opportunity to get away with it . . . a little feel-up under the table or a bit more. These are all the things that the men would try, and the women would go along with it to keep their men and themselves happy.

It's not natural to be away from your man or your woman for all those years without any sort of physical contact, and some women even went as far as to stick their skirt up in the air and plonk themselves on the man's lap and just sit wriggling and rocking around there.

I couldn't do anything like that. I couldn't go to that extreme. You lose your dignity. But it went on. All the cons knew what was going down and would discreetly look away.

There was nothing wrong with leaning across the table and having plenty of kisses. You had to show your love, and a kiss and a cuddle had to suffice. Men and women need that physical touch, and a little loving hug helps to keep a relationship going, you know.

Years ago, in the early days of prison, they used to put bromide in the tea to curb your sexual urges. They can't do it now. It used to work, all right. In those days, you couldn't make your own tea, so you got it whether you wanted it or not.

The idea of conjugal visits is most important. I hope it does come to pass, cos at least it will keep families together and stop the homes and relationships breaking down.

Tony Without a doubt. When you lock a man up for many years, you're depriving him of everything, which is why there's so much homosexuality in prisons. I never got involved in it, but you can understand why people do. They turn out more homosexuality than any other place, prisons. The obvious thing to do is what the Dutch do, and in some American states, and that's to bring in conjugal visits to keep the marriages together. It can only be for the better.

Fred If the men come home to nothing, then they're bitter and twisted and they take their revenge on society as a whole.

Tony Yes, a lot of them do.

Fred They've gone too far to be rehabilitated, then. Some of them do get marital visits in certain prisons, where they can be left alone if their marriage is going through a stressful period. The authorities are gradually coming around to it.

Tony   Or is this a little fairy tale that they put out every now and again?

Fred   The religious authorities understand the problem and the Church is saving marriages by giving private visits in the prison chapel. This has to be recommended by the chaplain and decided by the prison authorities.

Nothing's more destructive to a man in prison than to lose his wife, her loyalty and a family. A man comes out of prison with no wife, no kids, no home – but who can blame a woman, if she's gotta go ten years without any physical contact with her husband? It's hard for the relationship to survive.

Most of the long-term prisoners lay it on the line. 'You've gotta go off and lead your own life, and if you're still there, if we still feel the same about each other when I come out, we'll carry on.' You give the woman in your life the chance to walk away

Tony   I said it to my [ex-wife] Pat – 'There's the door and I'm advising you to take it,' because you can't ask a woman to wait years and years on her own. But she didn't take the door. We didn't split up until after I came out.

Fred   I said it to Maureen, my wife, and to my [current partner] Janice, and they both stayed the course. I take my hat off to prisoners' wives, you know. It's hard for them. But they've got children that show their love, and they've got parents. A man in prison, apart from his visits, can't come into physical contact with another human being.

Although there's a story about Gordon Goody in Wormwood Scrubs.

Tony   My old mate, Bluey!

Fred   Well, Gordon, he had a bad back. He injured his spine and he used to have to wear a corset round him. He was a big, powerful man, big shoulders and a very good physique.

Tony   All them Train Robbers were big men.

Fred   He went over to the prison hospital to have some treatment, and there was this physiotherapist over there. She was in her late forties, and she was a very attractive woman. She was a married woman, but she hadn't been ravaged by children and she had quite a tidy little figure on her.

Tony (*Laughing*) That sounds like Gordon talking there! He was a character, Bluey.

Fred She took quite a fancy to Gordon, and all of a sudden, it come to a little bit of kissing and a bit of fondling. And, of course, it was behind screens in the hospital. He used to sit outside, waiting, cos she used to leave him till the end.

She had lovely boobies, and he used to get them out and get his head in between them and have a little nuzzle around.

Tony (*Laughter*)

Fred And the evil, wicked bastards like us, we said, 'Well, get her to bring a bit of gear in,' you know, a bit of snout, cos that was currency. So she used to bring a bit of snout. And then it went from snout to steaks, nice fillet steaks, and pork chops with the kidneys in 'em, lamb chops and stuff like that.

We always had plenty of readies, plenty of pound notes, so we'd give her a shopping list and pay her to go and buy what we asked for.

When they search you when you go back into the wing, they just pull your jacket back open and they rub down your body. But Gordon had these poacher's bags specially made in the workshop and he had them under his coat. He used to load them up and come back with nice, big, thick gammon steaks. And we'd get some tinned pineapple out of the canteen to put on top. We had some lovely meals.

But then Gordon said, 'It's getting too much. Every time she's kissing me, she's got the tongue down my throat,' and he didn't really want it. He said, 'Can't someone else go?'

Tony He had the longest back trouble I've ever heard of! And his little sessions *didn't* straighten his back out . . .

Fred We used to have to push him to go over there – 'Now, Gordon, think of them lamb chops and think of them steaks for the weekend.'

Buster [Edwards] was a cook in the air force before he became a thief, and he used to cook this food we were getting. None of the screws used to see what he was cooking in the kitchen. He put metal plates over the top to keep 'em hot and we all used to go in the kitchen. He'd give us all our plates, still with the metal ones on top, and we'd take them to the 'dining out' area in the middle of the wing. At the given word, we'd lift the metal plates all off together and we'd get stuck in. You've got to eat it as quick as you can, cos you've got the screws walking up and down. You couldn't go and bang up with it in the cell, cos they was all locked up. If you were dining out, you had to stay dining out.

This screw came along one day, he looked, and he did a double take: 'Where the fuck did they get that food from?' We were all stuck into these lovely big steaks and things. I don't even think he got that at home. He reported it, and there was a little inquiry into where we was getting this food from.

Oh, it carried on for ages but, course, Gordon had to finish. He couldn't face it any more because he was getting molested and raped every time he went over to have his back straightened out. The old girl was having a right go at him. She thought they were going to set up home when he got out. Gordon should've got a medal.

Tony I've seen some of these little affairs spring up. And now they've got women prison officers, there's a lot more of it carrying on. I don't really see how that can work.

Do you remember the lady welfare officer in the Scrubs, Fred? She visited me all the time, and she was always calling me out to the welfare office, to my embarrassment.

Fred *No!*

Tony She was wanting to touch my leg and that . . . I didn't stop her. Certainly not! She was a nice enough woman. She was about fifty, and she was mutton dressed as lamb. She used to wear her hair long, with a little ribbon in it. And the perfume she used to wear!

She didn't proposition me, but I always thought she wanted me to give her one. In fact, I know she did. At that time, we all had long hair and moustaches and all that. She didn't fancy any of the other prisoners.

Of course, I enjoyed the attention and, yeah, I felt tempted, but it was an impossible situation. Everywhere you went in Category A, there was the big piece of glass so they could watch you all the time. They couldn't leave women alone with the prisoners.

You know, it didn't look good, and the screws started getting the hump with it, Fred. They were aware something wasn't right. Gordon Goody was getting very heated. He used to say to me, 'Well, why does she keep calling you out?' Very inquisitive, weren't he? He thought something was going on. Always questioning me about her. 'That boy's a dirty bastard,' they were calling me. But nothing ever happened – promise.

About a year it went on. Then I went down the block and that was the end of that. She died of cancer, you know that?

Fred Did she really?

Tony Yeah, about ten years ago.

Fred How about the new Spanish guy who come to the Scrubs? Gordon Goody was into anything Spanish. I don't mean that literally . . . he wasn't into any Spaniards! But he was into playing the Spanish guitar and studying the language. Now he's out in Spain, he's got his own beach bar, he speaks Spanish fluently and he plays guitar. That's after doing a thirty-year sentence.

Gordon's a proper man. They don't come any tougher than Gordon, but in his quiet way, he can be a really funny bastard.

On this day, someone said, 'There's a fella just coming through the reception and he's from Spain.' And Gordon kept saying, 'Where? Where? Where is he?' Gordon considered that cos he was Spanish, he could have helped him with the language.

So he's talking to him and he's got him up in his cell and he's making him tea and looking after him, and then the cons start fucking talking. They say, 'Oh, there's something going on between them two. He's always up in Gordon's cell.' They call it 'married quarters', when two guys are at it. So, all of a sudden, the Spanish kid's gone fucking berserk. He's running around shouting, 'Gordon is not my daddy sugar, he's not my daddy sugar. He's my amigo,' he said. '*He's my amigo*.' And he wants to fight everyone. That good old Latin, macho temperament came to the surface. We had to laugh.

Tony I gotta tell you a story about a screw in Gartree Prison. There was a screw called Lou who was doing the films and they called him Lou The Wanker.

Once a week, you were entitled to a film and, as well as that, you got a film card which the men contribute to. It's a private thing, so we're allowed films. And you always had the films on Saturday afternoon or Sunday morning.

It's like a proper cinema. They got the projector at the back there, and the men all sit in front. And this prison officer put the films on. He'd be standing there changing a film or putting another reel on and what he started doing is masturbating. It was a regular thing.

Fred Was it blue films they was showing?

Tony Nah, normal films. He got a kick out of it, Fred. I think it was over *us*. He loved it. Anyway, all down the front of this wall where the projector was, was all these semen stains.

So one day they set it up with the chief of security, and had him down there. And when they put the film on, the gym orderly waited for him to start and there he was, Fred, doing the old action, and who walked in? The chief of security. Took him straight out, sacked him on the spot. And he put it down to working with 'animals' in Gartree Prison. High pressure. 'Animals'. We were 'animals', us.

Fred We was really a bit pleased about what we did with the real animals in the nick. There was an Asian fella in the Scrubs called Raj. He was doing life. He had murdered his own daughter cos she was gonna run away with and marry an English kid. He actually chopped her body up. To do that to your own daughter . . . we was horrified.

Tony I remember that well. It was a big talking point.

Fred He had this terrible attitude. His family used to come on visits and you could see he was domineering. His wife wasn't allowed to look up at him and all this. He was laying the law down.

He never mixed with any of us, just his own people, and they treated him like a god. He was like a village elder. They sort of had to pay homage to him. He'd put his order in with them and they used to buy his stuff for him in the canteen. I'll never forget him. He had a very long, trimmed, grey beard and steel-grey hair.

Anyway, we had a couple of cells knocked into one where we used to cook and, round the wall, we had these little Belling stoves, the ones people used to have in bedsits. They had two rings on the top and a little oven inside. They've stopped making them now, I think.

There was 300 men and this was what we used to have to cook on, but we had to commandeer them. We'd put our pots of boiling water on them so we'd have, like, three of them for our table. And then there would be a big urn with constant boiling water, to make the tea with, just outside the door.

Raj used to make all these curries. He cooked for himself, looked after himself. He didn't sit down with other people, eating. We hated him, and especially what he'd done. We wanted to have a go at him somehow – arrogant bastard, you know.

You always had someone in the pharmacy you could straighten up, get what you wanted. In the Scrubs' there was a Belgian fella and he was all right – tall, glasses and a white jacket on. He used to come round with a screw, with a basket with all the medicines, to give the tots out, going all round the cells to give the cons their medication.

We got this Belgian fella to give us something to do Raj up with, put something in his curry, you know.

There was a couple of fellas in there who wanted to be women. They was trying to get the operation, over in the other wing. I used to see them walking around. They used to get, like, the cover of a red book, wet it and rub it on their lips to look like lipstick. And they had boobs on 'em as well. They was getting the hormone treatment.

Tony   One I remember clearly being brought in halfway through the treatment – they didn't know whether to put this person in a men's or women's prison. They wouldn't accept him or her in Holloway when they found a pair of nuts. And the wing of a men's prison was out of the question too, so this con ended up in the punishment unit in the Scrubs.

Fred   Anyway, the Belgian came over and I said, 'Get us some of that gear, that hormone treatment,' and he said, 'All right, I'll get you some.' So anyway, he left a packet of this powder.

Raj would be in there cooking and when he wasn't looking, or when he went to get hot water from outside, me and Buster would sprinkle some gear on the curry and give it a quick stir. We kept topping him up.

Tony   (*Hearty laughter*)

Fred   It went on for weeks and weeks and then, all of a sudden, my pal Frank O'Connell – he was doing fifteen for armed robbery

– he said, 'Fred, Raj has gone sick this morning. He was down to see the doctor.'

'Oh,' I said. 'Maybe we're getting some results. Phew!'

About another couple of weeks later, Frankie said, ''Ere! Get down in the showers lively. Raj is down there. Have a butcher's at him.' So I get my shower gear and go down the showers a bit quick, and he had his Y-fronts on in the shower. He used to shower with his pants on, but he was talking to another one of the Pakistani guys and he was saying, 'Ooooh, my chest, it really hurts. I don't know what it is.' When he turned round, he's got size thirty-six fucking boobs coming up.

Tony He had a right 'andful, they tell me!

Fred Big nipples on them and everything. And the nipples looked really red raw and rough, you know what I mean, as though they were just sprouting through the skin. It really worked. After that, he went missing and they said, 'He's in the hospital.'

Tony Well, you just don't grow a pair of tits out the blue. It doesn't happen.

Fred When he came back, he was all bandaged up.

When I saw where they'd stitched his chest, I thought we'd sewn up mailbags better, eight stitches to the inch. We spent years sewing mailbags in Wandsworth, but I reckoned these stitches were like kids done it. I was pleased to see they hadn't made a very neat job of it. I thought, You cut up a little girl. You deserve what you get.

Well, he got moved out of there to another nick somewhere, but I think they'd sussed out that we'd been doing him up with the gear, the powder. 'Ooooh, my chest, it really hurts.' Yes, you bastard, I bet it hurt when you was cutting that little girl's body up, you bastard.

2

Drink and Drugs: High and (not so) Dry

Conversation in Fred's kitchen, 1 March 2000

Fred You were the brewmaster!

Tony Oh, I made some of the best hooch.

Fred I drank plenty of it over the years, but I wasn't manufacturing it. I was one of the chief testers!

Tony The big problem is that you've got to do away with the smell of it.

Fred That's a fucking battle, that is. You can't have it in your cell. If you've got a couple of buckets of hooch under your bed, they're going to sniff it out straight away.

Tony But, I mean, what do they expect in there?

Fred They don't mind, really, but they still nick you if they find it.

Tony What you do is, you let them find one or two.

Fred And you've got the rest hidden away in the rest of the prison, up in false roofs and places like that, fire extinguishers, everywhere (*laughing*).

Tony If it's a good brew, you only want a cupful.

Fred You have to drink the first one all the way down, in one gulp, and then you get a little, warm sensation. And then you can get on with it. But it's no good sipping it. It's not that nice to sip.

I was watching that film a few weeks ago on the escape from Colditz. These were majors and colonels who'd come from Eton and Oxford and Cambridge, high-ranking, educated people, and they was going through the same things as what prisoners are going through today – boredom. And all they could think about was escaping – and making hooch. *You* made better hooch than what they was turning out by the looks of it.

Tony (*Laughing*) That's right.

Fred They couldn't have had the spot-searches that we had in Category A – 'Stand out on the landing!' Every strip of furniture in your cell comes out on the landing, every mattress, every sheet, every bit of clothing hanging over the side. And your cell was searched top to bottom. So when you look at the Colditz programmes, the things they got up to there . . . They had a man, a 'ghost', hiding under the floorboards.

Tony Did you see that?

Fred Imagine getting away with that in a Cat A prison? Having someone laying under the floorboards? And they built a fucking aeroplane up in the loft. How could you get away with that in a prison?

I got nicked loads of times in the spot-searches. Yeah, course I did. I'd get nicked and lose fourteen days' remission. But not for hooch. I never kept hooch in my cell. I got nicked for an extra pair of socks in Wandsworth and put down the block. How about that? I got nicked for a little piece of cannabis once, lost fourteen days, and I don't even smoke cigarettes!

Tony (*Laughter*)

Fred I don't smoke cannabis either. Some good-hearted fella, when I'm standing in Brixton getting my food, stuck a bit in my pocket.

Tony Thought he was doing you a favour.

Fred He gave me a little nudge and a smile and I felt something, but I didn't realize what he'd done. So I go back to my cell. I've got my prison uniform jean things, and they open me up early in the morning – search my cell. 'What's this?' I've got a little chunk of fucking cannabis in my pocket. I didn't even know it was there.

Five or six years later, when I got to Maidstone, I tried a bit of puff. Because I'm not a smoker, I used to put it in my yoghurt and I got a buzz out of that. I used to put it on a spoon and put a flame

THE RECIPE FOR HOOCH

Tony Well, a nice block of yeast, number one. It's like an ice-cream cube.

Fred If you can't get it smuggled in the nick, you've got to get it out the kitchen or somewhere.

Tony We used to get the old tea cans, cut a piece of yeast off and throw it in there. And that's alive. Yeast feeds off itself, but you must add hot water and sugar.

Fred Loads of sugar.

Tony And plenty of fruit. You can put in potatoes, anything that'll rot.

Fred Tinned fruit's the nicest.

Tony Didn't it give the game away a bit in the canteen, ordering five or ten pounds of sugar and tinned fruit?!

Fred So then it's got to ferment.

Tony You use warm water, because the yeast will feed the warmer it gets. So you leave it down for a night and then, the next day, you add some more sugar and – *whoomph*! It will start to fester.

Fred It bubbles. It's like acid.

Tony And you can flavour it in a lot of ways. My favourite was pineapple.

Fred I didn't care what they put in it so long as it did the trick! But I didn't like to see all that rotten old fruit thrown in the pot.

Tony You've gotta hide it from the screws.

Fred And then you keep feeding it. Every day, you've got to look at it and nurse it.

Tony Stroke it, talk to it. I'm telling you, I've seen men doing it!

Fred It should be down for five weeks. It's gotta be down, to mature, otherwise it takes all the enamel off your teeth. They [the cons] say, 'Oh, that's been down long enough.' It's only been down for a fucking week and they wanna drink it!

Tony But they're like that.

Fred And then you have to strain it.

Tony With a bit of gauze.

Fred A pair of your old pants or something, Tony. Or your slippers!

Tony (*Laughing*) Gawd almighty!

Fred (*Also laughing*) That would blow your head off! The things I could say about your slippers . . .

---

under it, cook it a little bit, and then sprinkle it in the yoghurt. You get the same effect without having to smoke it.

Tony I used to have a bit of puff. What you can get outside, you suddenly want in there, be it fish and chips, or a bottle instead of a cup of milk, or a bit of puff. Today, I understand that the heavy stuff, like heroin, is in the prison system. I never saw that when I was in the nick. I wouldn't even entertain the idea of getting involved with it. But anything goes for a peaceful life, I suppose. Anything can be got hold of.

I took LSD on two occasions in prison. I had to, because I wanted to know what the symptoms were like. I didn't want anyone doing me up and me not knowing what was happening. I made a point of not thinking about bad or depressing things before I took it. And it was fucking brilliant!

Fred Some funny things used to happen. One time in the Scrubs, the cons got a load of mescaline. Everyone got bored there and being locked up, you try these things, because you want to know what it's like.

We was all up on our landing and there was one big fella there, name of Martin Reid. He was about six foot four and he had a big muscle hump on his back. He was a very hairy beast with a sort of hound-dog face and these big rings under his eyes. He'd come back from Parkhurst, where they'd had the riots, Frankie Fraser and a few other faces, in 1969. And we all took some of this mescaline.

They bang us up at five-thirty, and about an hour, two hours, later, there's a terrible ruckus going on in his cell. There's furniture being smashed, and we thought, He's having a bad trip. He's gone off his head. They're calling out the windows, along the landing, 'It's Martin, it's Martin. He's gone into one.'

Both (*Laughter*)

Fred It went on for ages and then it all quietened down cos after ten o'clock, they switch your lights off. You had no control over the lights. They've changed it. You've got your own light switch now, but that's how it used to be.

And he came out in the morning. His eyes was sunken in and he looked in a terrible state. I said, 'What happened to you last night?'

Now, you remember the cell windows had just got one little pane that you slide across to let the air in? And he said, 'Something flew in last night, and it was bouncing off the walls.'

And he was on a trip, wasn't he?

'I'm trying to kill it and it's hitting me on the head and I can't catch it,' he said. He had to break up the chair to try and whack this thing.

It was a stag beetle, and he had it in a coffee jar. He said, 'That's what was in my cell last night.' Fucking hell, it was massive. It had big pincers on it, and wings. And it had flown straight in that little window.

It was taken over to the college, cos they had a college in there, and the students, the nature people, said they'd never seen one as big. I don't think I'd ever seen one before. This was a monster.

Tony Some people in Gartree, who shall remain nameless, gave an LSD trip to Jimmy Humphreys, 'The Porn King', who ran Soho. He brought half of Scotland Yard down. It was in 1976, and I remember it was a fine summer. They slipped a tab into his tea, and they put mirrors everywhere, under the bed and in his drawers. Then they got all the budgies that people had in their cells and put them in his cell. You can imagine – you're tripping and all them start flying about. About eleven o'clock, there was this hell of a scream – 'I'm being attacked by spacemen!' They had to take him out of there, cos once a trip takes off, you can't get off it. He flew for hours with the budgies!

3

Blood and Guts: Violence, Death and Destruction in the Nick

Conversation in the Brunswick Arms pub, Stamford Street, London SE1, 26 August 1998

THE PRESSURE COOKER: LETTING OFF STEAM

Tony Prison can bring out the worst in people.

Fred The violence used to start just out of nowhere.

Tony A little thing like the washroom in the morning . . . cos I find that to be a very temperamental time in a man. He's just got out of bed.

Fred And got the hump.

Tony You know, you see a dirty bowl. I've seen more men get bashed up . . .

Fred . . . over leaving a dirty bowl. They threaten to smash people's fucking sound systems up cos they've got them on loud. All these little things used to be going on all the time around you, fellas rowing with each other. There was always loads of fights and razor blades in the toothbrush . . .

And they'd meet in the recess and have a straightener, and we used to watch out for the screws. I mean, keep it fair.

Tony There was a geezer called Terry Twaites. You ever come across him?

Fred Yeah.

Tony He's in Australia now. I was with him in Hull Prison. And he had this habit of barging into people. As he come into the washroom, he just pushed 'em out of the way and the water went everywhere. One morning, he went to push me. I said, 'What's the matter with you?' Well, as he went to throw one, I shoved him back and he slipped and he's banged his head. I'm down the block for assaulting him. Assault! Not that he would say a word. Terry was a nice guy, but he had a bad attitude, Fred. Like Dougie Pidgley, 'Doug The Bug'. Come out of Notting Hill Gate.

Fred   Yeah.

Tony   He had cropped hair, to make him look meaner. And The Bug, basically, was harmless, Fred. And he was very pally with a man they called 'The Mad Butler', the one who poisoned all the MPs – Roy Fontaine.

Fred   Oh, Fontaine, yeah. I never met him.

Tony   The Queen of Hull Prison, he was (*laughing*). He had black hair and he used to wear a dressing gown . . . Anyway, Eric Flowers [armed robber] is very quiet, isn't he, Fred?

Fred   (*Amused*) Eric . . .

Tony   He used to be next door to me, Eric.

Fred   He's doing a ten, you know.

Tony   What, Eric?

Fred   Maybe he's finished now. I hope so.

Tony   He escaped with Biggsy from Wandsworth.

Fred   He climbed over the wall.

Tony   He had a little cup and saucer (*both laughing*), which tickled me. We had big, plastic mugs or something. But Eric, he was a very quiet, lovely man. And Doug The Bug used to come into his cell and smoke, which used to irritate Eric.

Fred   It would do, yeah.

Tony   And he used to go to Doug, 'Don't do that in here, don't smoke in the cell.'

Fred   Putting all his ash everywhere.

Tony   And I never saw that man lose his temper before, Fred, but this day, he lifted his flask and he said, 'If you don't fucking get out, I'll bash you with this.'

Fred   The prisoners used to go back to their cells and ferment all night about someone who'd annoyed them. They lay there tossing and turning and soon as they opened up, they was down the landing, they used to dive straight into that person's cell, and caught them before they got out of their bed, and they was on their chest. And they couldn't lift you off, and you'd fucking batter 'em.

Tony   Yeah. Yeah. Cos you gotta do it. I was in a couple of incidents, mostly up north. They're trying you out. You're in a different area, you're hated – you're a Londoner.

Fred   We was classed as LGs.

Both   London gangsters.

Tony   And I don't like that name. It's insulting. 'All you gangsters are the same,' that attitude. Because, at the end of the day, most of the major crimes are committed in the capital of any country. You know there's a lot of jealousy about this in prison.

Fred   There is, yes.

Tony   A lot of the disputes are all about standing. For instance, Tony Laing, 'The Monster of Parkhurst', bashed Connie Whitehead [one of the Kray firm]. He was sent a few quid to give him a right-hander in Wandsworth Prison. Now, we wasn't that happy with Connie Whitehead at the time, but when Tony Laing done that, he wasn't hitting Connie Whitehead, he was hitting one of us. And my brother Chris didn't want him thinking he could get away with that, so he gave him a whack in the toilet, and that was the end of the matter.

Fred   Guess who was in the next cell to me when I was down the block in the Scrubs after I bashed up Johnny Barry in the yard? There was this Nicholas Hoogstraten, you heard of him? He's a multi-millionaire – he's got one of the biggest stamp collections in the world. He's bought a mansion and he's been building a mausoleum with a surrounding moat and drawbridge, right outside of Brighton. He owns all these big properties down there. He was doing a bit of Rachmanism, getting up to all sorts of things to get people out so he could buy the property cheap.

He was a bit of a rascal, he was a rebel, and he used to go walking round with the tight jeans on, the open shirt and the gold chain round his neck, and his hair used to be all coiffed. He was a good-looking man.

I was in the block with my pal Frank O'Connell and another guy, a lifer. Then there was Hoogstraten, a young kid with an angelic face who was at Her Majesty's Pleasure, and a stranger we didn't know, who never spoke to us. He was a noncy guy.

We went to slop out one day and this stranger had propositioned the kid. I went into the recess and I hear terrible screams and this little nutcase, the young kid, had done the stranger from behind as he's washing in the sink. He's gone ssst, right across the face, and the blood's pumping out all over the sink, spurting everywhere, and the stranger was screaming, holding his face. The kid said, 'I just cut him, Fred, he's a nonce,' and he went back to his cell.

Now, the screws are looking me and Hoogstraten. They don't know who's done it, and we can't say anything, but they've tumbled it was the kid, and they took him to Broadmoor the next day. That's an example of what can happen over something really small. The nonce whispered something in the kid's ear, squeezed his arse, and got his face opened up from ear to ear.

Tony You know what it's like in them places, Fred. Everything gets magnified a million times over. It makes different feuds go on which really are nothing. I mean, it's so petty, some of it, but in there it becomes a very big thing.

Fred There's a book called *Dog Eat Dog* by [convicted American armed robber] Edward Bunker. And he says prisoners are like 'maniacs in hothouses'. It's a good description, innit? Things are boiling. And then you have the riots in there when the conditions get too much, and they explode. It's like a safety valve with steam blowing off, you know. You've gotta let off steam and smash fuck out of people. It's only discontent and frustration, isn't it?

But a lot of the time when you get yourself in the crap, it's other people's crap you're treading in, not your own.

Tony That's right, yeah.

Fred You've got to go along with the rest of the guys in the nick. You haven't got a choice.

Tony No, no choice.

Fred And you get swept up along with it all – the riots, the demonstrations, the protests, the fucking sit-downs and whatever. You have to be part of it because if you don't, you lose your credibility. Like you, in the riots in Gartree when it went off. You went straight in! Broke into the canteen and nicked all the fucking snout!

Tony That was 1972.

Fred They dig a name out, or a face, and they put you up at the front when you've got that notoriety. You have to negotiate with chiefs and governors.

Tony For me, it was obviously cos of the Kray thing.

Fred The Krays had nothing to do with it in my case. There were plenty of cons with much bigger reputations in prisons up and down the country. It was your standing with the cons and the authorities that put you into that position. Twenty years later, I was still doing the same thing at Full Sutton.

We had a big riot in the Scrubs. It started off in one of the other wings. They had a demonstration and they wouldn't go back off exercise. They all stayed out in the yard. We joined the strike in sympathy with them. We gave them food out of our cell windows. And then the screws stopped feeding us. And then the men was up and down on the roof like monkeys, and they was sleeping out all night for about a week.

Me and my friends, we wanted to keep the situation under control, but it broke out into a bit of a fracas, and chairs and toilets and televisions were getting smashed up. And there was Martin Frape, a guy who came from Parkhurst . . .

Tony I knew Martin Frape. A blond, curly-haired fella, a Leicester boy. He got battered to hell in the riots.

Fred He used to froth at the mouth. He tried to cut a screw's throat, and then he was trying to hang him, in Parkhurst. There was a riot down there. They sent him to the Scrubs, so he left one riot situation and walked straight into a new one.

And there was this old PO, a good old boy with a grey

moustache. He wouldn't do you any harm. And Martin Frape was gonna set about him and I stopped it. I didn't mind the dog screws getting beat up, but I didn't want to see the old screw get hurt, you know. He was like your father. Always listened to your problems and treated you like a human.

WATERING THE GRASS

Tony To call someone a grass is a very bad thing, especially in the nick. I was in Gartree Prison and you remember [bank robber] Dave Martin, Fred, don't you? He was a transvestite.

Fred He was the one who hung himself in the nick. He's the one they was trying to shoot when they shot the wrong guy, Stephen Waldorf, in a Mini.

Tony Yeah, in west London – 1983. They thought it was Dave Martin. They made a mistake.

Fred They was pistol-whipping the guy . . .

Tony Were they? Five bullets they put into him. Well, as they dragged him out of the motor, they was bashing him up. And the kid got 120 grand, weren't it?

Fred Compensation. He settled out of court.

Tony Yeah. And one day in Albany Prison, Dave Martin done Johnny Barry [who gave evidence for the prosecution in the Kray trial].

Fred Who I set about in the yard at Wormwood Scrubbs.

Tony Dave was standing in one of the wings one day with a tea urn, and Johnny Barry went, 'All right?' Dave's filled this jug up with water, and – luckily, it weren't boiling, Fred – he just give it to him in the face and said, 'You fucking grass.' That's the life that Barry chose. The minute he pointed the finger at us, the minute you done him, he was a marked man.

Fred Didn't that happen a lot, Tony? I mean, this was an easy way of hurting somebody, scalding them.

Tony Yeah.

Fred Them boilers was steaming.

Tony It sticks to 'em. *Oh*, it burns.

Fred The flesh just falls away, doesn't it? The layer of skin comes off. They go pink. Ohhh, I saw a black guy get done with it once, and with a black man, it shows up more. You can see all the pink.

Tony But the favourite weapons were those PP9 batteries or snooker balls, in a sock. Or a tin of beans. They was a good tool.

Fred When I was in Wandsworth years ago, there was a guy who rolled over and turned grass. He got some bird – but not half as much as his co-defendants. Jackie Kramer was there, Georgie Cornell and who was that little firm out in Notting Hill who used to do all the jump-ups, the robberies? They were there as well. There was loads of faces there and they said, 'This geezer, you can't get near him. He's sussed us, Fred. We're waiting to try and serve him up.' So I said, 'Well, I'll fucking serve him up.' So I got a tool and I'm going round to do him, and every time he came out on the yard, he had all his library books and magazines inside his shirt, wrapped all round him. He looked like Michelin Man and it stopped him getting served up. We never did get the opportunity to do anything before they moved him to another nick.

There were informers who would grass you up in the nick as well. They'd go to the suggestion box in the wing, right outside the PO's office, and they'd just slip a note in there – 'He's hiding snout under his bed.' It's just wickedness. Jealousy's one of the main things.

It was called sweet-grassing. They still do it today but they use the phone instead, cos they're all taped up! You would not believe what some of those idiots say on nick phones to their mates on the outside. The authorities must love it!

OFFENCES AGAINST THE SEX OFFENDERS

Tony There was a rapist brought down to the control unit in the Scrubs called Catino. Remember him, Fred?

Fred Yeah, yeah. He was 'The Beast of Bedsitland'. He used to follow these young ladies back to their bedsits all round Earl's Court.

Freddie and the Krays in their heyday.
At the gym with, from the left, Charlie Kray, Buster Osborne, Buller Ward,
Freddie and Harry Abrahams.

And here with (from left to right) Henry Cooper, Ronnie and Charlie Kray,
Red-faced Tommy, Reggie Kray, Freddie, Jim Wicks (Cooper's manager)
and Sulky, who managed the Aster Club.

Taken in 1968, this is the last photograph of the twins as free men.
From the left: Checker Berry, Ron Kray, Teddy Berry, Charlie Walker
(who was in the Firm), Charlie and Reg Kray.

Tony with Ron Kray, taken at the same time.

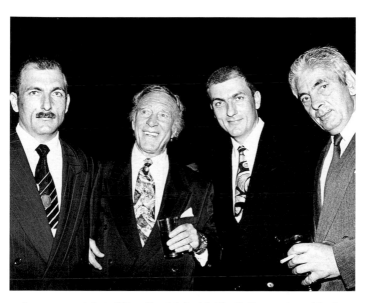

A more recent shot of Tony (far right) with Charlie Kray and two friends.

Freddie and Tony with Roy Shaw and young Joe Pyle.

Freddie Foreman

Freddie enjoying a drink with Great Train Robber Ronnie Biggs.

Freddie Foreman

Freddie and his son Jamie with crime writer Ed Bunker in the centre.

Jocelyn Bain Hogg

The Foreman family – Jamie, Janice, Freddie and Danielle.

Tony and Wendy
Lambrianou.

Sun

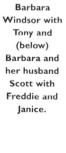

Barbara
Windsor with
Tony and
(below)
Barbara and
her husband
Scott with
Freddie and
Janice.

Tony Lambrianou

Freddie Foreman

Tony and Freddie with Freddie's brother George.

Freddie's exit from Spain, as portrayed by Charles Bronson.

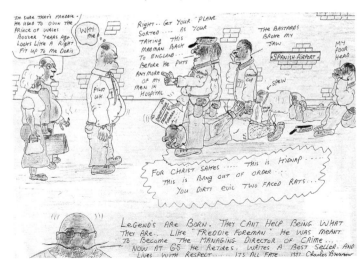

Tony and Sir Cliff Richard.

Freddie and Tony with Gillian Taylforth.

John Stoddart

Tony   I remember him being half-Italian.

Fred   Flat nose. Done a bit of boxing, and he served a few people up in there. He used to make out he was a Post Office bandit to all the inmates, but this guy, Lydon, used to keep every cutting from the newspapers and he fished out the stories about him.

Tony   Catino was brought down to the unit for a couple of days because Robert Carr, the Home Secretary, was coming for a visit. There were only two control units in the country, there and Wakefield, and they were for heavy punishment. The regime in there was so harsh they shut them down later on.

And they brought Catino down to tell Robert Carr how well they looked after the men in there. I was yelling through the door, Fred. We weren't allowed to mix with the other cons. And this day, I was having a shower and I remember Catino saying to me, 'Freddie Foreman had a go at me in the exercise yard.' And I went, 'What?' He said, 'Yeah, he done me.' (*Laughing*) I didn't know what you done.

Fred   I knocked his teeth out.

Tony   What happened that day, Fred? It was a game of football, wasn't it?

Fred   Yeah. It was a Saturday morning. There was a free ball, where the ref dropped the ball between Catino and me. He tried to kick the ball up between my legs, a bit fierce. And that was an excuse then to fucking do him.

I cut my thumb open on his teeth. And I battered him in the face, knocked him out. There were six screws standing around the concrete yard, watching the game, and none of them did anything or even said they saw anything.

Tony   You done Johnny Barry in that yard as well. They should rename it Fred's Yard!

Fred   The cons would do all sorts of things to sex offenders or anybody hurting women or children. They'd dive into their cells with buckets of water and soak their bedding. They'd throw buckets of water under their doors and flood them out. When the supper came round, they used to put razor blades in the buns and stuff. They'd tip barrow-loads of bricks and rubble in on top of them through the skylight in the bathhouse when they were having a bath . . . everything they could do to give them a hard time.

You had to say to yourself, 'I've gotta switch off from these people.' They'd all been seen to in the early part of their sentences. They keep them separate now, but, in those days, the rapists, sex offenders, child molesters and murderers of women used to be in amongst you, and you didn't know where to start and where to finish.

You know, there was one guy who killed his mother because she burnt the pork chops or something. Every time he went out in the yard, they'd all go, 'Mother killer' (*low, menacing growl*) and it used to drive him crazy. All psychological stuff. 'Mother killer . . .' He used to run around the yard like a crazed animal.

Tony   There was another man whose wife used to give him bread and jam every morning and one day she gave him marmalade, and he stabbed her to death. He said, 'It's one of those unfortunate things.'

Fred   Some of the stories are beyond belief.

THE SCREWS AND WHAT THEY DO

Fred   The screws could do some really vicious things. Did I tell you about the photo?

Tony   That was in Leicester, Fred. I remember it. Family photo.

Fred   It was sent in to me. It was a photo of Maureen and Jamie and Gregory and Danielle, this portrait. And they'd cut my head right out of the picture. That's how I received it. It was left in my cell. I found it when I came back off exercise. Whoever did it – security? – I don't know why. I think at that time, you wasn't allowed to have a photo of yourself. They always see the mail first.

Tony   I never put a photo on the wall after seeing that.

Fred   Another time, when there was the riots and different things, the screws went in and they smashed fuck out of people's cells. Smashed all their radios and cut up photographs and stripped their bed covers, their towels and anything personal that you had of value.

Tony Well, you expect that.

Fred I've seen screws run with a prisoner four-handed, an arm and a leg each. They make sure the con's head hits the fucking door on the way to the block.

Tony Nobby Clarke, Fred. Do you remember that day he says to me and you, 'They're talking about us in the office, the screws.' And I said, 'What do you mean?' He went, 'Well, what I'm gonna do is get all the snooker cues . . .'

Fred '. . . sharpen them into spears . . .'

Tony '. . . and as they come out, we'll spear 'em to death.' And he meant it.

Fred Some of the screws were all right. They'd leave you alone, you know, to do certain things. If someone was attacking a nonce, they used to turn their back and let him get on with it.

Tony If he's a bad one, they'd cover it up.

Fred They hated the nonces as much as we did. But they've got to protect them cos if they get hurt when they're on duty, they get called up in front of the governor. There was one incident in the Scrubs in the Seventies when a guy came into D-Wing, a barman from a pub in Blackpool who'd had an affair with the missus. She had three lovely little girls and he'd murdered them, impaled them on railings.

Everyone knew of his case and there was a terrible atmosphere in the wing, like impending fucking doom. You knew something was coming off. All the screws were on edge.

One day I came in from my job in the laundry to see the Governor. The nonce was in the wing while everyone was at labour, cos he hadn't had his work allocated yet. I was waiting outside the Governor's office, and all of a sudden, there's a commotion down the end of the wing. I see the screws all running down there and they found the geezer with his head nearly caved in. He's had a right fucking hammering.

All the cons come back from work, buzzing. 'Oh, he's got served right up. Lovely.'

It turns out that there was a Hell's Angels kid there, tattooed up, who's caught the nonce on the iron stairs going up, and he's battered him with a club hammer.

Tony   I remember that incident. He just done him.

Fred   The kid was with what they call a works screw – they're like civilians who come in doing little jobs around the nick. This screw, give him his due, took the fucking club hammer and washed it under the sink and then locked it in a cupboard with the rest of the tools, so they don't know who's done it.

Tony   It's a common cause there.

Fred   The nonce looked like dying. He was in intensive care in Hammersmith Hospital, although he did survive, which was a shame. But there was a big inquiry. The outside police came in, the CID, the murder squad, and the screw cracked under questioning. He told them everything.

One day, months and months later, I was in the mailbag shop in Wandsworth and there he was, the kid. I said, 'How did you get on, then?' He said, 'Ah, Fred, eighteen months, and worth every fucking day of it.' I said, 'Good on ya, son. You did well.'

Tony   Nonces are the lowest form of prison life. They hang around the screws and their own ilk. They never interfere in anything, never take part in anything. They're just complete outsiders.

They appear on the landing, they say they're serving sentences for robbery, but you know full well they're not.

Some of the less high-profile prisoners try to get themselves in a bit of limelight when they occasionally batter a nonce, because they want to impress 'the boys'. They'd want us to do 'em a few little favours. It's all about standing.

There was a PO in Wandsworth who hated all cons, and used to piss in the soup, everybody's soup. 'Flavour that up,' he said. 'Do 'em good.'

THERE WERE MURDERS . . .

Fred   Nobby Clarke was in doing a double life. He'd committed a couple of murders.

Tony   (*Laughing*) He was accused of so many, they lost count.

Fred He looked like John Carradine, the actor, with a parting down the middle and all the hair hanging down his face. And he was mopping the floor. The first time I ever saw him, he was bent over. He was all, like, bony . . .

He went to Broadmoor and he wound up killing a young prisoner. He strangled him and he had a flex round his neck. They found him dragging him along the corridor, trying to put him in a cupboard. He done one in the bath as well.

Tony He harpooned him in the bath, and the rumour was that he done it because the guy never cleaned the bath out. I'll tell you what. One of the most educated men I've ever come across, you know him well, was Tony Dunford. He got degrees.

Fred A double lifer. He was with us in Leicester. He was a very intelligent boy. He studied a lot in there. He was self-taught, wasn't he? I really liked Tony.

Tony He was a good man, he was.

Fred Tony stabbed and murdered another prisoner, a kid called Buckingham, cos he didn't really know how to fight. I got him on the punchbag we had there, and I taught him how to punch.

Tony You did.

Fred And I said, 'Now you can defend yourself and you know how to fight, it won't happen to you again, cos you're a big, strong boy, and if you can use your hands in a fight, you won't use a tool so you won't get yourself in any more trouble.' He was much more confident after that.

Then there was Duggie Wakefield, who killed another prisoner and hid him under his bed. The screws were counting and there was one missing, and they kept going round all the cells, checking. He had him under his bed all the time. He was a weird bastard, he was.

He was doing life. He was built like a brick shithouse and ugly with it. He used to run round the sports field wearing these tiny, black shorts that looked like a skirt, with splits up each side.

His job was to look after the centre garden in Full Sutton. Lovely, it was – loads of plants and flowers, and a small greenhouse. Someone upset him one day and he dug the whole garden up and smashed the greenhouse. It was like a bomb site. I saw him years later when I was in Springhill and I went into the Grendon Underwood psychiatric prison, where they had the dental facilities. While I was in the waiting room, Duggie walked in with a cup of tea for me.

Another con, a young lifer called Mark Edmond who was a good friend of mine – he was with me in Full Sutton – had told Duggie I was coming into the nick to see my dentist, Leo, who'd come from Harley Street.

I had a very pleasant conversation with Duggie, and then he sashayed out the door. I later heard that he'd come out the closet after all those years. Good luck to him. That may have been the cause of all his problems. And I still go to Leo. He's got a practice in Aylesbury – a Harley Street dentist not charging Harley Street prices.

THE HANGING SHED

Fred   I always remember when I was in Pentonville and they hung someone; I'd like to remember who that was now, back in the early Fifties. He was one of the last guys to be hung, and we all made a right racket on the doors and the bars with the old tin cups, the stamping and the banging and the kicking the doors. It was horrendous, you know, the morning it happened. It was the same in most prisons when they hung someone.

Tony   Terrible. Terrible.

Fred   What an atmosphere over the whole prison. And some time afterwards, I was on a works party and they wanted a hosepipe. They unlocked the enclosure to let me in to where they had the unmarked graves. The ground was like limestone in there. The earth was white. All new grass was growing, like young seeds springing up.

Tony   I was in Bristol at the beginning of the Sixties when there was a hanging. Didn't have a coffin, Fred. He was in a big bag. And in Bristol, the hanging shed was down by the gate on its own, and he was left there for an hour, and I always remember the screw. He come into where I was working and he went, 'How's your day been – swinging?' and I went, 'You horrible bastard.'

Fred   Oh, he made a 'joke', did he? Very funny.

Tony   And they brought him round in a barrow, two work screws, both smoking a fag, pulling this barrow. And the Godfreys, [music star] Tricky's relations, were there – Arthur and Martin Godfrey, two of the hard boys in Bristol at the time. And he started going into one, Arthur Godfrey – he's dead now, Big Arthur – 'You don't talk like that, it's not nice, it's non-religious.' 'Yeah, fuck' – the attitude, Fred. I'll never forget it in my life.

The atmosphere around any hanging in prison was shocking.

Fred   You can't believe it. It's a powder keg. It's ready to ignite. I mean, the wrong thing said can spark off a riot. They keep you banged up.

Tony   Everything's done an hour earlier.

Fred   Before they have you up for breakfast, it's all, like, over with.

Tony   I don't think there's a case for capital punishment, because they can't put it right, and they've made too many cock-ups.

Fred   I think, you know, in certain cases with these fucking people like [Moors murderers Ian] Brady and Myra Hindley, they should live every fucking day till they die and make them suffer. Killing them is too good.

Tony   That's exactly what I think. Make 'em suffer.

4

Sick Jokes

Conversation in the Brunswick Arms, 26 August 1998

Fred   Did you ever hear about the old arsonist, Fred Bishop? Oh, this is funny.

Tony   I've read that most arsonists have ginger hair.

Fred   Have they really? Well, the guy, he was a lifer. He was in his late sixties, getting on to seventy or something like that, and he spent all his life in prison cos he couldn't stop setting light to places. He was a pyromaniac. He used to work in the Scrubs for the Governor, Howard Jones, and the chief and the POs. He used to take their tea in, and biscuits on a tray.

   Anyway, we'd be sitting in the wing – it's all open, with a few tables and a television at each end, for 300 men. So you're watching a film and, every now and again, the bell used to start ringing for a fire engine, you know, or the police. And Fred would come out of his cell, and he's got slippers on – they were worse than *your* slippers . . .

Tony   (*Laughter*)

Fred   And he couldn't stop what he was doing, drying his cups up with a teacloth or something, and he'd come shuffling up to watch the fire engines come running. When it was over, we were more interested in the film, and he'd just shuffle back to his cell. And he always had a little old dog-end on his lip, and he'd talk to you and it was still there, you know, the dog-end, as he's talking.

   I used to have a day off sometimes, if I was pissed off with the laundry, where I was working. I'd make out I was sick. And you'd have your door open, and you could wander around the wing a little bit, just for a change of scene.

   And I'd be in the wing. 'Want a cup of tea?' That's what he used to say. I'd say, 'Yeah, yeah. All right, Fred, yeah, I'll have a cup of tea,' and I used to have a little chat with him. And all of a sudden, this day, he's gone over in the wing, walking to his cell. He's gone into an epileptic fit, and he's lying on the floor and all his body's going into spasm. So me and someone else, I don't know who it was, we run up, got hold of him and we picked him up, got him in his cell and laid him on the bed. And I'm looking after him on the bed, and he's gone out completely. And I'm all worried about him because I'd heard about it, but it's the first time I'd seen anybody have an epileptic fit. It's frightening. And I got his little hand, and I'm giving his old hand a little (*slapping noise*). You know, I'm very concerned about it cos I liked the old boy.

And as I looked at him (*laughing*), he's still got this fucking dog-end on his lip, it's stuck to his lip, and I'm going, 'Fred? You all right, Fred? You all right, mate?' And all of a sudden, his eyes opened. 'Want a cup of tea?' he said. First words out of his mouth.

Both (*Laughter*)

Fred I'll tell you another little thing which was funny. Probably you won't remember it, but this was after I came back from Spain, and it was in Brixton. Same old place, you know, with the same stains on the bath and everything, hadn't changed in twenty odd years. Still the same poxy place.

And I'd been upstairs on the landing, and next door to me was a little Canadian guy who was nicked over a big drug bust. They called him 'The Bear', cos he was like a little teddy bear. He was a nice little fella, very dark.

And he comes out this day. We were walking round to slop out in the morning, and there's the screw, sitting on the chair, dozing. He's half-asleep. And as The Bear walks by, he's got this newspaper and he went like that (*loud bang*) on the screw's head.

Tony (*Laughter*)

Fred He said, 'Wake up!' We walked straight into the recess and when we came out, I went back and the screw was going (*loud snoring sound*) like that, and I thought, He's not right, him, he don't look like he's asleep now. (*Snoring sound again*) Big dribble coming out of his mouth. I called the other screws who were in the PO's office – 'Your mate out here, better come and have a look at him.' They come out, and he was having a heart attack. Like the shock of the newspaper had brought on a heart attack.

So they put him in the office and they got all the chairs with no arms together, and they made a bed and they've got him laid out on there. And they kept ringing up for an ambulance. They get the doctor over.

The doctor was geriatric – he must have been eighty-nine. Can hardly walk. And it must have taken him twenty minutes just to get across the prison. Then he comes in, locks the door, and he's shuffling towards the staircase and we're all watching him. Fuck's sake. You wouldn't want him in an emergency. And he can't get up the fucking stairs, and he's pulling himself up with two hands, one over the other. He walks in and he's so slow it wasn't true. And I said, 'The screw'll be fucking dead by the time he gets to check him out.'

I said to the PO, 'What's happening, Mr Jardine?' He said, 'He's had a heart attack. We're trying to get an ambulance for him, but it's the ambulance strike. The army have got the Green Goddesses out. It took hours before they got him to hospital.'

Both (*Laughter*)

Fred You know Jardine. He was one of the screws used to take us to the Old Bailey all the time. He was on our escort during the Kray trial.

Tony Yeah, Jardine. He used to read war comics, didn't he, Fred? He used to relive the war to us.

Fred Anyway, the screw made a full recovery. He got bored at home and he come back a month later. It was a happy ending. I think.

5

Prison Food: In One End . . . and Out the Other

Conversation in the Brunswick Arms, 26 August 1998

Tony Bread and water, Fred. Now, that went out of the prison system a long time ago. And the first dose of it I had – I was doing three years in Bristol Prison – you got three days on, three days off. They could never give you more than nine days.

Fred No, nine days was the limit. I first got mine in Brixton in 1953.

Tony It's meagre, innit, Fred?

Fred We used to have a cob of bread, just like a little cottage loaf with a knob on the top, and a jug of water.

Tony A lot of us wouldn't eat it.

Fred Cos it used to just bind you up.

Tony Yeah. And what used to get me, the medical officer would say, 'Is everything all right?'

Fred After three days, you're not hungry. Your stomach shrinks. First couple of nights, you can't sleep because it's rumbling and grumbling and hunger pains, and after three days, it's gone. Then you go back, and that's a type of torment cos they put you on a Number Two Diet.

Tony Just the basic meal. Plain meal, no sweet, no drink with it. All weighed.

Fred They weighed it, yeah. They used to weigh the bread.

Tony You had a plastic knife and fork.

Fred That was after the tin knives.

Tony That came in about that time.

Fred They used to have a bit of tin, and they just turned the ends over and hammered them down.

Tony That's right, yeah.

Fred And all the food used to be corroded in the bend where it had been hammered down. The bacteria in those bloody knives . . .

Tony Rotten. Filthy. Yeah.

Fred And that was what you used to cut your food with. All of us used to suffer with bouts of diarrhoea with all that bacteria. That was years ago.

Anyway, I gotta tell you this, about these two screws in Leicester in the early Seventies. They'd position themselves right opposite the toilets, so they were looking into the recess. There was eight cells on either side, weren't there, eight rooms – a TV room and a kitchen and a room for the weights and a unit. One of the cells was a shower, and there were offices at the end, and you went through the office into the punishment block, the bulletproof glass, all that.

Tony Known as a submarine.

Fred Yeah, submarine. Anyway, these two screws were sitting opposite the toilets, and I remember one day with John Duddy – this is the bloke who shot the three coppers with Harry Roberts in 1966. He shot one of them and Harry Roberts shot the other two.

Tony Nice guy.

Fred Yeah, John Duddy. Scotchman, lovely guy. Annie Oakley couldn't have taken a shot like his. He went down on one knee, fired at a moving target and shot the driver in the head. If you tried it a million times, you'd never pull it off.

Now, he badly wanted to go to the toilet, but I beat him to it and I got in. You can see over and under the door, it's like a stable door, so I've left the trousers there with the slippers on the floor, looks like someone's on the toilet, and then I've crept out and left them there and slipped back to my cell. And John's breaking his neck to have a crap and he can't hold it, you know, and he keeps shouting, 'Fred, come out of there, I want to go!'

He's pacing up and down the TV room and the kitchen, cos all he wanted was tea. You'd never see him without a mug of tea in his hand. The screws were fooled as well, thought I was still in there.

Anyway, they reprimanded me over it. They think you're, like, leaving a dummy in the bed or something. You know, you're supposed to be there and you're somewhere else. No sense of humour.

Tony Yeah, yeah.

Fred These two screws used to bring their sandwiches in with them, and they would sit there opposite the toilets and have the sandwiches with a cup of tea. One day [Great Train Robber] Charlie Wilson's gone in the toilet, and they was sitting there eating their sandwiches and suddenly Charlie walked across to them, he's bent over and pulled his shorts down, and his bare arse is right in their faces. And he says, ''Ere, have a look, I think I've fucking shit myself.' And he's got mustard pickle all up his arse (*laughing*). And they went, 'Uuuuuuugh!' and they spit their sandwiches out.

Tony Do you remember the cook in there, Fred? They tried to teach us to cook. I don't know why they were doing that.

Fred Well, I asked to get the food up, didn't I? I said, 'Send us our own food up and we'll cook our own.' And that's when they said they'd show us how to cook.

I was still on trial after you was all finished. Then I was acquitted of the [Frank 'The Mad Axeman'] Mitchell murder. I went straight into Leicester and that's where I stayed for a long time. They never moved me around a lot like they did the others. I think they really wanted me there, cos I was a bit of a sensible head. And Steinhausen was the Governor. He said to me, 'You can have what you like. Anything you need?'

I said, 'No, actually, I don't want nothing that nobody else can't have.' He said, 'Well, let me know.' I said, 'What about food? We can get our own food in and we can do our own cooking.' And so he did that, the Governor. He sent over some meat, beef and stuff, and we used to cook our own dinners and make our own pastas and it was all right. Eggs to do our own breakfast. Give us something to do, you know.

Tony He was a little bloke who come in to give us these cooking lessons. They got him out the university up there. And the screws must have said to him, 'Be careful here with knives.' So he don't leave no knives about. And when he gets this big carving knife out, the screws were saying, 'Watch that knife. Don't turn your back. They'll cut your throat.' They must've terrified the life out of him. But we just wanted the grub.

Anyway, you were personally very funny about your food, weren't you, Fred? You didn't like people touching it. Where hygiene is concerned, you've got that standard. It's very, very important.

Fred Course it is. When you're banged up in a cell and they shut that door, you've got no toilet.

Tony There's a pot.

Fred And you've gotta use that if you've got any problems. It's bad enough having to piss in it.

Tony Some of them ain't too fussy, and they get bad habits. Fortunately, I never got bad habits.

Fred I got Hate 'Em All Harry [Johnson] to do the veg, cos he was always washing his hands.

Tony Always.

Fred Washing his sins away. He'd polish his floor in his cell and everything was in the right place. He was fastidious with the veg. He'd have the tap running, and every little leaf, he'd be washing it under the tap and putting it in – 'Ah, there won't be no dirt on these.' And he'd spend hours just getting the veg ready and peeling the potatoes.

Tony I liked him, Harry.

Fred He was all right, but he did hate everybody. He hated women, he hated children, old people, young people, priests. To him, everyone was a possible grass, so he didn't trust anyone.

Tony 'Everyone is wrong.' I first met him when they moved me into Hull Prison. And the day after I got there, he stabbed a bloke on the landing and just stood there. I don't know what it was about.

Fred He got into the special unit cos he was dangerous.

Tony Yeah.

Fred I think they thought he'd get served up and that would sort him out, being with the big boys.

Tony Anyway, to go back to what we were saying, I knew you were fussy about your food. You were 100 per cent right. You like your grub, but if certain people served your food up, you didn't eat it. I wouldn't eat it.

Fred In Full Sutton, my friend Mark Edmond, the young double lifer, used to cook for me. He'd get the food out of the canteen. One day he comes tearing into my cell, all agitated. He said, 'I've just had a row with these black guys who I lent some food to last week. I can't cook you your meal tonight cos they haven't paid me back.'

The rules are, if you borrow food this week, you pay it back next week.

He's jumping up and down with anger and frustration, Mark. He's got a tool behind his back, and he's given me one, which I put in the back of my trousers.

All of a sudden, I've got three blokes in my cell with duffel coats and woolly hats on, so I know they're tooled up. They're on a mission. They won't get recognized walking across the yard or the sports field. You know all these moves.

I know one of these guys. I said, 'Now, look here, you know the fucking rules.' We're nose to nose. He said, 'Here, I've got your food.' He pulled a plastic bag out of his duffel coat and he's got a tin of peas, three potatoes, an onion and a Fray Bentos steak and kidney pie. I looked at it. I said, 'This is it? Your debt's paid?' There we are ready to stab each other over a fucking two-quid dinner.

They was going to rip Mark off, but not me. They thought I was gonna react very badly. There would have been bloodshed there, so they've gone and got the food off somebody else.

Some time after that, the guy I was nose to nose with was being released and he had a going-out party. I was the only white fella invited. I was in the room having a drink of hooch with all the black guys.

It just shows you how ridiculous prison life becomes, where you look like pulling out the tools over a bit of veg and a meat pie.

But it's typical of the rows over food, no matter how bad that food might be.

What used to annoy me, Tone, was when you'd see the newspapers, the *Sun* or whatever, and they'd put, 'Oh look at that Christmas dinner for the prisoners – soup, chicken and turkey and baked potato.' The menu used to look lovely.

Tony   Don't it sound nice?

Fred   I'll tell you what. The Christmas dinners I've fucking had – I used to come out of the canteen, going along the hotplate, and I used to tell people, 'It's crap, everything's crap. Go straight over the fucking bin and throw the lot in and get yourself a couple of eggs out of your cell and cook yourself an egg and chips.' That's how good the food used to be.

Tony   In some prisons I was in, especially the long-term ones, the cons never served the food. The screws did it, which I think is better.

Fred   I'll tell you this little story which they put in *Nil by Mouth*, the Gary Oldman film. They took me up to Wayland Prison [in Norfolk]. You're going through the system, and they reduce you gradually. You move to less secure prisons as your sentence goes on. I was at the tail end of my sentence for the Security Express, and I'd been coming down in category all the time, going out to work, getting weekends out and not having to wear a uniform. But then they caught me attending Buster's funeral, and on another occasion they found me coming back to the prison with £400 in my pocket, which was well over the limit you were allowed, so they sent me up to Wayland. It was like starting all over again – no job, back in prison uniform, banged up for twenty-three hours a day . . . Not many London guys there, and I'm queueing up at the hotplate. As we're going through – you know where they do all the eggs, the poached eggs? They put an egg in the boiling water and it comes out like a little tadpole. It was like a round ball with a little tail on the end of it. They were the smallest eggs. They were like marbles. They were the cheapest they could buy.

Then they get the bacon and they throw it in the fryer and it goes *sssssss*, it curls up into a ball, rolled up, and then they get a bit of bread and they throw it in the fat and then, *shhhhht*, turn it out – fried bread. And then they always had them great big tins of plum tomatoes. So I go through on the hotplate and I've got the tray and as you said, they're all screws serving up the food. I said to the screw, 'OK, I'll have one of them eggs and a bit of bacon. Don't want the fried bread.'

'No,' he said. 'Egg *or* bacon.'

'You sure?' I said. 'What do you mean, egg or bacon? Bacon and egg, egg and bacon, they go together. That's what you call a breakfast. Egg and bacon.'

So he said, 'No, you've gotta have the egg or the bacon.'

I said to the other cons, 'I've never heard nothing like that in my fucking life. You fucking stand for this up here? Has no one been down to the governor's? You call that a fucking breakfast, one poxy little egg?'

Now they're all lining up, the screws. They had a barrier there. They go, '*You*, go on then, move along, Foreman.' I said, 'Put me down for the Governor. I'll see him in the morning.' Course, the cons are all kicking off now. They were all screaming, 'Yeah, we want egg and bacon! We want egg and bacon!'

Tony But you're marked down as a troublemaker.

Fred What happened was they moved me back to Maidstone. They did think I was a troublemaker. I don't know if they ever did get the bacon with the eggs, but what a fucking liberty.

This is where all the trouble starts, on the hotplate. I've seen more fights and rows on the hotplate. And this PO years ago, over the food in the Scrubs – remember the chief with the hat and the braid? And he's standing there, and they used to cut the ham so thin, with, like, a razor blade. You could see through it.

And I got hold of it and I said, 'Do you call this fucking food?' A hungry prison is an angry prison. The kitchen was on the other side of the fucking nick and the food used to have to come over on them trolleys across the yard, whether it snowed, rained or whatever. They put it on the hotplate, you know, to try and warm it up a bit, but you used to get it stone cold. It was atrocious food in there.

I got this ham and I threw it at this PO and it was all over his face like a mask or a silk fucking stocking. It was like a film. He had a moustache and you could see it moving underneath. And all the cons were laughing. How he never nicked me I don't know. He was too embarrassed by it, probably.

Tony And the kitchens. I went in the Scrubs kitchen with a screw one day to get a mug of tea or something, and he turned the light on and the cockroaches . . .

Fred Oh yeah. The floor would be black, and then all of a sudden, they'd disappear.

Tony How were you supposed to live on what they give you to eat? They've put the wrong people in the kitchen. You don't know who's touching your food, or what they're doing with it.

Fred If someone came in there and he was a chef, they'd put him on the fucking bricklayers, or they'd put him on the garden party. And a fucking gardener they'd put in the kitchen.

Tony Or a painter and decorator, or something.

Fred Plus all the screws was running round . . .

Tony Well, they were nicking everything. Tins of corned beef . . .

Fred They were seen putting the fresh fucking gear in the boots of their cars. What we're supposed to be getting, we're not getting any, you know.

Tony You know where Hull Prison is? You know the docks there? It's one of the few last fishing ports we've got in this country.

Fred All the seagulls coming in.

Tony The prisoners see the boat, and they know it's fresh fish coming in, but they're not getting any of it. They give you whiting. It's a very cheap fish.

Fred Yeah, whiting.

Tony And it was off one day, and [Great Train Robber] Jimmy Hussey made a noise about it.

Fred Screamed about it.

Tony There was me, Jimmy Hussey, Eric Flowers and Danny Redman [both armed robbers]. Jimmy said, 'That's off. I'm not eating that. Would you eat that?' And this PO, Lane, he ate a bit of it and he said, 'You're right, it's off,' and he gave them another meal.

Fred Let me just tell you about one guy, [post office and bank robber] Micky Kehoe.

Tony Micky Kehoe. Good man.

Fred What about the screw who was out in the night, under Mick's window in Durham E-Wing? The screw was screaming out, 'Who's fucking your old woman tonight?' Cos she was a lovely-looking girl, his wife, coming in on visits, and all the mini-skirts were in then. And, course, Mick was in love with her and he was going ape.

When you're a young fella and your girl's outside, you're thinking all sorts of things, ain't you, and it's driving you nuts. And this screw was outside his window saying, 'Who's fucking your old woman tonight, Kehoe?' and giving him a terrible time. And Mick knew who it was, though he didn't declare it, the screw. Mick tumbled who it was by his voice.

But there he was in the workshop this day, this screw, sitting on the chair, leaning back against the wall, and he had his hat on the back of his head, reading the newspaper.

Tony (*Laughter*)

Fred And Mick went in the toilet, had a crap in some toilet paper and he just walked by him and he went smack! Smacked it right into his mouth. The screw's mouth opened with shock and surprise at being attacked, and as he opened it – aaargh!

Tony You know who told me that story in Durham? [Lifer] Joey Martin.

Fred And they all jumped on Mick, the screws, and dragged him out down the block, and he was shouting out, 'Who wants some Richard the Third?'

Tony The screw had six months off with it. Psychologically, he had to get over it.

Fred He would do, yeah.

Tony He had, like, a funny face. I'll always remember the screw, cos Joey Martin says to me one day, 'You know who that is there, don't you?'

Fred 'That's Shitface.'

Tony That's what he was known as after that.

Fred Every time he walked across the yard. they always used to call out, 'Oi, Shitface!'

Tony And the funny thing is, after his six months off they put him back in the same wing, which was unusual. Every time he'd be about, the cons would go (*loud sniff*). Joey Martin used to go, 'There's a terrible smell in here.'

Fred What about when we was in Brixton, coming back from the Old Bailey, that guy that was underneath us, and he had a terrible tear-up? He potted up the screws. What was his name?

Tony Barney Ross. I saw the mattress . . .

Fred That's where they charged in on him.

Tony He was hurling pieces of shit over 'em as they charged in the cell to batter him. So they used the mattress as a shield.

Fred And after, there was this screw standing there serving up the food and I'm looking at the shit over his collar and his tunic where it's splashed all over him from the tear-up. He didn't realize he had it all over him.

Both (*Laughter*).

Fred I went, 'I can't eat nothing here. There's shit all over your shirt.'

Tony Another example. Christmas time is a funny time in prison, and the censor takes the stick. You know, cos they accuse him of not giving them their cards, nicking money out of them.

Fred Yeah, the censor gets a lot of stick.

Tony And what they did, Christmas Eve in Maidstone, a lot of them who didn't get cards and that, they got his mac and they took it in the recess and they crapped in his pocket and hung it back up on the hook.
    They knew he had a habit. Every day as he came out, he locked the door, he put the mac on, the collar up and the first thing he did – they were all waiting for it as he came out . . .

Fred Put his hands in his pockets.

Tony As soon as his hands hit the pockets, he knew what had happened. Bruce Reynolds was there, everyone, and we were all waiting. And all of a sudden, like, he went 'Aaargh!' and he ran screaming out the wing. Six months off, standard issue. If they have excreta put near 'em or on, then they get six months' full pay. Psychologically, think about what it does to you.

I can tell you another one. Mick 'Shitty' Evans in Wandsworth. Have you ever heard of him, Shitty Evans?

Fred No.

Tony What he used to do in Wandsworth, he'd have a funny turn now and again. He'd go in the recess at about quarter to seven in the morning and he'd strip off, cover himself, and go back to his cell. He had a potful in there too. Soon as they opened the door, he'd jump out and start kissing them, the screws, covered in crap. Covered with it. And every now and again, they'd clean him up. Down the block he'd go, come up, but it was regular.

Fred I used to work in the wood shop in Wandsworth in the early Fifties. Later on they done away with it. We had long benches, and the noise, the buzz and screaming of the electric saw cutting up the log sleepers, the *chop chop chop* of the prisoners on the benches, was driving me fucking insane. One day this screw was having a cup of tea, up on his pedestal, and I ran across and I buried the chopper in his fucking desk and I went, 'Get me out of this fucking shop.'

And he went, 'All right, son, take it easy,' and opened the door and got me outside. He sat me on the garden wall, and I was hyperventilating. The noise – I couldn't stand it. I was only in my teens, eighteen, nineteen, something like that.

He pressed the alarm and a few other screws came, but they didn't treat me bad. They didn't want to upset me any more, and I was a powerful man. I was young and fit. I was up before the Governor in the morning, and a screw comes in and they said, 'What work would you rather be in?' I said, 'Anything but that fucking wood shop.'

So they put me in the shop, where we used to stuff mattresses, in the summer. Rays of sunshine were coming in through the bars, showing up all these particles of dust and floating fibres. I got paranoid again. I went and sat down by the gate and I got my head in the bars and I said, 'I'm not breathing all that shit in my lungs,' and I'm trying to breathe in fresh air through the bars.

Next thing I know, I'm down the block, and then I was put down the hospital wing for fucking observation. The screw could see I wasn't mentally ill and he got me a job as an orderly in the hospital.

It was a good little job, but I got all these fucking nut-nuts down there throwing shit about. It was sticking to the walls of their cells. They had it in their porridge . . . and they was eating it.

They'd block the toilets up, and I used to get one of the nut-nuts to come out and I'd say, 'Get your arm down there and unblock that toilet.' There would be crap floating in the toilet, and he'd put his arm down and he'd bring it back out, all covered in shit, with the paperback book or whatever was blocking the toilet. I'd say, 'Throw it in the fucking bin.'

It was a very short stay, again. I told the screws, 'This is all down to you putting me in that fucking wood shop.' I went on to be a cleaner on the landing, and that was the best job.

Tony The cons all used to walk about with parcels of shit as protection. I often saw Shitty Evans come into the TV room, sit down and put the parcel beside him. You got a bag of that with you, they ain't gonna come near you.

Fred Some prisons, they used to throw shit parcels out the window, so you had loads of rats outside and things like that. They'd give prisoners a bucket and a rubber glove and, every day, they would walk round each wing picking up shit parcels. It was a disgusting job, and the cons who took it on were slaves to nicotine. They got some extra wages to buy more snout. A very degrading job for a few fags.

As you know, the prison cells had no toilets and the screws would not open cons up to use the recess. The cons may be three in a cell, they would be locked up from four-thirty or five until the next morning at eight o'clock, so if nature called, there was only a pisspot. If it had to be used, then that would stay in the cell all night.

Tony   When you think of the unhealthy lifestyle of it all and how you come out of it pretty fit . . . I mean, some of the stuff you see in there is shocking, innit, Fred?

Fred   Yeah.

Tony   Absolutely shocking.

6

Doing Your Time:
A Lifer's Guide

Conversation in Fred's study, 12 October 1999

IF YOU CAN'T LAUGH, FORGET IT

Tony   Remember John Bindon, Fred?

Fred   Yeah, course. John [actor and gangland friend] used to come
to Maidstone when I was in there to visit a mutual friend called
Alan Stanton, who was doing a twelve. He was a big, stocky bloke,
John, but he was losing weight rapidly at that time. He looked
worse each month. He died of cancer.

Tony   Yeah. He got nicked with a friend of mine out of Battersea.
But he was known in the nick for one thing, weren't he?

Fred   His dick. He used to whip it out and flash it at the drop of a
hat.

Tony   The only other one I saw near him was Jackie Marsh. He's
dead now.

Fred   I remember him. Oh, it used to hang down to his knees. He
used to tie weights on it and walk around in his cell of a night. And
then he used to slap it on the table and get the HP sauce bottle and
belt it. He used to beat the fuck out of it, break all the blood vessels
in it . . .

Tony   Any new screw or governor coming through – 'I've got
something to show you!' He'd show 'em it.

Fred   Yeah. Flasher. What about 'The Thug'? He had something
tattooed on his one. You're all showering together, you all see each
other fucking bollock naked . . .

Tony   Do you remember Charlie Manley? He was doing life. Come out of Plymouth. And he used to walk about with two canaries on his. He used to have a grey prison coat on, white towel which he'd use as a scarf or round the head, and he'd walk around with his coat open with two canaries balanced on it.

Both   (*Hearty laughter*)

Fred   That's a party piece.

Tony   Chirping and singing their heads off. Had me in stitches, Charlie. They used to call him 'Chirpy Chirpy Cheep Cheep'.

Fred   Talking of pets, there was Johnny Cooper, a lifer. He was the only guy in the nick who was allowed to have a cat. And everywhere he went, from prison to prison, he took this cat with him. They were allowed fucking canaries and birds and things like that, but Johnny Cooper was the only man I knew had a fucking cat.

Tony   Till Bubba got his hands on it one day, didn't he, Fred?

Fred   Bubba's slippers ran a close second to Tony Lambrianou's!

Tony   (*Laughter*)

Fred   Bubba was doing fifteen years for shooting a guy called Farmer who was a pimp and a grass. Later, when Bubba got released, he went to live back in the East End in the Cable Street area, in the top flat of a building. And someone set light to the house and burnt him to death. They proved it was arson . . .

Tony   Yeah. Terrible.

Fred   Then there was Mungo Jerry – Jerry Swain. We used to have a drink up on the 'Fours' [the fourth landing]. We'd have this little party from half past five to bang-up, eight o'clock at night, so you had to get as much down you as you could. When they used to come out, Jerry would go down the stairs, cos he lived on the 'Ones' [the first landing], and he used to have to run the gauntlet. All the young guys used to get jugs of water and throw them down the stairs. He used to hesitate, see who was about before he went down.

One night he's gone out with his duffel coat on, and as he went down the stairs, he put up an umbrella. And they was throwing water over him and he was laughing, going down with his umbrella. Fuck knows where he got it from. Who has an umbrella in the nick?

Must have nicked it off one of the probation officers or something.

Tony (*Laughter*) Do you know who I seen a little while ago? You'll know him well, Fred – Jimmy Cochran.

Fred Oh yeah. He shot a geezer on his doorstep.

Tony Jimmy Hanmore. One of the Hanmore brothers out of Hoxton.

Fred Well, well, he was out of his head.

Tony Do you remember that night they brought him into Brixton?

Fred Yeah.

Tony He said to me one day, 'See that tea urn there? We could make it into a rocket.' He was into spacemen and all that carry-on. He said, 'With that steam coming out, I can convert it so it can take off.' Oh, it took off, all right. It took off in his head.

Fred Oh, the poor little fucker. He was doing a life. He couldn't cope.

Tony He was harmless.

Fred He wasn't harmless – he went and shot someone with a fucking shotgun.

Tony Well, yeah. I tried to help him a little bit, but what can you do? Another name came back to me just now – Georgie Smith, you know, the boxer?

Fred Every time you said something about anyone, Georgie would say, 'Oh, I know him.' We used to get fed up with him knowing everybody we mentioned, so we set him up. We'd say, 'What was the name of that tobacconist on the corner of so-and-so street?' and he'd go, 'Oh that was old Mrs . . .' and he'd come out with something, guessing, and you'd say, 'No, it was so-and-so,' and he'd say, 'Oh, that's it, that's right,' and it was fucking complete rubbish, but he'd agree with everything.

One day we're sitting down watching television and the cartoons come on, and we was saying, 'How is he getting on, that old Fred Quimby?' and we were taking all the names off the television in front of us as the credits are coming up – 'produced by' and 'directed by' this one and that one. We're just digging all the names out as they're going past on the screen, and he's going along, 'Oh yeah, I know him.' In the end, he tumbled it (*laughing*).

'You bastards!' he said.

Oh, we had loads of laughs in the nick. You've gotta have a sense of humour.

Tony　Very big. If you don't have a sense of humour, forget it.

Fred　I mean, just looking at your fucking slippers gave me a laugh every day. Let's get a pair made up – have them gold-plated or something – and then we could auction them off at the next boxing do, couldn't we? Fetch a lot of money for charity.

Tony　(*Laughter*)

Fred　You used to shuffle about in those slippers, and they was them grandad ones, the old-fashioned tartan, with the bobble on. And they used to follow you across the fucking wing, behind you. I used to say, 'For fuck's sake, get a new pair of slippers, Tony.'

Tony　I did, eventually.

Fred　I think they was about two years overdue.

Tony　(*Laughing*) You was gonna get a pair sent in for me.

Fred　You know when you came out of the nick and that woman slung you out of the house and into the caravan?

Tony　Oh yeah, yeah.

Fred　(*Laughing*) I reckon you had your slippers with you then, in your overnight case. You took them everywhere. That's why you had to go to the end of the garden. She couldn't stand the slippers. She could smell you creeping about at night!

Tony　(*Laughing*) You say that, Fred . . . I sit down some nights at home and – my [wife] Wendy must think I'm potty – I just burst out laughing. Something really funny will come back to me, some of the antics from the nick. Do you do that, Fred?

Fred　Yeah, a little bit – when I think of you!

Tony You've gotta have a sense of humour about it.

Fred Fucking hell, you'd go off your head if you didn't. When you're in there, you have to turn a nasty situation into a funny situation. You know the London cockney, he's got the best sense of humour that you could ever fucking dream of.

Tony Which makes you not liked in a lot of prisons.

Fred The screws, you can't let them see that they've got you, that they've upset you. It's impossible to do it all the time, but you've gotta try and laugh about everything and take it all as a joke.

Tony No matter what the punishment is, you've gotta laugh about it.

Fred When I came out the dock with that nine-stretch and I was going down the stairs, they were all standing with their fucking guns and their shoulder holsters, and they were looking at me for my reaction, the robbery squad, and I went thumbs up – 'Fucking good result.' You couldn't let them see that you was gutted.

Tony Dignity. You never, ever show feelings.

Fred They were trying to get me twenty-two years. They've got me nine. I've had a result, and I'm going, 'Lovely.' They're all going, 'What's he fucking laughing about? He's just got nine years.' But that's the attitude you've gotta have.

Tony I've never heard you complain. You see, you accept it as a hazard of the game.

Fred Course you do.

Tony It's an unfortunate hazard, and that's the end of it.

WHO'S RUNNING THIS PRISON ANYWAY?

Tony When I first went into the Scrubs, you were on D-Wing and I was in the control unit, at the bottom of A-Wing. They'd got two cages at the back there, for exercise. I haven't seen you, but there weren't a screw every day who didn't come over and tell me that you had control of D-Wing.

Fred   Well, they wanted us to run it, cos it saved them a lot of work. They wanted it to fucking run smooth, and it did. A prison will only run smoothly with the cooperation of the prisoners. We got away with a lot of perks there. The screws had to recognize our 'authority' to a certain extent.

Table Four, where we sat down to eat, was like the top table at a wedding. We were good friends, all of us on Table Four. We was like a strong flower in the wind, you know.

I already had friends down in the Scrubs when I came in, and they got me straight on to Table Four. When you first arrive, the screws know if you're somebody, cos all the cons rally round and start getting things for you. They get the cups, your chairs, they get you a nice mattress with good springs – everybody gets bits and pieces to make you feel comfortable, to help you settle in.

There was lots of cons in there who would have liked to sit with us on Table Four, but nobody could unless we invited them on. And that was only if there was space, if one got moved to another prison. It was all democratic. We just discussed it amongst ourselves – 'Who do you think we should have on here?'

It was a prestigious move to get on our table. They was only people who really had respect and credibility, people like [robber] Billy Gentry, Gordon Goody, Buster Edwards, Jimmy Hussey, Alan Gold, Frank O'Connell and one of my old pub customers, Roy Hilder. There was other tables with good people on them – we was all pals – but the number-one table was Table Four.

Everyone came to us for advice, if they wanted any help. Any little scams going, they'd put us in it, stuff like that.

There were no real problems in that wing when we was in charge. When they split Table Four up – I left and all the chaps went off to different prisons – then they had terrible trouble. They smashed fuck out of the wing, didn't they?

Another 'promotion' was to go up higher and get a cell on the four landing. And you had to have one of those cells that looked, not into the prison, but out into the roadway – and the nurses!

All us guys had those cells. And I never knew it for a long time, but the screws had a little personal thing which they used to pull on the new screw.

The old screws know the worst thing they can do in the morning is to throw your cell door open. Then all the noise of the wing comes in on you. It's like opening a door on to a big scenario of noise and fucking smells, people walking by with their pots, slopping out. And all the old-timers, they just throw the lock, they go 'click', and they leave the door barely open.

So when they used to get a new, young screw on, they used to say, 'Go up there, and when you get to Foreman's cell, get him out of bed and throw the door open.' It happened to me about three times in the Scrubs. I was out of bed like a fucking shot, like a lunatic, and while I'm chasing the screw round the landing, he'd be running for his life and I would be giving him all the verbal – 'I'll throw you over the fucking top of the landing,' and all that.

Tony (*Laughter*)

Fred But that was just a sort of initiation, breaking them in. I tumbled it after a while. And another thing when you're a long-term prisoner is when you go in your cell, you never let the screw lock you in. You always kick the fucking door shut behind you – bang yourself up, not him banging you up. *Crash*. Then they just come along and look in the spyhole, see you're in there, and 'Goodnight'. You have to give yourself a bit of dignity. And all them screws accept that. If you was to go back in there now, they would all act the same way. All the old-timers, there's certain things they pass on.

Tony And we all used to keep to our own company, but you would always stand by the underdog if you had to. There are times when you have to be seen to come out right against authority.

Fred Well, it was everyone's enemy.

Tony A common enemy. So you stuck up for the underdog. But, at the same time, you were very cagey at that time, Fred, about talking to anyone you didn't know.

Fred I wouldn't talk to no one.

Tony I remember that as clear as anything, you saying, 'Be careful what you say, on the yard or on visits.' The visits were all through the glass.

Fred You was a young fella then, Tone.

Tony That's right. I was listening to advice.

Fred You talk to someone on them exercise yards walking round, you think you've got something in common and the next thing, they're up in the box giving evidence against you. You've got to keep really schtum. You mustn't talk.

Even your depositions and defence notes that you might have been working on with details of your witnesses or any evidence that you might have, you'd put inside your shirt and take out on exercise with you in case the screw let outside coppers in your cell to nick your paperwork and photocopy it. They used to get up to all those tricks. I used to leave traps to see if anyone had been in my cell while I was on the hour's exercise and things had sometimes been moved about. You had to be extra careful. Your fucking life was at stake.

Do you remember those visiting boxes in Brixton? They put us into certain numbers and you had to shout to be heard. I'm sure they were bugged. I used to hold notes on small pieces of paper, then eat them afterwards.

Tony For all that, you could always depend on your own people to look after you. Down in the control unit in Wormwood Scrubs, you had nothing to read. Now and again, a Bible might be in there, and they always sent the vicar round.

Fred 'Repent your sins.'

Tony And this governor had this cell painted all in grey, and they had a grille over the window, you had no chair – you had a block – and your bed was taken away during what they called working hours, weren't it, Fred?

Fred Yeah, and they brought it back in at night, after work, after tea.

Tony Cleared out everything. And now you've got a day to fill. And one day, having a smoke, I was looking at the light socket, and it just didn't seem right to me. That night, when they brought the block back in, I get up and I unscrew the whole thing, and inside it was a half ounce of tobacco, papers and a few matches. And I know someone's left it – 'This is for the poor bastard who's in here now.'

Fred Yeah. 'Next!'

Tony You always done that. Whatever you had left, you'd leave for someone else.

YOU'RE SO VAIN!

Tony Most of the time in prison is boredom.

Fred The football on Saturday mornings was the big event of the week at the Scrubs. There was so many injuries, cos it was all concrete, the yard. You'd go over, you'd break knees and fingers and shoulders. And there was a con acting as a newsman there, writing up the matches for the newsletter. But there was very little to do at the Scrubs.

Leicester was even worse. *You* know that. I was up there for about four years, isolated with eight people who you might not even see from day to day because they kept in their cells. It was like church (*whispering*), wasn't it? Couldn't hear no sounds. It's very unusual in a prison, because there's always a lot of noise, people milling about, but there was nothing like that there. There was nothing for us to do.

And once you've been with people for about a year, your conversations dry up, you know every story they have to tell because they've repeated them time and time again, and you get to the point where you just go in your cell and bang up.

We used to work out there, so we kept ourselves reasonably fit. But they only had a cage to go out into the open. And the bars on the windows, you couldn't see daylight through them, and the cells were small with reinforced walls and ceilings, and they had extra doors and extra locks.

It made us all environmentally friendly, didn't it, because you never saw a fucking leaf or a blade of grass.

They had the all-night light, and if you didn't show yourself above the blanket every fifteen minutes, they'd flash it on. It was sort of sleep deprivation. You was really on the edge all the time. It was new methods they was trying on us. We were sort of guinea pigs.

When they eventually moved me out of there to Wormwood Scrubs, it was like going into Waterloo Station with the noise and the banging and, like, 300 cons running about. And you *still* got bored.

Tony That's why so many men used to be in the gym all the time.

Fred I used to say, 'I never want to see another fucking gym as long as I live when I get out of here,' cos I spent so many hours in it. I've been to the gym since (*laughing*), but it did bring back memories.

Tony A lot of inmates who've done a long term in prison, they're pretty fit. You haven't changed that much, Fred.

Fred I've lost a bit of barnet, that's all. I had a bit more hair when I first knew you.

Tony One day, Ronnie Bender in Leicester Prison – do you remember it, Fred? He got that solution.

Fred Oh, yeah (*laughing*), the hair tonic. I had Ronnie Bender putting the old Regain on and massaging my head for hours while we sat and talked. It didn't work. There was just a fine, downy fluff – sort of baby hair.

Tony (*Laughing*) You said to me one day, "That's grown a bit, you know.'

Fred I said, 'I think I'm sprouting a few.' And right in the middle of my forehead, there was a few hairs come sprouting out, and I would never let anyone cut them. I had one sticking out there for years. Janice pulled it out eventually. She said, 'It's gotta go.'

Tony There was worse than you, Fred! This geezer, Tony Laing, 'The Monster of Parkhurst' – they done an operation on his head, tried to implant some hair, and it's made it even worse. You know what the operations are like in them places.

Fred Oh, a fuck-up, yeah.

Tony I mean, I've seen some cock-ups. Personally, what I think they were doing was experimenting. He got a septic skull and most of the hair went, and he had a bit left that he tried to comb over.

Both (*Laughter*)

Fred They was probably on the golf course in a half-hour . . . 'Stitch him up and send him back to the nick!' I bet they had a right laugh about it over a drink in the clubhouse.

THE BEST OF INTENTIONS ...

Fred When you start any sentence, whether it's a long one or short, you say to yourself, 'Well, Fred, let's get through this one nice and easy, try and stay out of trouble and don't get involved.' But with the injustice of the prison system, petty-mindedness, the stupid rules and regulations and the way they're carried out, the everyday violence, the atmosphere of intimidation and fear, nothing is natural or normal. It's not a nice way to live out your years.

If you're a kid in a young offenders' prison doing a few months and thinking it's just a laugh, wait until you're in the big league with men doing lifes, sentences with no release date.

I was considered by many to be a sensible head, but I still got involved in riots, arguments, attacking other prisoners and screws, going down the block, losing remission. I was outraged at injustice, not only for myself but for other people ... You get sucked into situations and riots, and if you've got a bit of a sensible head about you, you find you're being pulled in just to fucking keep the peace or to talk some sort of common sense, and say, 'You're not going nowhere, you're just making the situation worse, so, like, be fucking sensible, get what you can out of the situation now, and say, "We'll settle for this, you settle for that, and we'll all go and bang ourselves up and we'll start again." You know, be sensible with it.'

Tony Half the disputes in prison, really, they're so petty.

Fred They're a fucking load of crap. Nearly all my nickings were down to other people's problems, and it was left up to me to sort it out. Other cons looked at me and waited for my reaction to any situation. I did defuse a lot of trouble, but then again, I started quite a few incidents that turned violent myself, so, you see, my fear was that I might start off with a ten-year sentence and finish doing a life, or 'nutted off' completely.

I'm an easy-going person, I can see the funny side to a situation where others may not, but when some idiot rattles my cage – you'd better fuck off a bit rapid and head for the hills. But that's only on very rare occasions. Most of the time, I really try hard to be the perfect gentleman.

USING YOUR HEAD

Tony You don't go into the TV room in a prison to watch *Coronation Street*, because that's a bit of a taboo. You join what they call 'the flock' when you do that. They used to sit and watch the spot go out.

Why do you think they put televisions in prisons? It's a sedation. None of the boys used to watch the usual crap. They liked the educational programmes on TV.

Fred Oh, yeah. They love it.

Tony Travel, all them type of things.

Fred They used to bring in films sometimes about digging for oil and exploration, and stuff. When you're in the nick, you find you're interested in these sort of things.

Tony A lot of criminals go for education, for degrees, in prison. They do Open University courses. It's a very big attraction.

Fred I took advantage of the educational opportunities . . . well, when it was allowed, when we was through all the special units and special wings. We didn't get nothing to help us there.

Tony Nothing.

Fred I mean, all that they did was cage you up like animals and wake you up every fifteen minutes through the night. So the only time I was able to go to a proper education place was when I went to Full Sutton [Yorkshire prison] and I've signed on there straight away. I did everything I could put my hand to. I did the art school, the pottery, I did the general knowledge, I studied Spanish, and yoga, for two years.

Cos all the classes are full up, you have to wait your turn. You might have to wait for six months, but in loads of cases, before you sat the exams and got your qualifications, they'd move you on to another prison.

Tony So you were back where you started.

Fred You couldn't finish any degrees, unless you were lucky.

Tony I've seen them do half a course and get moved.

Fred But I did *learn*. Of course, I used to read as much as I could. I think every book will teach you something, even if the book is crap. So anything I can do now is self-taught.

Tony When I came out of the system, I started going to Category C in a place called Acklington, a prison up in the north-east. And I was told, 'Look, you're coming up for review. You've got three and a half years to do – get something down on paper. Talk about getting your A and O levels.' Did you ever see the certificates I got? Maths and English. So they was impressed with that. You've got to give them something. Cos the board are going to say to you, 'What have you done in the last fifteen years?'

Fred Well, it's just common sense. You have to try and keep your head down and get through the prison system as quickly as possible. I'll show you what I made, in the other room. I've got two big flowerpots in there. They're all I have to show for my years in prison. They still have one in the office of the education department at Full Sutton.

Leslie Grantham [*EastEnders'* Dirty Den and convicted murderer] got into the drama, doing a play in the Scrubs.

Tony Yeah. I met him in there. Quiet fella. Liked his game of cards.

Fred Oh, Les, he was all right. He was a young fella with very long, blond hair in a ponytail. And that's when he got into the acting game.

Tony To tell you the truth, I went into education to laze about, Fred. Cos it was cold up in the north-east, and I went to classes to get in the warm, but then I started to enjoy it. And I came out of prison and I travelled the world with Wendy, as you know. We went everywhere. It expanded my mind a lot.

Fred Course it does. It's the greatest education, travel.

Tony I've been in the wilds, I've been to the best places, and I enjoyed it.

Fred So you did learn something out of being in prison.

Tony Yeah. That came out of it.

Fred And you know yourself as a person there as well. You can get to your inner thoughts. You can digest things. And you get to know your true values in life. You know you're only here on this earth for a short period of time.

Tony You want to expand on it, enjoy it, and I did.

Fred And you put your priorities in order.

Tony Professional criminals seem to be the ones to want to learn and expand. Not the lowlife. No. They see crime as a way just to live. I believe that in prisons now, if you can't read and write, the facilities are there. But it's still a bang-up system whatever way you look at it.

Fred Yeah, I mean, Wandsworth – a twenty-three-hour day.

Tony But if a man can't read and write when he comes out, what chance has he got? None.

Fred It doesn't give them a chance to go and get a decent job, does it?

Tony No chance. I'll always remember signing on at the labour exchange – 'We've got nothing in your line!' If you've got a conviction, who's gonna employ you?

Fred The only people who interviewed me when I came out was the fucking tax office. They was asking me for ridiculous money. I said, 'Well, give me a shotgun and a pair of gloves and I'll go out and get it for you.'

Tony (*Laughing*) Do you know what, they once asked me to go and speak to a police college and enlighten the cadets on the life of crime.

Fred That would've been the funniest thing. Their brains would've scrambled if they'd listened to *you* for two hours.

THE TROUBLE WITH TATTOOS

Fred Did you get any tattoos when you was in borstal or anything?

Tony   Never. I would never have a tattoo, Fred.

Fred   No. The authorities, they love to see the young kids do the needle and ink in the nick, don't they, cos prison tattoos are different to the professional ones.

Tony   You're a marked man.

Fred   You're branding yourself a criminal wherever you go. One look at you in a restaurant or in a bank or anywhere, any business place, they see them tattoos. You've gotta wear long sleeves and cover your hands up, and your arms, cos you're saying, 'I'm a criminal, I'm a thug, I'm an ex-prisoner.' You're waving a flag: 'Watch me, I can't be trusted, I'll rob you, I'll nick your purse or I'll mug you.' And it's an identification. People can say, 'Oh, yeah, the guy who robbed me had "love" and "hate" on his hand' – all the kids had that – or, 'He had a JC, Jesus Christ, down his back.'

And then there were the cons who got tattooed with an elephant with big ears? You know, their dick was the trunk.

Tony   The best one I saw was the hunt. The fox tail's going up your behind, and the hounds and the huntsman are chasing it in. Have you ever seen that. Fred?

Fred   No.

Tony   I've seen a complete hunt, with the dogs right at the legs. Coming up the thigh, you've got a huntsman on a horse, all done in red with a black cap, and the fox in the anus with the tail hanging out. How can you tattoo that? I could never have it done, Fred, never.

WHERE'S MY JUMPER?

Tony   The only thing I ever kept from my prison days, Fred, and it sits in the kitchen to this day, is my radio, the Hacker.

Fred   You wasn't anyone unless you had a Hacker. They're Fifties radios. They still make 'em.

Tony   You know, I look at it all the time. I clean it. And one other thing – I had a Marks & Spencer pullover, V-neck. It was dark blue, and everyone had 'em, and it hangs in my wardrobe.

Fred   Do you remember how we used to get our jeans cut in flares?

Tony   (*Laughing*) With wedges! And long hair! We tried to keep up with the fashion.

Fred   And we had these little short collars, didn't we, that they used to cut off for us in the tailor shop in there. You couldn't bring in your own clothes, but you were allowed to get a jumper sent in, like the one you just mentioned.

They was pure wool, nice-cut sweaters to go over your blue, striped shirt. My George tells a story of it, because they was very hard to come by, and he was doing a three-stretch in a cell with our pals Terry Murphy and a bloke called Big Ron.

Terry's son is Glen Murphy, of *London's Burning* fame. And Terry's got a record company now. He used to run a live music pub called the Bridge House in Canning Town. He was a terrific middleweight fighter – the only fighter in history to chin the referee, at the Albert Hall. I fucking saw it.

He was a young man then, in the nick, in the Sixties. And the three of them were in the cell using a bucket. I was still using the fucking bucket in my cell in 1995.

Tony   Is it still going on, Fred?

Fred   They still never had no toilets in Maidstone when I left. But anyway, getting back to George in the cell. And he's keeping on, Terry Murphy, about this nice, soft, woolly, blue jumper of his, and they ain't got none. So George and Big Ron prearranged something, for after they'd had their fish dish on the Friday.

You would always wait till the morning if you needed a crap. You would not use the pot if you was on your own, let alone if you were with two other people.

Tony   Never use it.

Fred   You've gotta suffer all night. And first thing in the morning, you're out like a shot, you know, cos the food was never that fucking clever and you'd have upsets.

So the light's out now and George says to Big Ron, 'Fuck me, how do you feel, Ron? My guts is killing me.' He said, 'I don't feel too clever, George, I've got a bit of a gut ache.' So he's lying there, and they always used to talk and have a little chat before they went to sleep, like you do.

Tony Yeah.

Fred Might have a singsong, tell little stories, as you went to sleep, if you was in with proper people. If you was with mugs, you couldn't fucking talk to 'em, but it was very rare that you got three people who knew each other on the outside.

They used to talk about the old club George and I had, the Walk Inn in Lambeth Walk, cos he was a regular customer, Murphy was, and we had some great times down there.

Anyway, George says, 'I'm sorry, lads, I've gotta go on the pot, I can't wait till the morning.'

'Oh, George, can't you hang on? Can't you wait?' That's Murphy.

'I've gotta go, I'm sorry.'

And Big Ron: 'George, if you've gotta go, mate, you've gotta go. There's nothing you can do about it. You can't have your guts ache all night.'

George said, 'I'm sorry, I'll be as quick as I can.'

So George has got out of bed and he's sitting on the pot. He said, 'Oh, it's fucking cold down here, Terry. Can I borrow your sweater?'

He's give him his sweater. 'It's just to keep me shoulders warm,' George said. He's sitting on the pot and he says, 'Oh, finished now. Pass that toilet paper.' Murphy gives him the toilet roll.

Then George gets up. 'Oh, fucking hell! I've dropped the jumper in the pot!'

'Oh, my fucking jumper!' Terry said. Course, he's out the bed, ain't he, Murphy. *'What you done with my jumper?'*

Big Ron and George are killing themselves laughing cos George ain't done nothing in the pot at all, has he? They did like to get Murphy at it.

FRONTING IT OUT

Tony I remember I was sitting there watching *Inn of the Sixth Happiness* on the Christmas, Fred, and I've turned round, this is a very sad film, and they're all sitting there, the boys, with tears in their eyes. If the public could see it . . .

Fred All these hardened criminals on murder charges and God knows what, and they're all sitting there crying their eyes out! You know, whenever I go to a funeral, I'm really determined to hold out and not get emotional, cos men look on it as a weakness if you start shedding a few tears. 'He's supposed to be a hard case – what's he crying for?'

I do get emotional, but it can work both ways because if someone fucking upsets you, you can be over-the-top emotional when it comes to violence. Emotion is not one-sided, it doesn't just apply to sympathy, it applies to anger, and I'm inclined to overreact. It cuts both ways.

7

Crime Pays . . . Or Does It?

Conversation in Fred's kitchen, 16 February 2000

Fred If I was a young man now, I wouldn't want to go into crime for a living. Nah.

Tony We knew no other life. But looking back on it, I would have done things in a different way.

Fred I mean, you was up against it all the time – your nerves was fucking on edge.

Tony Always in danger of going away . . .

Fred You're worrying about knocks on the door in the early hours of the morning.

Tony Even now you worry about it.

Fred Let's face it, if I'd been educated as a boy, if I'd gone to a decent school. I would never have turned to crime. I would never have done anything wrong.

Unfortunately, when I was a kid, most of the schools in my area were bombed cos they stood out as big buildings and the Germans thought they was targets. They could've been munitions factories or something. They didn't want large numbers of kids in one place in case they all got killed, so, like, cinemas were closed and you didn't get any schooling at all during the Forties.

I've left school at fourteen. I haven't got no qualifications to get a decent job. All I'm gonna do is carry hundredweight sacks up ladders and dig trenches – that's the only sort of jobs that was offered to me. If I could bring home a good wage packet, I wouldn't need to turn to crime.

I was man enough as a kid to want to have a good standard of living and to put a bit of money in the home and help my parents, cos they were struggling.

I wanted to pay my way and to better myself and my standard

of living, get married, own a house of my own and get my kids into good schools and give them a chance in life, which I managed to do. The way I did it was through thieving.

Tony   Most of us came from very poor, working-class families, and when we was growing up, the education was still very limited. They learned you the Three Rs and that was basically it. The bomb sites were our playgrounds. I left school at fourteen, like you, Fred, and the first job I had was at the Sleepy Valley bedding company in Bethnal Green. I got two shillings an hour.

You didn't have a lot of choice but to go into crime, especially if you come from a big family that needed money. That's why you had so many brothers coming up into crime together in that area.

Fred   I had to go out and get it the best way I could. And my main objective when I did make money was to give my two sons and my daughter a private education. Then when they had that, they wanted to go to stage school and I paid for that. My Jamie has been involved with acting ever since.

I went and risked my liberty to give my kids the opportunity that I never had, and to provide for Maureen, my wife. She lived fucking high, holidays in the South of France and Spain, the best clothes, best restaurants, best hotels ... we never went in a cheap gaff. Always had to be five-star. I gave her the best motor cars, the best make-up, hairdressers ... she had the best of everything.

I couldn't have provided these things if I'd been a nine-to-five worker, getting just an ordinary wage. And this was what it was all about.

And you get into that way where you can't settle for anything less. You've gotta have the best, you know, and that's how you go through life. Once you get used to it, you want it all the time.

PRISONS: COMPOUNDING THE PROBLEM

Fred   'We're going to build fourteen new prisons next year.' The Conservatives, that's all they used to say. It's all kickback, they're all earning money out of it. Somebody's getting the contracts and jobs to build these places, when they should be spending the money to stop crime at the root. The cause of crime is not having good living conditions and education. Education's the main thing to learn a person not to turn to crime,

Edward Bunker says in *Dog Eat Dog* that they fill the nicks up, 'with damn fools on nickel and dime drug cases'. They're in the nick for petty crime, and all they do is learn how to commit bigger crimes than they would have done before they went in. They're nickel and dime when they go in, and they come out big, major robbers. This is what all prisons do.

Then the nicks turn 'em loose on the public after they've destroyed them and made them bitter and twisted. I've seen people in prison saying, 'Society's gonna pay for this when I get out of here. I'm getting my own back.' And they won't take no prisoners when they do something.

Like with a dog – if you keep beating a dog and chaining him up against a wall, he's gonna be a vicious dog. If you show him a bit of love and affection, he's a lovely dog. And this is the way they treat people.

With the opportunities that children have got now, there's no need to go into crime at all. They've got all the facilities to study. They say they're hard done by, kids today, but they're not as hard done by as we were. They've got more opportunity than we ever had. I mean, look at the computers, the things in the home.

Tony I was talking to my grandson the other day about a computer. He's eleven years of age and he knows more about it than I'll ever know.

Fred They can learn by just being indoors. My grandkids, they can work a video recorder better than I can.

Tony It's like the Internet. You can sit at home and order anything you want now. So the bottom is going to fall out of the stolen property market.

Fred You still have to pay for it! But look at computer fraud, where they're nicking people's names and you gotta buy your own fucking name back. They done it to Bruce Reynolds.

Tony Yeah.

Fred They done it to Ronnie Biggs and they wanted seven grand to give him his name back. We got it back for him for nish.

Technology has changed the whole face of crime. Fucking hell, a guy was telling me the other day . . . he's in his new car, a Mercedes. He's got the map-finder on his dial and he's driving down the motorway with his wife and kid, trying to find his way to London from up north, and his little boy had a nose bleed or something. He pulled off on to the hard shoulder and the fucking map on his dashboard went, 'You're on the shoulder – get back on the road. Don't stop here.'

Tony (*Laughter*)

Fred He'd just gone over that white line on the side of the hard shoulder, and this is on a satellite. It's pinpointed him coming along that motorway – it's fucking frightening.

Tony It's changed everything.

Fred Can you imagine trying to do something, some villainy, if that's what you can get in your own car? What have the other people [police] got? We know already they've got cameras everywhere, CCTV video and stuff. It'd put anyone off – anyone with any sense. It's fucking put me off since I came out the nick . . .

I mean, you walk out on that street, you walk down a few turnings, you're on twenty-five different fucking cameras. If a robbery went off, you don't have to be sitting in that street, you can be three streets away and you're on camera. 'What are you doing in that vicinity? Why are you there?' You can't win. That's why these robberies don't take place any more. Because it's impossible to get away with it.

Tony It's all gone now.

Fred You just can't do it.

Tony I kept hearing you on about computers. I've been missing out! But I've got one now. I'm buying the name for my website, and I've got the e-mail sorted out.

Fred I've got a website. Well, Frankie Fraser's got one, so why can't I? It's a whole new ball game, so we got to get with it, Tony, or get left behind.

THE PRICE YOU PAY

Fred When you get your sentence, you mustn't show your feelings but, inwardly, you feel despairing, just seeing all the years in front of you and things you'll miss out on. Will things still be the same when you come out – relationships with wives and girlfriends, families and kids? You'll miss their growing-up and their birthdays and Christmases.

That's the hardest part of it, the thing that hurts the most, taking your liberty away from you. The hard conditions they keep you under are not necessary. Because they're taking the most important thing away. That is the worst punishment. Don't matter what else they do to you. If I had a choice between two years down the block or fucking six years in an ordinary prison, I'd rather do the two years down the block and get it over with. So it's not necessary to treat you bad. They could give you a bit of decent food and clean conditions.

The cells are filthy, fucking infested with cockroaches crawling over your chest, over your bed, oh, all that stuff. In Wandsworth, I had a longtail, a rat, in the cell with me. I'm looking at him and he's looking at me, a big, fucking grey and black sewer rat. And he'd been coming in my cell for about a week and I didn't realize it, eating off my tray.

The food wasn't no good, so I used to put the tray on the floor and then I used to hear this scratching noise in the night, and I thought the geezer next door was bloody well digging out.

It turned out it was just longtail creeping under the door every night. But you wouldn't dream of complaining to the screws. They would laugh – 'Terrible. Bad luck. Hard cheese.'

Janice (*Serving dinner*) 'That's your five-star accommodation.'

Fred (*Laughing*) Yeah.

Tony When I was in the Scrubs, came down from Gartree, I was in the control unit at the back of the prison. You've been in there. And you know, they've got a plastic dome over the window to save anything being passed in to you. And I used to lie there in the summer, and I could hear the kids playing.

Fred Cos there was playing fields out the back.

Tony   Yeah. And there was a little exercise yard, and I used to walk round it, listening to all of this activity on the other side, thinking to myself, One day I might be doing that. It hit me bad there.

Fred   You can hear the football matches.

Tony   You could hear Queens Park Rangers playing.

Fred   In Leicester, we could hear the football crowds roaring when someone scored a goal.

Tony   You used to think to yourself, If I walked over there and got over that wall, there's reality there.

Fred   There's life there. It's going on. And you wanna be shut off from it, really, cos that's tormenting you.

Tony   You don't wanna see Christmas.

Fred   The worst time when you're doing bird is Christmas and New Year, for people who've got families and relationships outside.
   You're banged up at eight o'clock at night and you're thinking of all the parties, 'Auld Lang Syne', wishing the New Year in, and it fucking breaks your heart.
   In the Scrubs, they had a concert hall and every Christmas we used to get people coming in there. George Melly used to come, and that singer Clodagh Rodgers, and the harmonica player, Larry Adler, he used to come in regular as clockwork. They was very good, they used to put on a decent little show.

Tony   You can stay in bed a bit longer at Christmas, can't you, Fred? And the food might be a little better.

Fred   But none of that went anywhere near making up for what we was losing. I used to take a sleeping pill – somebody somewhere would have them – on Christmas Eve and New Year's Eve, and just get into bed, have a read or listen to the radio, crash out and, hopefully, I'd sleep till the next day, and it's over. I used to be in a sort of drugged state, you know, over the Christmas, but that's the way to get through it.
   But you get to the New Year and twelve o'clock come and you were in a nice, deep sleep and some bastard would get up at the window and go, 'Happy New Year', and he'd start rattling the

fucking bars on his window and start off another mug over the other side, and then he would start shouting, 'Happy New Year', and then the whole fucking wing would be up going, 'Happy New Year!'

And then you were awake, you were angry, so your adrenalin's pumping away in your body, and you're laying there for another two or three hours. You can't sleep, and I laid there till fucking daylight, you know, when I wanted to forget it. You don't want to be visualizing your family having their little drinks, the little kiss under the mistletoe and all that sort of thing.

Tony   You can't.

Fred   But these mugs torment you all fucking night, so you're awake listening to 'em till the fucking dawn chorus. And then you're knackered for the whole day.

Tony   I found there was a build-up. Two weeks before, you start to think about it and you try to block it – 'It's just another day.' It's a very explosive time in prison.

Fred   When you first get your bird, for the first two years of your sentence, your mind is half in the nick and half outside.

Tony   Yeah, yeah . . .

Fred   So you're not really acclimatized to the prison routine. It takes two years at least to get settled into prison life. You gradually switch off from thinking about outside and what your family are doing, what you would be doing today as opposed to what you're doing now – 'I'd just be going down to get a newspaper,' you know.

So when you've got to that stage, your time becomes a little bit easier, but sometimes I used to dread a visit, especially with your kids. Cos it took a week to get over 'em. You was in a terrible state.

Tony   For the last few years of my sentence, I didn't really want a visit. It was the build-up and the let-down afterwards.

Fred   We had a few nice visits in the Scrubs.

Tony   Yes, it was good because it was straightened out, Fred.

Fred There was all our own, London people and they always used to smuggle in a drop of wine, and the old baby's bottle used to come out and they used to give us a drop of gin or vodka or whatever in orange juice.

Tony And the screws turned a little bit of a blind eye as well.

Fred They did, cos we used to get a little bit rosy-cheeked, a little bit mellow, you know, and there was no problems. And then on the next table there'd be Jimmy Hussey's wife, on another, Buster's wife, so it was not only with your own family but other people's families, and it was a really social visit.

Tony You knew everyone.

Fred And they used come over and say, 'Oh, hello,' and smuggle across a nice little ham sandwich or a beef sandwich. And the screw's sitting up on his pedestal looking down. Someone might walk up to the screw and say, 'Where's the toilet?' and then, soon as he's not looking, everyone was passing gear across . . .

Tony It was a good atmosphere.

Fred But now they've got cameras everywhere. It's a pity it's not the same. It's all drug-related now, you see, but drugs didn't interest us in those days.

Tony I used to love the visits there.

Fred They was nice visits. When I'd done eight years of the ten-stretch, they sent me back to Wandsworth, and it was like starting all over again. Maureen came to visit me, and all of a sudden I'm in a cell with a screw sitting either side and Maureen trying to talk to me. And they've got notebooks and pencils, hanging on every word we're gonna say. And I said, 'Maureen, it's not worth coming on the fucking visits here, people writing things down that are said between us. Forget the visits. Don't come here any more. I've got six months left before they move me back to Brixton, and we'll have a visit in Brixton.'

She was upset, but she said, 'Yeah, you're right, if that's what you wanna do.' Really, she still wanted to come but I said, 'I can't handle this cos I'm gonna kick off.'

Tony Yeah.

Fred I didn't encourage my pals on the outside to come and visit me either. Even today, it doesn't do my friends in prison any good to be in contact with me, ringing me and having me on a list of phone numbers, or getting visits from me, cos the authorities say to them, 'You're still associating with known or ex-criminals. You've not got away from them.' All that stuff's looked at, you know. It's logged on the computer. It's the worst thing you can do. It's quite a new thing, isn't it, in prisons, being able to use the telephone? It's a privilege. I never experienced it until my last sentence. And I never used to ring anyone up but Janice and my immediate family. I would never ring another person.

THE
FREEDOM
YEARS

1

Freedom: It Can Be a Strange Thing

Conversation in Fred's kitchen, 11 January 2000

Fred You know, years ago, when a fella came out of prison, he'd stand in a pub and you'd look at him and you knew where he'd been.

Tony Oh, instantly.

Fred Not so much now. I'm talking more about the Fifties and Sixties. The guy would have no weight on him for a start – he'd be hard-looking with chiselled features, and he'd be very, very pale. It's a prison pallor. It comes because you never used to get out in the sun too much in prison. You used to spend all your time in either a workshop or in the cell, and you just used to walk around for an hour – half hour in the morning, half hour in the afternoon – exercising in the fresh air. If it was raining, you had to stay in the wing and walk round the landings instead. It gives you that grey look, you know.

I'll give you an example. I'll bring it in. (*Leaves the room and comes back with a photograph of himself*) I'd just come out of Wandsworth that morning, and I've got that look. You see what I mean? Your face is gaunt, your clothes are too big for you where you've lost weight. You might as well have been on a strict diet.

Tony I bumped into someone yesterday who'd just finished ten years. He was standing at the bar in a pub, and everything about him smelled of a con. Like you say, Fred, the clothes he was wearing were ill-fitting, out of proportion. And if a man has done a long time, quite often he'll stand back, keep quiet, like this guy. He seemed uncomfortable, he kept glancing around, and he kept looking at his watch.

Fred At the same time, people can look pretty good when they come out. In *Dog Eat Dog*, Edward Bunker says, 'Prison preserves a sucker.' It does. People age well when they've been in prison because of the austerity of the routine – not overeating, not staying out late at night, early to bed, early to rise, and although we all have a little drop of the good hooch in prison, you don't get too much booze. You know, it's moderation in everything, and it's the regularity of it all that preserves you, keeps you in a glass bowl, in a way.

Tony It does preserve you. And you can keep yourself very fit in the nick. Some of them I've seen coming out look great. I looked very fit and slim. But then you start having the things you missed in prison, the drinking and the rich foods, so within a year, it catches up with you. You balloon.

Fred You know, when you leave the prison, as soon as you get out on the main road, or in the town, you smell the petrol fumes and the oil and the diesel. It hits you straight away. Cos when you're in those prisons, you're not getting all that pollution around you. The only thing you're getting is the smoke from cigarettes and stuff, but you don't get the petrol fumes and all them smells, and it hits your nostrils right away once you come out.

Tony Just walk by a bakery! Smell decent food!

Fred After a week or two, you're attuned to it. You get used to it. But one thing that's sad is that not everybody savours their liberty or really *wants* it. They don't know what to do when they get it. These are young kids from deprived backgrounds, going into prison in their teens. From little kids, they grow right through the system, and that's how they keep on.

In the Scrubs in the Seventies, you'd see these guys in there on small sentences, maybe doing a five, and they'd release them at half past seven in the morning. Come back at twelve for your dinner, look out your cell and you can hear 'em outside the prison, over the wall, calling up to their mates.

Tony They're back. We've seen it, Fred.

Fred The mates are shouting back from the cell windows, and the screws have to go out and send them away – 'Go on, fuck off. You're out now. What you fucking doing here, still?' you know.

Tony   Yeah, tell 'em to go away.

Fred   They've been hanging around outside. They've gone out the gate, they've got a few quid in their pocket, whatever the authorities used to give them, they've got nowhere to go, they've just got the clothes they're standing up in and they've got no friends, only the ones they made in the prison during that five years. They had nothing to do. These were young fellas, and, already, prison was their life.

Often, they go and do another crime just to get back in the nick again. Cos, there, they get three meals a day, a roof over their head, clean linen, clean clothes to wear and their mates. And no responsibility. That's what prisons breed. They're unfortunate people, let's put it that way. They haven't got any families, they haven't got anyone who's worrying about them, and prison is a life that they're quite happy with. Because they got nothing else outside. They're incapable of going and getting a living, and they don't want to.

Tony   I've seen that many, many times.

Fred   Lazy bastards who don't wanna fucking do anything. They wanna lay about in their cells, fucking smoking a bit of puff and getting stoned, or shooting up smack, which they do. I mean, everything's available in them places. So they couldn't give two fucks about being out with their families and missing them. They don't miss no one cos no one misses them.

Tony   For example, we were in Bermondsey at a friend's party. I've known him a long time. And you know what he said? His wife was sitting there, and we was all chatting, and this is the words he said: 'The best years of my fucking life.' With *us*. Never mind about his marriage – 'The best years of my life.'

Fred   What, in the nick?

Tony   In the nick.

Fred   *No!* Well, this just illustrates what I've been saying.

Tony   Yes. And Wendy said, 'Is he serious?' He was, Fred. Because he felt a bond there that he'd never had anywhere else.

Fred This goes back to what I was saying about the young kids. I mean, what sort of life has the man had if he thinks that's the best years of his life? He must have meant the people – that's what he had. He obviously never had any good friends before he went in prison. What's he doing now?

Tony He phones me up and he misses us. He misses the comradeship, I think. That's what it was about.

Fred Yeah, the camaraderie. But it doesn't say much for the life he led before, does it?

Tony You sit in a pub with people you knew in the nick, and everybody wants to talk about prison for some reason. Do you ever find that, Fred? Weird, isn't it?

Fred They've done so much bird, that's all they can talk about. I suppose it's therapeutic to them, to get it out of their fucking heads. You get flashbacks all the time, don't you? I do.

Tony Oh, yeah, yeah.

Fred I always get them in the morning. You're laying in bed, you wake up and – 'Thank God!' You're not looking up at the prison fucking ceiling, or the walls, or the bars at the windows. All sorts of things trigger off the flashbacks. Music . . .

Tony Yeah, music does that to me.

Fred And sounds. You know, certain sounds, like the clanging of doors and the rattling of keys and that.

Tony You know what reminds me of '69? That song 'Two Little Boys'. Do you remember it? Rolf Harris. Whenever I hear that song, it takes me back to Christmas in Leicester. Is there any one song that brings it back to you, Fred?

Fred I don't know. So many . . .

Tony Every so often, one'll catch you out.

Fred A morbid thing – I can't stand to listen to 'The Little Drummer Boy,' cos that reminds me of them fucking animals, Hindley and Brady. They played that when they was killing that little girl [Lesley Ann Downey]. When I ever hear that record, if it's on the radio or something, I will turn it off. I can't bear to listen to that.

The Sixties pop songs – they all remind me of the pub, and the clubs in the West End. They bring back good memories because that was before we were nicked. But post-fucking '68 and right into the middle of the Seventies, they're not good memories, those songs. Everything reminds you of the nick.

Tony You know what? I've got the habits. Prison habits. I don't know if you do this, Fred, but I come out of my house in the morning and look down the road and I know what's going on. I'm watching out for every little thing.

Then when I'm going out, to a pub or something, I'll often stand at the door, hesitate for a second, before I go through it. A lot of the boys do it, because you're so used to waiting for the screw to open the door.

I go home of a night and I can't go to bed unless that kitchen's spotless. I can't leave a cup. Can't do it. If I've forgotten a cup – which doesn't happen often, I assure you – I'll get up in the middle of the night and wash it. That's the way I live.

Insomnia comes into it, too. I can't sleep till it's very late – three or four in the morning. I'm trying to make more of the day. When I first came out of the nick, I used to go to bed at nine o'clock at night. And I didn't want to go out for about a year. I was too unsure of myself. I didn't want to make a mistake.

Even now when I'm at home, I always stay in the kitchen. Everything I do, Fred, is in the kitchen. I feel more secure in there. Just little things like that can affect your life.

Wendy knows, and I'm sure Janice would say the same thing if they was to talk about us – we like to get our own way. It's because we've fought authority all the way through our lives.

And do you find that you tend to keep to a routine out here? I'll do certain things in the morning, like the phoning. Lunchtime, I like that to be a bit free, take the dog for a run. Then in the afternoons, I like to just pop down and have a bet or whatever. But it does that to you. When you've done long periods in prison, you like the routine.

Fred You like the regularity of things.

Tony I've gotta make the bed the minute I get out of it.

Fred You've changed! You never did that in the nick! But, yeah, it's like children – they want a bit of order in their lives, don't they? They want special times to come and have their tea and a time when they go to bed.

Tony You have all these habits you learn in prison, a lot of them to do with food. I like stews. And if it's not stew, you tend to cover food up, mix it with gravy. In that way, it always looks presentable. Dry food never looks presentable because it was so tasteless in prison. I always eat with a fork and a spoon, very rarely a knife. Prison habit. I'll always drink a mug of tea, never a cup. Prison habit. In a way, it's a form of institutionalization.

I mean, what's a man gonna do after fifteen or twenty years? There was one example, a fella in Maidstone. I remember him as clear as anything, and it frightened me, Fred. Done twenty-three years of a life, and he arrived at the hostel the week after me. I'll always remember him walking down the middle of the road, the first time he's been out of the nick after all them years.

He was using this pub down at Maidstone, and he was a fucking, raving nutcase. I just wanted to get away from him, Fred. He thought everyone was following him.

Fred Yeah, paranoid.

Tony Paranoid like I've never seen. He was stood in the pub and he thought everyone was a copper! And I just didn't want that round me.

Fred No.

Tony He lasted four weeks.

Fred That's a long time for a man to survive in that condition. They get paranoid to fucking stand in the toilet with someone. They think everyone is dodgy, and they're likely to attack when they're in that state.

Tony Fred, he was bad. You could see it in him.

Fred When they hit the pub and start getting a few Scotches down 'em and getting pissed, then they're dangerous, aren't they? A wrong look, the wrong word, will kick them off. It's not funny. Those are the sort of men the prison system turns out on the public.

2

The Reggie Kray
Freedom Campaign

Fred They shouldn't be arguing about, 'Should he be let out?' They should be arguing about, '*When* is he gonna be let out?' It's thirty-two years now. Why isn't he released? How much fucking longer do they wanna keep him? Till he comes out in a box?

Tony I seen that programme on television [*Reggie Kray – Thirty Years And Rising*, on Channel 4 on 17 February 2000]. It's asking, should Reggie Kray be released?

Fred I thought it did help Reggie.

Tony It probably was one of the fairest programmes I've seen on the subject.

Fred I thought that your brother Chrissy spoke well on it, even though I don't like the man. And also the psychiatrist.

Tony Yeah, he done a good job.

Fred And so did [author John] Pearson. He said some positive things.

Tony I thought Pearson came over well, yeah.

Fred He said that the strong influence was Ronnie, and without that strong influence behind him, Reggie wouldn't have done the things he did. And Ronnie's no longer here, so there's no fear of it happening again.

Tony I thought they made Roberta [Kray, Reggie's wife] look a bit too much like a fan, although she come into her own later on when she was interviewed properly, just sitting there. But you can see their motivation.

Fred You know, they edit these things. They can't understand the fact that she's married someone like Reggie, you see, and they're looking at her a bit spiteful, like she's a groupie instead of a genuine woman who feels for and loves her man.

Tony Spitefulness, yeah. I think that.

Fred Some people looked on it like it was a marriage of convenience.

Tony Exactly.

Fred And it wasn't. Course not.

Tony No. I think she's done more for him than anybody else had in a long time. His public image now is a lot better since she's handled that side of it. You know, he was a free target, wasn't he? Everybody coming out the nick would write a story on him. And that don't do no good.

Fred He handled himself very well at Charlie's funeral.

Tony Yes, he came out of that very, very well. I thought he looked great, and he handled it with a lot of dignity.

Fred He did very well when he spoke to the TV interviewer. And I loved the poem he chose. It wasn't one of his own, thank God! It's a classic poem ['I Am Not There', recited by Reggie on a tape which was played at the service].

Tony He handled himself with a lot of composure considering the strain he must've been under. It took a bit of doing, that.

Fred It's not a thing you can get used to, but Reggie's been through that a few times now. Funerals are the only experience he's had of the outside world in the past thirty years. You know what I was thinking of afterwards, after he got in that van and he left?

Tony I felt gutted.

Fred I know what the procedure is, going back to prison. They take them cuffs off, take your clothes off and you go through the formalities of reception. You go back to your cell and close that door . . . How did he feel?

Tony   I felt sick. I don't know how he does it, Reggie.

Fred   I don't know how he stands it. He's a very, very strong man.

Tony   Yeah, gotta give him that.

Fred   To see his whole family buried, and the only time he comes out of prison is to go to another funeral . . .

Tony   And he's still locked away. It's very sad.

Fred   They went one by one. He's the only one left. But he handled himself well. He really did.

Tony   You know, he called me to the grave, he called the right people to the graveside, and I admire and respect him for that. I'd like to say thanks, you know. I got a little kiss from Roberta.

Fred   I've never actually met the girl. He asked me to the graveside too, and he asked to see my Jamie. I liked the fact that the police had him cuffed to a woman instead of making a big point of cuffing him up to giants who dwarfed him. And the police kept a good distance, they didn't interfere. I thought they handled it very well.

Tony   Yeah, they did.

Fred   It was done discreetly, and it was thought through. Because, I must admit, things got a little out of hand outside the church at Ronnie's funeral. The crowds were so enraged about Reggie's situation, the way he's been treated over the years, that at one point there, it looked like they were going to spring him. They were gonna get those cuffs off of him and take him away with them. And I can understand the police being concerned, you know. They must've crapped themselves, with an angry crowd like that.

But he didn't do himself any damage at all at Charlie's funeral, in terms of his campaign to be released.

Tony   He done himself no harm here, considering the pressure he must've been under.

Fred   But, you know, you've gotta help yourself in every way you can. You've gotta go through the system. You've gotta go to places like Springhill, get your day release and do a bit of community work. He hasn't even started that yet. How can they let him straight out the gate into the street? He's got to go through that system of release, step by step by step.

Tony They give you a plan, Fred.

Fred When he volunteered to go to Wayland, I thought that was the biggest fucking mistake he's made. I couldn't believe that he'd asked to go to a poxy place like that, cos I couldn't get out of there quick enough. I was sent there for punishment, from Latchmere. I was in a good nick and, to punish me, they sent me to fucking Wayland. Who wants to go there and start over again? It's like turning the clock back.

I told him when he phoned me up. I said, 'What the fuck did you do that for, Reg? Going to Wayland of all places.' And, well, he didn't give me any answer.

Tony From Maidstone, where he was before that, he really should've gone to an open prison.

Fred He should've gone to Springhill or Blantyre House or Latchmere House. They're semi-open. You're locked up, and you've got a perimeter fence, although it wouldn't be hard to escape because you're walking out the gate to work in the community, going to old people's homes, or houses where people are isolated. You go and do their gardens for them, do their odd jobs in the house – decorate, paint something up, that sort of work. That's what they do in Blantyre. They give them bikes to go out and do these little jobs in the community round the area. So there's no reason why Reggie shouldn't be allowed to do that.

Tony I helped to build a hospital when I got out of Maidstone. My job was building the mortuary.

Fred That was handy, wasn't it? Building a mortuary! I was looking after people in an old people's home. I was running 'em up and down the fucking hill in these wheelchairs. (*Laughing*) And I couldn't help doing wheelies on the back. I couldn't hold them, when they came down, a couple of them big old boys, you know. There was a South African old boy. He was a heavyweight, he was, and I couldn't keep hold of him going down the hill. We used to fucking tear down the hill . . .

You had to pay to be in them prisons, didn't you? You had to take them back forty quid a week to stay there.

Tony   Yeah, for your keep.

Fred   They reckon you can get money back now for that.

Tony   Everything I paid in, they gave me back. I had full employment, see. But getting back to Reggie, he's gotta do two things. The Local Review Committee is one, and the Parole Board. What the Local Review Committee recommend to the Parole Board, the Parole Board carry out, and the Home Secretary signs it. Now, where Reggie Kray comes into the equation, the number-one problem is his name.

Fred   Who wants to sign?

Tony   Now, I understand from what I know, he has done nothing, Fred, to help himself.

Fred   Well, he's not shown any remorse. That's one thing that you've got to do if you're working to try to get out.

Tony   They asked me that question, the Local Review Committee.

Fred   If you were sorry for what you did.

Tony   'What was your view of the crime?' My attitude was, 'I'm sorry someone had to die.' I went down that road with it: 'It couldn't happen again.' You tell them what they wanna hear. I said it was wrong that a man should lose his life.

Fred   Anyone that was involved in it has got to be sorry.

Tony   That's right. It was a bad thing.

Fred   It's something that needn't have happened, because if they'd left it a bit longer, somebody else would've fucking ironed Jack ['The Hat' McVitie] out. Probably it would've been me! At least then it would've been done right!

Tony   It was destined. I've always said destiny comes into this.

Fred   Oh, Reggie was, like, on a death wish.

Tony   And it's what he's saying now that's important. I mean, these are the people who hold the keys to the door.

Fred　And you can't even have an attitude or a look. I heard that on the last Parole Board, he gave the geezer a dodgy look or something.

Tony　Well, he acts up. He played up a little bit: 'What am I doing here? You're not gonna let me out the gate.' They're not gonna let him out the gate until he goes through the system.

Fred　So, really, it's a waste of time him sitting on them Parole Boards.

Tony　Technically, yeah.

Fred　It is. It's a sham, cos they're not gonna let him out the gate. They're not gonna let him walk out into society after thirty-fucking-two years.

Tony　Can't do it.

Fred　He's got to go to an open prison, and he's gotta come out maybe once a week to start with. Then twice a week. They go into the local village or town with a screw escort. And they go into fucking McDonald's and they go to the library, the shopping mall, a bit at a time.

Tony　Exactly right.

Fred　They do a bit of shopping, buy a bit of gear and back again . . . and that's how they try to familiarize him with the outside world. That's how a man's gotta be treated. You can't just throw him out the gate into the wide world. So if you don't go along with it and you don't cooperate to the extent where you play their fucking game, what chance have you got of being released?

Tony　It's a game.

Fred　That's all it is. You just play their game, and you go along with what they want to do and say what they want to hear.

Tony　He's never done that.

Fred　You have to work the system through.

Tony　It's still gonna take a minimum of two years to get him out.

Fred　I can't see them releasing him out into the wide world. He's gotta go to another prison and he's gotta do his work without high walls and fucking wire fences and cameras all round him. He's gotta go to an open prison and work on a garden party where he's wandering about on his own and he don't run away, he don't abscond and he gets on with it. And, gradually, they give him another job further outside the perimeter of the prison or up to the officers' mess or somewhere.

Tony   That's right, yeah.

Fred   And then they cultivate you, see how you react, see if you're a responsible enough person to come back and you ain't doing a Frank fucking Mitchell, legging it over the fields and fucking off. And once he's had a year of that, he'd go to a freer prison where they work in a proper job outside and get weekends out.

Tony   But, Fred, do you know anybody who's done that length of time and come out?

Fred   Well, it's only Joe Martin.

Tony   He's the only one I can think of.

Fred   He was in a semi-open prison, wasn't he? It's hard adjusting to society again.
    When I first come back out, I'd only been away for a little while – eight years of a ten-year sentence [over Jack 'The Hat' McVitie] – and I stood in a phone box trying to put money in a fucking box which only took cards. I mean, these are silly little things but they were new, you know.

Tony   He's never applied for a course to help himself, has he, Reggie?

Fred   What, education?

Tony   Yeah, I did. They asked me to do it.

Fred   He don't watch television, does he? I never seen him watch any television.

Tony   He sits in his cell, writes a lot of letters and stuff.

Fred   If you're not watching television, how can you keep in touch with what's happening in society? I can understand it in the early days. In Leicester, I used to try to get him to come and watch the television. I got him out a couple of times, he sat there for a few minutes and fucking went back to his cell.

It's like you're shutting your mind off to the outside world. That's what he was doing. He was bringing a barrier down to say, 'I don't want to know what's going on outside that wall, cos it's gonna drive me fucking nuts. I've got a thirty-year fucking sentence here. I'm not going to be interested in that, this is my life in prison.'

Cos whenever a man goes away in prison, it takes him eighteen months to two years to settle down. During that time, half your mind's in prison and half your mind's over the other side of the wall, imagining where you'd be and what you'd be doing if you were outside.

But once you get a couple of years into your sentence, you're just focused on prison life. That makes it easier, mentally, to cope, to get on with it. Once your mind starts switching outside, you're unsettled. You're half a person when you're laying there trying to go to sleep at night, your mind starts ticking over and you're thinking of every bad scenario. So you want to switch off from all that, and that's what he did at the beginning of his time. I mean, we're sitting here analysing Reggie and trying to see the way he thinks.

Tony   To work it out, yeah.

Fred   Just trying to work out what other people maybe can't, you know, unless they can see it more clearly than we can. But, I mean, if Reggie comes out, let the man fucking live a normal life. I should think he wouldn't want a lot of attention, I think he'd fucking want to get in the country somewhere, out the way.

But he'll be like a superstar walking round. He'll have the crowds round him everywhere he goes, won't he? Autograph hunters and weirdos and fucking nutters.

Tony   But what do they want to see? Are they expecting a thirty-four-year-old Reggie to come out? He's sixty-six now, and we've heard that he's ill. I think what also comes into it is the business side of it, running a business from in there with headed note-paper . . .

Fred   Yeah.

Tony   You've all that going on there and he's earning money. What's he gonna do when he gets out?

Fred This is another reason why they won't let him out. It isn't fair that he's still in there, but, you know, they've got a dilemma. I know the prison authorities and I must say, if they put him in an open nick, they're gonna have all these photographers taking photos of him walking round in the prison when he's doing his everyday work. If he's out on the garden party, for instance, they'll be sneaking in the bushes and round hedges taking pictures.

Tony Someone's gonna phone up and tell the papers. Give a bit of a tip and get payment. 'Reggie's gonna be here or there at a certain time,' you know.

Fred I had it myself. *News of the World* got me slung out of Latchmere. They got me thrown out of there with one silly photograph. They said I was at the pub. I was home on my weekend leave, so it was up to me where I went, anyway. But I wasn't even in the pub. I parked in the car park of the Bull and Bush, in Golders Green, for convenience, and I went into the park nearby. I had coffees and a meal in the cafeteria there. I walked back to the pub car park and that's when they smudged me up.

That's just to show you the sort of attention you can get. And I wasn't the high profile that Reggie is. Nobody had fucking heard of me then, not like they have now. And they're taking photographs of me just fucking getting in a car. And that got me slung out of Latchmere – that and the fact that I was found with more than £40 in my possession, which was against the rules. That's how I ended up in Wayland.

Tony I remember that as clear as anything.

Fred That's it. I mean, what will they do with Reggie? The prison governors hate it. They don't want people creeping round with cameras, taking photos of the prisoners when they're working. You know, they've got enough to get on with at prison, so they don't want twenty or thirty photographers hanging around the gate, do they? That's the problem they've got.

But, at the same time, Reggie deserves the same treatment from the system as anybody else. Course he does.

Tony Even the Home Secretary won't comment on him. I've never heard the Home Secretary mention his name. He'll condemn Brady and people like that, but Reggie is a worry because the arguments to release him are very big. But the publicity and the business dealings weigh against him. They do.

My brother said something on that programme – Reggie has done double the time that we did. That takes a bit of getting your head round. Therein may lie a problem. From my own experience of seeing men who've done a long time, going out is a frightening prospect, a very daunting thing. So I think you've got to bear that in mind.

I mean, you gotta look at the whole picture here. You have got to see what his family's been through. A cursed name, unfortunately, and everyone has suffered with it. It's funny. Whatever way you look at all this, it has been a curse on all our lives. It has affected every one of us. No one or nothing has come out of it any good.

3

Sixties Villains Today: Friends and Foes

Conversation in Fred's kitchen, 6 May 2000

FRANKIE FRASER SUPERSTAR

Tony Frankie Fraser . . . I mean, they had him coming out with the pliers and that, pulling people's teeth out for the Richardson gang.

Fred Nah! I don't know any witness who actually said that he had his teeth pulled out. I might be wrong. Frank would know.

Tony I don't know anyone who actually saw anything. Well, of course, you get accused of these things, and there's nothing you can do to rebuff it. You go along with it. You start to live and breathe it. And then, I suppose, you're so used to hearing it that you start to believe it yourself and play on it.

He's got no other choice. He's Frankie Fraser. He's legendary – that's where this lies. The heart of the whole thing is the spirit and the legend around it. There's no escape from it. We're the high-profile ones. Me, you, Frank, the twins . . .

If you ever talk to Charlie Richardson about it, he'll tell you he got fifteen years for a scratch to someone's foot. In the so-called torture trial of 1967, they said he tried to nail the guy's foot to the floor. All they found was a scratch. Roy Hall – what did he do? Because he was friends with Charlie [Richardson], he got ten years.

Ironically enough, for all this war that was going on between the Krays and the Richardsons, they put us all in the same prisons, in the same maximum-security blocks.

I think they did it deliberately to see what would break out, what would happen. And nothing did.

Fred We may have had a few differences on the outside, but the common enemy was the screws and authority, so you had to support each other.

Tony It looked good, didn't it? South London, east London, pulling together against the system.

Fred And the police, they love to spread the disinformation that gets one rival gang to fight the other. Divide and rule, you know what I mean? It's to create fucking problems.

Tony It creates their jobs. And the newspapers helped. They really did prey upon it. I mean, they were falling over themselves. I remember going to Leicester [Prison] with you, Fred, and Charlie Richardson and all them were there . . . They [the authorities] didn't know what to expect. They were testing the water.

Fred It's like the IRA and the UDA. In prisons all over England, they're all mixed together. It's just a truce, isn't it? They're in a no-win situation, so what's the point in carrying on fucking old feuds and stuff? Not that there was really any serious feud with the Richardson gang. I mean, I lived in south London, like they did, and I never had no trouble with them. I never crossed swords with them in all those years. Well, a few words on one occasion but it never turned to violence.

We go back a long time, me and Frankie Fraser. All his family are close to me. They look on me as their Uncle Fred. Frank's with Marilyn, my god-daughter. She's the daughter of Tommy Wisbey and Renee.

And he's been running these tours of London, Frank, stopping off at all the famous crime spots of the Sixties. They showed a bit of it on the telly. I was laughing my bollocks off. I mean, Frank . . . he ain't got his name ['Mad Frankie'] for nothing.

Tony Yeah, that's right.

Fred He's been a villain and he's done more fucking bird and time down the block than most prisoners.

Tony (*Laughing*) Character.

Fred It is true – he's a great character. He's fucking brought the old scene alive – everyone's getting a living now, all the old villains, and he's a little shining star now, isn't he? A superstar.

Tony What is wrong with it? I wouldn't deny him, at his age, a little bit of fame and easy money.

Fred What you wanna do, do it, as long as you don't harm anyone. It's all bollocks anyway.

Tony Whatever you want. I mean, you're right there. 'Don't deny me my little bit of pension.'

Fred Fucking right, yeah. Enjoy it.

Tony And he laughs it off, Frank, in his own way.

Fred Of course, yeah.

Tony And he suffered, Fred, didn't he?

Fred He suffered.

Tony He gave evidence for us at our trial.

Fred And Charlie Kray's last court case. I mean, Frank would shape up for anything.

Tony What they should do is build a memorial outside the gates of Wandsworth, when he goes. He'd like that.

Fred Yeah, a statue of Frank throwing a petrol bomb at the gates!

Tony That's Frank! You've got to admire him because he's never wavered, has he?

Fred Nah. He's solid as a rock. Be with you till the death. And he's, like, the same as us ... people like my old mate Joey Pyle with his book, raising money for Zoe's Place in Liverpool, that children's hospice. We all went up there, didn't we, Tone, to help and support it? Poor little kids – breaks your heart to see them. Roy Shaw, Johnny Nash, Alfie Hutchinson, us – a coachful of villains all gave their time and money to a good cause. So we're not as bad as people make out, especially where kids are concerned. We all have children of our own, and grandchildren.

Tony You know Frank did a benefit?

Fred Where?

Tony Thomas A' Becket [legendary pub with boxing gym in the Old Kent Road].

Fred Who was it for?

Tony Gary Davidson, the boxer. Cos he died – did you know that?

Fred Oh yeah.

Tony He had a massive funeral, apparently.

Fred He used to run the Thomas A' Becket. That's an unlucky pub.

Tony Yeah, some people died in there. Beryl Gibbons and all that.

Fred Beryl died, and Tommy Gibbons, her husband. And now Gary's died.

Tony Very unlucky pub that. It's still going.

Fred Well, they put a Thai restaurant in there a few years ago and they closed the gym. I don't know if the bar ever closed, but I had heard it was open again. They should've kept the gym going. I used to work out, train up there, and there was one poxy shower in the corner and the place was so small, when it got busy, you had no room to skip or shadow-box.

Tony But it should've been kept on just because of its name.

Fred It would be nice if a boxer came over here for a world title fight that he could rent the place, just for his personal use with his own sparring partners and that. But then, they'd have to improve the facilities.

Tony Beryl Gibbons was the first woman boxing promoter.

Fred Well, yeah, she was good at promoting shows. Beryl was like one of the chaps. I was pretty close to her in those days. I had pool tables in her three pubs. One day at the Thomas A' Becket, we had an exhibition of paintings from guys in different prisons. Lord Longford was to be one of the judges. Beryl was upstairs getting ready for the show and Longford was waiting with all the press.

Beryl put on this skirt, black, and a white see-through blouse. She was one of the first women I knew to have a boob job – nipples like a baby's dummy. I said, 'You can't go down dressed like that.' She said, 'All right, I'll change.'

I went down to the gym and waited with the other fifty or so, and she made her entrance with the see-through lot on. Longford's eyes popped out. Beryl looked at me and she had that naughty twinkle in her eyes. The press had a field day. She was a smashing girl. Everybody loved Beryl. A shame she died so young.

I went to shoot one of her ex-boyfriends who broke into her house, robbed her and beat her up. I looked everywhere for him. I think he emigrated.

OLD SCHOOL TIES

Fred People like the Train Robbers, Bruce Reynolds, Bobby Welch, Tommy Wisbey and Jimmy Hussey I see regular and drink with, you know. Gordon Goody, he's out in Spain. He was on the phone to me only the other day.

Tony I liked him, Gordon, I did.

Fred I sent him over the copy of that programme on the Train Robbery that Channel 4 did a while back, cos he hadn't seen it. And the old faces in London, we meet each other all the time. We're friends, aren't we? We meet at benefits and functions and boxing shows.

Tony And if we have a get-together, people generally find it very interesting to see us turning out, the names in the underworld from that period of time. The public, they have taken to it. They know the names and the faces. It's like being the reverse of a pop star. Nicky Reynolds [sculptor and son of Train Robber Bruce Reynolds] summed it up very well a while ago on a TV programme. He said, 'Through no fault of their own, they became heroes.' Well, I don't know about the 'heroes' stuff . . .

Fred It's like being in the services in the war – they have reunions, don't they? Criminals have reunions and they get together and it's all, 'Remember that?' and 'Remember them?' and 'Where was you . . .?' Not, 'Where was you stationed?' but 'What nick was you in?' It's not, 'Were you in Italy or Normandy?', it's, 'Was you in the riots at Gartree or the Scrubs or Full Sutton' or, 'Was you on the twelve-day hunger strike in Leicester?'

I mean, they was in a battle or in the trenches or wherever, and they've shared those times of danger, the grief and the hard times, and the funny incidents as well.

Tony It *is* like being in the army.

Fred Yeah, there's a bond. You've all got that in common, suffered in that way. You know what it's like to be in the Old Bailey and walk down them steps with a fucking lump of bird to get on with. And them fucking trips from Brixton in the old meat wagon – tearing through the streets with the sirens going. We've experienced that, you know?

Tony I've still got some very good pals around me from those days.

Fred They're forever.

Tony Yeah, without a doubt.

Fred There's lots of arseholes you meet in prison, and if they walked in one door, you'd want to get out the other. If you're not a respected criminal, no one gives a shit who you are when you arrive in the nick, and you have to scavenge for yourself. But if a dozen people know you from the out, you've had drinks with them, you've been to work with them, socialized with them, and then you're in there in a different environment, you do get a lot of bonding. You form relationships there that stay with you for the rest of your life.

These are people you feel comfortable with today. You've seen them at their worst, you've seen them at their best, you've seen them under duress and stress when they first get their sentence, you've seen them when they stand up to it and get on with it, and you've seen them when they come off their visits and they're fucking breaking their heart about their kids.

You see them at their most vulnerable. You share the summers when you know everyone's out on holidays, going abroad and stuff, and you're stuck in there, walking round a concrete yard. Then the Christmases come, and you're sharing the Christmases. You make the best of it with the other cons.

Going back to Edward Bunker and his book *Dog Eat Dog*, he says, 'There were no other facades between them, nor any need, for neither judged the other for anything: they were friends as only thieves can be.' That's what I was saying about the relationships.

You might not see someone for ten, fifteen or twenty years, but when you do meet again, you just take up where you left off. It's an unusual relationship.

In business, if you was in a factory or in an office block or something and you left there, you would drift away and you'd never see your colleagues again. If you did happen to see 'em, you'd have nothing in common.

With criminals, the friendships are special because they suffer together, you know. They go through all the highs and lows. I mean, you've gotta experience the pain and sorrow to appreciate the joy as well.

They live life to the very extreme. And this is what makes their relationships so strong.

Ninety per cent of the cons have come from the same sort of background of poverty and lower standard of education and not had the opportunities in life, probably, you know.

But we were still selective. Our best relationships were with certain people that we've gone away with over our crimes. There's nothing bonds a friendship more than cutting up a bit of money when you've had a touch. You go, 'That's yours,' and, 'That's yours.'

Tony Yeah, that's a smile on your face.

Fred You're putting your little bag down and putting your readies in it. That's a lovely bond, you know.

Tony And when you come out of prison and you've kept your name clean, and you can go and mix with the boys, it's a very proud thing to be able to do. We've all come on a long way, and we're a lot older, and yet, for all what we've been through, we can still get together and have a drink and a laugh about it.

BUT NOT EVERYONE'S IN THE CLUB . . .

Fred Up until this week [beginning of May 2000], when we was all at the premiere to relaunch *The Long Good Friday*, I hadn't seen Ronnie Knight since he came out of prison. I didn't know where he was or what he was doing or who he was mixing with, so I was really surprised to see him there. I was a bit disappointed in Ronnie, because he hadn't bothered to get in touch with me or Micky [Regan], who had been his partner at one time. We was the best of pals.

Tony　He's up for a quiet life now, living in north London somewhere.

Fred　Well, it's up to him if he wants to drop out of the scene and go his own way. You know, if it suits him, good luck to him. People do change. I asked him, 'Where you been? Why ain't you been in touch?' He said, 'I didn't know where you lived, and I didn't have your phone number.' I said, 'It's not hard to make contact with me or Mick.' He had no real answer.

Tony　I first met Ronnie Knight around 1961, '62 in a club in the West End, somewhere around the time he met [his wife-to-be] Barbara Windsor, and I bumped into him over the years – once in the nick and then out in Spain at your club, the Eagles. Like you, Fred, I hadn't seen him for a long, long time until this week. And he was very friendly to me. I was talking to him for about a half hour, and Joey Pyle spoke to him too. I had a few photos done with him, Roy [Shaw] and Frank [Fraser].

Fred　I didn't have time for a proper conversation with him. He was on his way out when I bumped into him. It was nice to see him, but we didn't exchange phone numbers.

Tony　That's the first function I know of Ronnie Knight attending since he came out of the nick. I think it was to see what our reaction would be. And he had aged. He looked jowly.

Fred　He was a handsome boy. But time takes its toll on all of us.

Tony　It had caught up with him.

Fred　One person I really changed my mind about was John McVicar [armed robber turned journalist].

Tony　I knew John.

Fred　They brought him to the Special Wing at Leicester. He was all right when he arrived there. I mean, he was giving it the large, playing the part of the Public Enemy Number One title he had on him.

Tony   He was very well liked then.

Fred   Course we liked him. When he escaped from Durham in 1968, friends of mine were harbouring him and looking after him. He didn't seem to appreciate things very much. He's obviously moved over to the establishment side, and you've only got to read his articles to know what I think about him now.

I spoke to him in Spain and I said, 'You know, you can't sit on the fence. If you're a journalist and you're gonna report on criminals, you can't expect them to open up to you if you've changed sides. You've got to be balanced in what you're talking about.'

He said he was gutted that people thought he was doing anything wrong. But he was writing about things that shouldn't be mentioned.

Tony   What I thought was bad was the way he done Charlie Kray. There was no need for that.

Fred   I rarely read his articles.

Tony   It was shocking. I've got the article indoors, and he rips into Charlie as a has been who's ponced off his brothers' names. Really ran amok, went to town on him, just before Charlie died.

Fred   And he's wrote some articles on the Irish situation for *Punch* magazine and mentioned my name in it, regarding my friendship with certain people – which I'm not going to deny or be ashamed of.

Tony   Shouldn't do that.

Fred   He was saying I was a friend of Brian Keenan; that he was close with the underworld criminals, namely me, in Full Sutton. Well, I've met many of the Irish terrorists in prison.

They're solid, staunch and they're loyal to each other and to other cons. If there's a grievance, they stand with you and they are decent men to live with. They're clean and they abide by our prison rules, not the authorities' – you know, the way we live. And they're all right to do your bird with. They're nice people, they also make a good drop of hooch.

I always told them at the beginning, 'As long as we don't talk about religion or politics, we'll all get along together.' They was doing lives and thirties, and I don't wanna name them all, but Brian was one of them. We'd talk about everything other than the Irish situation, about what was going on in the nick.

Tony They're educated people.

Fred And they're not criminal-minded. You can't talk about bank robberies and things like that with them, cos they saw themselves as political prisoners who was only aware of what was going on between England and Ireland. They wasn't interested in any other form of criminal activity. They was all just doing their bird as best they could.

When I was in Brixton, there was two who got nicked in Wales. They got thirties apiece, and I used to play draughts with them. We got on all right.

The prison authorities dressed them in trousers halfway up their ankles with no flies and no buttons on 'em. Wouldn't fit 'em. And it's winter, and they wouldn't give 'em any sweaters or warm clothing. They had shirts on. Snow and sleet coming down – freezing their bollocks off out on exercise. I gave them some of my sweaters, just as a bit of human decency.

Tony I met loads of them, and they were very loyal, polite men, mainly young. But I'm not a politician. I didn't really get involved in that side of it.

Fred You don't want to.

Tony They've been brought up with it. They're not criminals as we know it, and they was loyal in the demonstrations and that. But feelings sometimes did run high in nicks.

Fred They could touch a nerve. If they started talking about politics, we'd say we didn't wanna know.

Tony And there we were, all in the cesspit together.

Fred It's obviously a very sensitive subject, and McVicar was spiteful to bring it up in such a superficial way. We all tried to get along with everyone in prison, including the Irish, and he knew that by singling my name out, it would alienate people. He mentions me quite a lot in his writing. I'm just good copy for him. In a way, I suppose, it's a back-handed compliment.

He's not a criminal at heart. He had a good education to start with, and he had his claim to fame for a few years when he got nicked and went off the rails. But it didn't last very long, did it?

Tony   He took a university degree in prison.

Fred   He's clever at what he says. When he puts things on paper, he's very articulate. It's a pity it has to be at the expense of the people who helped him once upon a time.

11 December 2000
FRANKIE FRASER: A CHANGE OF HEART

Fred   A week or two ago, I was flying out to Cuba. My son Jamie got stranded out there. He was having a ball, him and his pal Tony from Liverpool, and he overstretched himself. We couldn't get any money to him out there, so I was on a mission of mercy to get him home, and Janice and I decided to make a nice week's holiday out of it.

The morning I left, I got a phone call from my old pal Micky Regan. He said, 'Fred, have you read Fraser's book?' This is *Mad Frank's Diary* (published by Virgin in 2000). I said, 'No, should I?' He said, 'Yes.'

At Heathrow, I noticed it in Smith's. On the plane, I started flicking through the book. I noticed my name, and I read one little chapter. Immediately, I was very, very upset at the things he had written about me.

Janice said, 'Don't read any more. Don't spoil your holiday. Wait till we get back,' which was the sensible thing to do. I didn't look at it again till I got home.

I read it, and my immediate emotion was rage. Later, I realized he's a silly old piece of shit. I'm not getting in the gutter and digging the dirt with Frankie Fraser, but a lie uncontradicted becomes an accepted truth, so I can't ignore it. He's took the gloves off with me. If there's anybody who can substantiate the crap that he's written about me – man, woman or child – let them bring the evidence.

Tony   There are things in this book that everybody knows are lies. All the chaps are shocked and disappointed in Frankie.

Fred I always thought he was a sound man and a friend. The family have been friends of mine all their lives, but I realize now that he's not been a friend at all. It's been a pretence, and he's a wicked, evil, little bastard.

I think he wants to go out in a blaze of glory. He probably wants me to go round and put one in his nut. He would feel content to die leaving a feud between his family and my family to continue for years. That would make him very happy. But I wouldn't do a day's bird over him. What anyone else does is nothing to do with me, cos he's upset a lot of people.

Tony None of us have ever said a bad word about him. We've all spent years in prison together. He gave evidence for us!

Fred He did that to safeguard himself, cos the twins and all of us were going into prison. He had to pal us up so when we see him in prison, there's no animosity.

Now he's accusing me of losing people's respect because of the programme I did [Carlton TV's January 2000 two-parter, *The Krays*]. The idiot thought that I went on the programme with Albert Donoghue, because it was edited to look as if we were on an escalator at the same time. The last time I saw Albert Donoghue was in 1968 when he was in the witness box giving evidence against me.

Tony Do you think for one moment he would want to be within a mile radius of you?

Fred And if Frankie's talking about losing respect . . . look at that article he did with his lovely Marilyn, running a massage parlour –

Tony And there's a video to prove it.

Fred In the last ten years, all he's done is get shot in the head and done fuck all about it, even though he knows who did it.

He turned into a tour guide of the East End, which he was never a part of – cos there was no friendship between him and the Krays. They hated his guts, and he was at the top of Ronnie's famous hit list. That's why he ridicules Ronnie Kray in all his lectures and speeches, talking about his homosexuality in a really vulgar manner. And then he's up visiting Reggie, who never knew the way he was talking about Ronnie.

Another accusation. He states that my pub was always full of coppers. There was only one police officer who was ever allowed to drink in my pub and that was Frank Williams. If it was always full of coppers, why does Fraser say, 'I used to go in [Fred's pub] a lot; took my mum and dad in once or twice.' He only came in my pub on one occasion – when I wasn't there.

He's also suggesting I was responsible for the trouble in Catford. He alludes, 'Now it makes me wonder about Mr Smith's Club. There's always been stories that he [Fred] set it up as a favour to Reggie and now, after seeing him on telly, I'd believe anything.'

I was invited to go to Mr Smith's that night [in March 1965, when there was a gun battle arising from a dispute between the Richardson gang and the Hayward brothers, who were involved in the club, leading to the arrest of quite a few of the Richardson men]. But I had the club, pub and casino to run. No one knew what was going to happen that night, in hindsight it would have suited if I'd been there, there'd have been a few more casualties . . .

Frankie tries to prove his allegations by saying I helped Billy Hayward get his head stitched up afterwards. That's true. I'd help any man who was in trouble and I'd get him medical help if he needed it.

What else? Oh, Frankie's sister Eva was nicked for conspiracy to pervert the course of justice, and he's accusing me of not helping her when I could've. We didn't even know Eva had been arrested.

Tony I think a lot of people have come to disrespect him for what he's said about you. By attacking you, he's attacked everyone. Frank's been ostracized by all the chaps, cos they've realized what a piece of shit he is. He tells the world in this book that his own sons are drug dealers – 'Am I sorry my boys have gone into drugs? I can't rightly say I am. That's the culture now . . . and they're just supplying a need.' Is that not grassing up your own family?

Fred In another part of the book, he slags off Dodger Mullins, Charlie Kray and my pal Alfie Gerrard for not participating in any of his sit-downs or organized demonstrations in the nick. They had more sense than to be manipulated.

In every prison, it took us ages to get everything running smoothly for all the cons' benefit. As soon as he arrived, he'd upset the applecart by creating problems for everyone and the whole prison system, resulting in people down the block losing remission and doing extra time.

Frankie is a man who, in his early days, couldn't do his bird without self-mutilation. That's a man who was looking for sympathy – 'Look at me, Mummy, I don't like it in here.' He even showed the scars at one of his lectures to students . . . To be proud of slashing yourself? No person in his right mind would give himself eighty stitches in each arm. What does that tell you about a man's character?

Tony　What does that achieve? I find it embarrassing. Since I've read this book, it sheds a different light on everything. I still can't believe what he's written about you. None of us can. You don't talk about a man in public like that, whether you like him or not. Everything he's said about you smacks of jealousy. Everything that Frankie Fraser wanted to be, you *are*.

Fred　He was only a nick-face, someone with a reputation in prison but not outside it.

Tony　He's certainly not observing the code that we've always lived by. The minute he done that to you, he was finished, in my eyes.

Fred　Another thing is, he's trying to insinuate that it was because I was with Duke Osbourne and 'Scatty' Eddy Watkins [in the customs trap] that they got nicked. Make no mistake about it, there's an insinuation there. 'Freddie was lucky again.' *'Again'*. He doesn't say that I had to leave my home and businesses and go on my toes to America for four years, only to return and get arrested when one of his close friends, Frannie Daniels, put the finger on me in a club in Soho. After I stood trial at Winchester Crown Court, where the prosecution dug up all my past regarding the Kray trials, I was treated very leniently – for the first time in my life.

I mean, this book even accuses me of making a mistake when I shot Ginger Marks, saying it was the wrong man. There was no mistake, believe me. When Ginger Marks knocked on my brother's door for the second time, he stepped to one side and Jimmy Evans stepped out of the shadows with a twelve-bore shotgun. The reason I couldn't shoot Evans was because he held Marks up as a shield to take all the flak, and only one bullet went through Evans' clothing when he legged it for his life. So the two of them should have disappeared that night. Ginger Marks was as guilty as Evans. He was an accessory to the attempted murder of my brother. Believe me, there was no fucking mistake.

4

The RIPs and the
Not-So-Wells

Conversation in Fred's kitchen, 20 April 2000

LENNY MCLEAN

Lenny died of lung cancer in 1998.

Fred He used to fight Roy Shaw in these illegal fights. They had about three fights, didn't they, Roy and him? He fought other people as well, and some of the chaps earned a bit of dough there, so they had a business arrangement with him. They went to his funeral, obviously, cos they knew him personally but, I mean, I didn't really know him at all.

Tony He could handle himself; he was a violent man. He come out of Oxford. I didn't know him all that well, but I went to his funeral because any time I met him, he was always polite and he made me welcome in his company. I mean, I speak as I find.

Fred When I went to the fights, I supported Roy rather than Lenny McLean.

Tony Oh, obviously, we're very close to Roy Shaw. I like Roy. He's a nice guy. But Lenny McLean, he speaks well of me in his book [*The Guvnor*, published by Blake in 1998] and he speaks well of you and all the boys.

Fred Well, he was good to us people, you know – respectful.

Tony I met him first of all at the Camden Palace. He'd make a fuss of you.

Fred Yeah, always. He was a minder and a bouncer and his job was looking after people. If you was out in his company, he'd be looking after you all night.

RONNIE BIGGS

Fred He is a folk hero, definitely, and he's carried himself well over the years. He's a lovely character, a fucking diamond. And I'm very sad that he's ill at the moment [having suffered another stroke]. Please God he pulls through it.

I went over to see him in Brazil, and his son, a year ago, and he'd just got over a stroke then. I was with him for about a week, and he was getting better every day. We had a great time talking about old times.

It's amazing how our paths crossed in so many different ways before the Train Robbery, and yet I never knew him in those days. He could have been walking in one door as I'm walking out the other, in different pubs and places. I knew so many people that he knew, and he knew so many people that I knew – and yet we never met, until the day he climbed over the wall at Wandsworth.

Tony The villains are all known to each other, even if they don't know each other in person.

Fred So we had a great time out there. Janice took some good footage on the digital camera. We're talking in Ronnie's apartment, a real character apartment it is, and I'm at one end of the table and he's at the other end. Janice is filming, she's got the camera pointing towards me, and I said, 'It's Ronnie you wanna film.' But there's a big mirror behind me and Ronnie's over my shoulder as I'm talking. His reflection is clear as anything, so she knew what she was doing.

Tony Clever, yes.

Fred Artistic. She got the two of us in one shot instead of swinging from one to the other.

Tony Would he like to come back to England, ever?

Fred I think he would, but what's he got to look at? I mean, when I was in Wandsworth, a couple of cons in the reception said, 'Come round the back and have a look at this.' And there's Ronnie's box, still with his clothes in – the suit that he arrived in, the shoes and the shirt and everything. There's a half-finished mailbag in there. And the screw makes a quip – he's probably said it a million times – 'This is for Ronnie when he comes back. He's gotta finish this.' Cos for him to escape is a right smack in the face for the people who run the prison system.

Tony A kick in the bollocks. I met him in Wandsworth. I only spoke to him a couple of times. I mean, everybody knew he was up there for thirty years.

Fred A thirty-year man, fucking everybody's looking at him . . . but, no, he won't come back here. Malcolm McLaren, fucking little rat-faced thing, will be happy to hear that, I'm sure. He and Ronnie and his son had a falling out over those recordings they done with the Sex Pistols.

Ronnie Biggs performed with the Sex Pistols and made a video with them for the single 'No One Is Innocent' [a Top Ten hit in 1978]. The B-side was 'My Way' by Sid Vicious. That sold well, that song.

Tony Very well.

Fred It's a sort of a classic. He thought he should have got more out of it than he did. And then McLaren took Ronnie's son Michael and his band on tour while they was out there.

Next thing, McLaren's being pulled about it by a reporter at a launch of some kind. He's on a video which Ronnie Biggs has got, looking at the camera, and he's saying, 'Well, Ronnie, if you want your money, you better come home and get it, hadn't you?' and laughed, knowing Ronnie can't come home.

I don't think Ronnie ever thought it was bad to get mixed up with the Sex Pistols, but it was bad to be fucking mixed up with McLaren [their manager]. He was the bad news, wasn't he?

Tony He's had some bad things happen to him, Ronnie Biggs, with people pulling strokes on him.

Fred Raimunda died, his wife.

Tony Has she died?

Fred Yeah, yeah. Couple of years back.

Tony Was it sudden, Fred, or what?

Fred Yeah. He went round and found her dead. He didn't go into what she died of, or anything else. She was an entertainer and a dancer and she went on tour round Europe. So she went her own little way for a while, and when she came back to Brazil, she never went back to live with him, apparently. She had her own flat, so he only used to see her every now and again. The relationship was a bit open.

Tony   Do you know what's happened to Charmaine?

Fred   Well, she came over to Brazil to try to get back together as a family, cos he lost his son in Australia.

Tony   Yeah, that's a shame.

Fred   His boy got killed in a car crash. Well, she was in the car with him, wasn't she?

Tony   Shocking. Shocking.

Fred   She was his first wife, and he had another son by her.

Tony   Didn't she go through hell with him, Fred?

Fred   Well, she stuck by him right through that period.

Tony   She stood by him.

Fred   And, of course, when he had to leave, he couldn't take his family with him, and she had to stay behind in Australia. He had to get out very quickly and she didn't have another crooked passport to go with him.

BUSTER EDWARDS

Fred   Oh, I couldn't believe it when Buster committed suicide.

Tony   He wasn't that sort of person.

Fred   Nah. Never. I would never have dreamed of him doing a thing like that in a million years. I was in shock. He was a troubled soul somewhere along the line. I still miss him, you know.

Tony   We used to go down and see him regular, me and Wendy, down at his flower stall at Waterloo. He always had time for you. I met him in the Scrubs with you. Very down-to-earth, genuine bloke, weren't he?

Fred   Yeah.

Tony And now and again, if I was meeting Charlie [Kray] at Waterloo Station, cos he lived in Croydon, we'd pop in that pub opposite where Buster's stall was. He always used to say, 'I'll be in in a minute.' And he always spoke about you, Fred.

Fred Ummm.

Tony I would say he was your best pal, Fred. Even in prison, him and you were always together.

Fred Oh, he was. One of my best pals.

Tony Always with you.

Fred Yeah, yeah. Do you remember, everyone hooted the hooter when they went by his stall? I mean, he didn't even look round half the time.

Tony He made me laugh. He'd always be bending over, doing something.

Fred He'd be serving somebody, and up would go the arm to wave. It was hard to park there, wasn't it? And I still feel bad about it, cos I only saw him a week or so before he died. If I'd stopped and had a chat with him, I might have found out how he was feeling and spotted something.

Tony Perhaps you might have known, yeah.

Fred I introduced Buster to crime. I used to move around that little area down The Cut, and I used to get into The Spanish Patriot. That's the pub where I was asked to take part in the Great Train Robbery. It was next door to Adie Warner's florist.

He was a character, Adie. And he always wore a trilby hat, cos he was a bit bald. He was gay. And we used to meet up at different parties and have a laugh. He had a good business head, and Buster worked for him, selling the flowers, at one time. They had stalls in the market as well. Then Buster became quite proficient at making wreaths and bouquets and stuff like that, so he had a trade at his hands. We just struck up a friendship.

And they used to buy all the crooked gear at their shop. I used to serve them up with all the hot stuff. I was out with the keys then, clearing out the electrical shops, all their TVs and radiograms and washing machines. It was a booming industry in the Fifties, when every home wanted and needed these things, but couldn't afford them – unless they came to me!

So Buster moved quite a bit of gear when all the locals and market people used to come in to buy flowers. Then he progressed with me – you know, 'Do you want to come out and we'll do a couple?'

I felt fucking terrible when he died, cos I was in the nick, in Latchmere House, and I was getting out a few hours a day. It was on the tail end of my nine-stretch, just finishing off.

The Governor made me sign this bit of paper to say that I wouldn't attend Buster's funeral. Course, I still had to be there. I couldn't go to the house, cos they had cameras there, I would have been spotted, and they'd have slung me straight out of Latchmere cos I'm disobeying a fucking order. So I thought, Well, best bet is to go into the crowd at Buster's pitch at Waterloo and mingle. Cos the cortège was going past the pitch. So I went there, and fucking hell, someone came straight over and put a microphone up to me . . .

Tony   (*Laughter*)

Fred   'Have you anything to say?' One of the newcasters there. And I said, 'No I've got no comment.' I went, 'Oh, fuck it.' And I was so depressed. I couldn't go to the cemetery. I saw my wife and my kids go by in the car – they spotted me and I waved to them – and I'm standing in the crowd while the fucking funeral procession goes by.

Tony   Everyone was there. Everybody.

Fred   I met a couple of other faces standing about, and we went in the Wellington across the road and had a couple of drinks. From there, we went to the pub where Buster's family was going afterwards. It was safe cos they [the authorities] didn't know where it was, and there was minders on the door. It was private.

RONNIE KRAY

Ronnie died on St Patrick's Day, 17 March 1995, from a heart attack, aged sixty-one, having been rushed to hospital from Broadmoor. His horse-drawn hearse led a procession which travelled from the English funeral

*parlour in Bethnal Green to the Kray family grave at Chingford Cemetery
amid massive crowds.*

Tony   He'd never let a screw touch him on the shoulder, Ronnie,
while he was on a visit. Five minutes before the visit ended, he'd
get out, to avoid that tap. And he was always immaculately dressed,
weren't he? He didn't like you going up there without a suit on.

Fred   Didn't like that.

Tony   I liked that in him. He never changed. What he was out
was the same as what he was in. You know what always hurt me –
I used to say to him, 'Ron, you'll get out,' and he'd say, 'Tony,
help me get Reggie out.' He worried about him.

Fred   They were sending money backwards and forwards to each
other, stamps and stuff like that, weren't they?

Tony   All the time, yeah.

Fred   Reggie was buying him a watch at the time he died. I was
in Maidstone when we got the news. Joe Martin and I went over
Reggie's cell and sat with him all day, just the two of us. They
banged us up together in there, and we're drinking a drop of green
hooch, cos it was St Patrick's Day.

   I'd been sent down to Maidstone from Wayland. I'm in Kent
Wing and Reggie's in another wing. As soon as I arrived there, he's
waiting, but they wouldn't let him in the wing. So I go down to
the gate and he's all excited to see me. Like a little kid, he was,
jumping up and down. They let me go out to say hello to him, and
he's brought me over a box of hand-made chocolates, and he's
given me about half a dozen phone cards. This was my greeting.
So, course, I go back and I see him regular. I see him over the gym
and I walk round with him on exercise a few days and things like
that, so we was meeting up all the time.

   Then, all of a sudden, we get the news that Ronnie's died.
Another prisoner told me. He heard it on the radio. And that's how
he found out, Reggie. Nobody told him. He heard it the same as
Charlie heard it, on the news.

Tony   I was got out of bed with the phone calls – did I know
Ronnie Kray had died? I couldn't believe it.

Fred I went to the PO and I said, 'Quick, let me get over there cos I wanna, like, comfort Reggie and help him through it.' They let me up to his cell. Oh, he's crying, and people just kept coming in one at a time, paying their condolences and leaving these jugs and sandwiches and stuff, and we was just getting pissed, me and Joe and Reggie. We stayed there all fucking day. And Reggie's got a magazine out with all these watches in it, and he said, 'That's the one I ordered for Ronnie, to send him,' this particular watch. He said, 'He won't get it now,' and he was right emotional all day. So I said to him, 'Well, be strong, cos while you're alive, Ronnie won't be forgotten.'

So then Reggie wants me and Joe to be pall-bearers at the funeral. They wouldn't let Joe out and they would only let me go under an escort. Don't forget, I've already been in Latchmere, going out to work every day, even having weekends home to spend with Janice, and I've been slung up to Wayland in a closed nick again. Now I'm in Maidstone and they want me to go to the funeral in handcuffs. I said, 'How can I fucking carry a coffin with a screw handcuffed to me? Be sensible.' So I said to Jones, the Governor there, 'The only way you can get around it is to get me a bit of parole. I've only got, like, a few weeks left before my release date. So he said, 'OK, leave it to me,' and he rung up the Parole Board.

They gave me these few weeks out early. So Ronnie, in his death – he got me out of the nick. You know, he done something nice even when he died (*laughing*).

Tony Yeah, yeah. That was the way he was.

Fred Cos I wouldn't have got it without him. They'd always blanked my parole.

Tony He was a very honourable person. That always stood in my mind about Ronnie Kray.

Fred And he kept his word, didn't he?

Tony Kept his word to a T. I remember the first time I seen him after I came out. I went on a visit with Charlie and our pal Wilf Pine. He was delighted, Ronnie – the smile on his face throughout the visit! He couldn't believe seeing one of us come out. It meant a lot to him.

CHARLIE KRAY

Charlie died on 4 April 2000 from complications due to heart trouble, and received a spectacular East End turn-out at his funeral on 19 April, leaving from the English funeral parlour in Bethnal Green. Charlie was buried in the family grave at Chingford Cemetery. He had received twelve years' imprisonment in June 1997 for organizing a £39 million cocaine deal, a charge which he always denied, claiming entrapment by undercover police officers posing as friends.

Fred   Everyone thought well of Charlie, didn't they? How could they dislike him? It's all right these people slagging him off in the press – they didn't know him. He had his crosses to bear by being the older brother of the twins. I mean, cor blimey! What an unfortunate thing for anyone, to have the twins as your fucking younger brothers.

Tony   He always tried to be nice and to defend them.

Fred   As best he could.

Tony   Which must've been very difficult.

Fred   It's not an easy job, is it, to make a case for them? But he tried his hardest all those years.

Tony   I never heard him say a bad word about them. Never.

Fred   Or anyone else, for that matter. I've known Charlie Kray from the Fifties, and in all them years I've never seen him raise his hands. I've never seen him fight or punch anybody.

Tony   He'd never see a visit through with the twins. He'd say, 'Gotta go.' That was Charlie's way.

Fred   He was getting too much stick all the time. He couldn't win with them. Anything he did, if it never worked out, he'd get the blame. And if it did work out, he didn't get the credit for it.

Tony   That's the life of an older brother!

Fred   Yeah.

Tony   I think, in his way, Charlie, he felt responsible for them.

Fred Course he did. I wouldn't have met the twins if it wasn't for Charlie. He introduced me to them when they was young fellas. One of the first times I met them, they were out in the back yard, punching the granny out of each other . . .

Tony (*Laughter*)

Fred . . . You know, having a straightener in the yard, and I remember their old man said to me, 'I can't fucking separate these two out there.' I said, 'I'm not going out to separate them. I can't interfere in family rows.'

Tony Let 'em get on with it.

Fred Because if you do try to stop them, they both turn on you. It's like fighting one person.

Tony And you've gotta respect that.

Fred I just found them very amusing. I knew they was gonna be an 'andful for the rest of their lives. I felt pity for Charlie and his mum and dad straight away, cos you could see what the future held.

When I opened my gym, there was two little twins from south London, and they reminded me of Ronnie and Reggie so much. As soon as they've got in there, they've rushed to the ring. They've put the fucking boxing gloves on, the two boys – never bothered to lace them up, never even took their coats off. They've just tore into each other. I thought, There's the twins all over again.

Tony You couldn't dislike 'em, the Kray twins.

Fred Oh, no. We had a little chuckle at some of the things we used to hear. Charlie used to say, 'You'll never guess what . . .' and I just used to wait for the story to unfold. All I could do was laugh, you know. He used to unload on me, Charlie, tell me what they done. 'What you think happened last night?' and that. And, 'What do you think I should do about it?'

Tony Charlie could never say no to no one. That was his problem.

Fred Yeah. I went to see him at St Mary's Hospital near Parkhurst on the Friday before he died, with Wilf Pine and [Charlie's girlfriend] Diane. I must say they was really looking after him well there. And the two police officers who were sitting there were gentlemen, very decent guys.

Charlie was in a wheelchair, he had the drip on him, and I could see the way he'd deteriorated. I was shocked. And we was left on our own for a period when Diane and Wilf went for a cigarette outside.

He was talking about old times and his mind and his brain was really sharp, very, very clear, and we had a really good visit.

Diane come back in, talking to him, and she was holding his hand and leaning his hand on his upper leg. Then, when she took their hands away, there was that indentation where they'd been resting on his leg. The fluid was gradually creeping up his body to get to the vital organs, you know.

He had two blocked valves in his heart. It was diagnosed when he was up in Durham Prison. What they should've done was to unblock the valves when he was strong enough to withstand the operation.

But, course, he got a chest infection that developed into pneumonia, so then they didn't want to operate on him. All I think they was interested in was getting him back in prison because of the expense of the hospital and having two officers sitting with him. So they got him back to the prison too soon, before he was over the pneumonia.

Why didn't they get him healthy and give him the operation? In my opinion, he's a man of seventy-three, and I suppose they can't be bothered, so they pass the buck. They send him from the extreme north to the extreme south, which was Parkhurst on the Isle of Wight. He did an eight-hour journey when I don't think he's fit to travel, and he was freezing cold in one of them thin, red boiler suits. He travelled all the way down to the island and he collapsed. Then he collapsed again.

Tony He's always smoked and drank and so, I mean, that comes into the equation.

Fred By the time they got him into St Mary's, his condition was so feeble that they didn't want to operate because they didn't think he could survive it.

So, now, because the heart's not pumping the blood round the body properly, it's not reaching the far extremities, and your liver and kidneys are not working because they're not getting the blood supply. Your body's slowly dying.

When I saw him, both his legs were full with fluid, it had almost reached his pelvic area and he was swollen something terrible. He couldn't have had an operation. But I think he should've had one in Durham at the time when they could've done something about it.

Tony Prison's not geared for really old men.

Fred In Holland they put them in secure units, like nursing homes.

Tony See, seventy-three years old – apart from the fact that he shouldn't have been there in the first place, they cocked it up with him.

Fred I think if they'd kept him in the hospital up in Durham and built his strength up, then they could've performed the operation. But the other thing is that you can't get treatment just like that because of the NHS, can you?

Tony That's right.

Fred You have to be on a waiting list, and because you're a prisoner, you're not gonna jump the queue. But I reckon if they'd done it then, Charlie would've been alive today. He would still be fucking among us.

He knew how serious his condition was, but he was putting on a brave front. He was no idiot. We was keeping his spirits up to let him keep fighting, you know, rather than giving up, and he was agreeing with us. He was laughing and joking, the same old laugh and sparkling twinkle in the eyes.

Tony He had that twinkle about him, didn't he?

Fred But the eyes could only light up for a little while and then they went dead, you know. He knew in his heart he was on his way out.

Near the end of the visit, I said, 'I'll leave you, you're getting tired now. Let Diane have the last half hour with you and I'll wait downstairs.' I was choked up when I left him.

I gave him a little hug and a kiss. And as I said goodbye to him I thought to myself, That's the last time I'm gonna see you, Charlie. And I was right. I told him that I would see him the following

Wednesday with my Jamie, as Charlie asked to see him, but he died that weekend.

Tony I didn't see him in his coffin. I wanted to remember him as he was. I went to see him just a few weeks before he died, with Albert Chapman and Keith Smart, and he didn't look too bad to me. He looked underweight in the face and a bit grey, but he was laughing and joking about this, that and the other.

Fred He deteriorated in the last few weeks.

Tony He was, very, very pleased to see us. They're good people, straight people, aren't they, Fred?

Fred Yeah, Albert and Keith. Two of the nicest fellas I've met in years. Travelled all the way down from Birmingham to visit Charlie.

Tony But he didn't want to die in prison. He wanted to be out for that. It's a sad thing that happened to him, but I didn't want to start to feel sorry for Charlie. I didn't think he'd want that, you know?

Fred He didn't want pity. He was a proud man. He wanted fucking fair treatment.

Tony He got the funeral he deserved. He would've known what the reaction of the East End people would be after his mother and father's funeral, and Ronnie's. They did love him. They proved it by the way they turned out that day.

Fred He brought the good weather too. The sun came out for him. You felt he was looking down on you.

Tony But everyone was still very sad, including the general public.

Fred I mean, he could walk down them streets of the East End, and all you'd hear was, 'Hello, Charlie.' He'd stop and talk to them and shake their hands. He had time for everybody, and he did a lot of charity work, which he didn't shout about.

Tony All his old friends were at the funeral.

Fred There were a lot of strangers sitting in the service who probably didn't know him that well, but the real, true, old friends who've helped him out all these years and took care of him . . .

Tony We were there for him.

Fred We were there. I thought that the vicar was absolutely brilliant.

Tony Bang on.

Fred His words hit the spot. He knew exactly how people felt. And my Jamie got up. He had a little speech already mapped out, but they were the same words as what the vicar had been saying. So he had to cut that out, because you couldn't top what he had already said, that vicar. So Jamie just read out the messages.

Tony Charlie's character, his personality, were the things I'll always remember.

Fred He gave himself to people. He cheered them up. They immediately came to life.

Tony People genuinely liked him as a person. He was a very friendly type of man.

Fred With everybody. Old girls loved him.

Tony Oh . . .!

Fred I mean, he was a charmer. He could work a room.

Tony He could.

Fred He was never a drug dealer.

Tony And I believe very strongly that that sentence put him in his grave.

Fred Course it did. That fucking killed him, that twelve years. To make him fucking live like that . . .

Tony I know Charlie sat in that nick and didn't know what he was doing there.

Fred That's a death sentence they gave him. The people who were arrested with the drugs wind up getting five years [Bobby Gould] and nine years [Ronnie Field] – and Charlie gets twelve. It took the undercover police officers nine months to set him up.

Tony Shows how naive he was, to let them get that close.

Fred They never stopped pouring champagne down his throat. He was fucking trapped. It was entrapment. Fucking £39-million coke deal every month! I don't know anyone in the country who could fucking do that. Charlie, for sure, wasn't able to. Even the Colombian cartel couldn't put a deal like that together every month. Fucking hell, it's ridiculous.

Tony He was obsessed with what happened to him, and I'm convinced they got it wrong here, with him. Anyone could tell me they were innocent of a crime and I'd be the biggest disbeliever there ever is. But with Charlie, I always believed him. He didn't do it. There's just no way. And it affected his health when they sent him down. It seemed like he just wanted to throw the towel in, especially since he'd already lost Gary [his son, to lung cancer].

Fred It would've been so easy to target Charlie. He had no idea of how to go about getting cocaine, but when you've got two undercover police officers trying to get you to commit a crime . . .

They was on at him for about nine months, working on him to go out and buy drugs. And to get them off his back, he went and found somebody who was handy with a bit of drugs. He put two people together. All he did was say, 'There's two people who might be able to get it for you after all,' when he was drunk.

Tony Probably forgot all about it.

Fred Yeah. Never even thought about it.

Tony The drugs weren't even on Charlie or anywhere near him.

Fred Charlie was the fucking scapegoat once again. He probably made promises – 'Yeah, I'll do it, I'll get that straightened out for you.'

Tony That was Charlie. Try to do the best for anyone.

Fred But sometimes it was impossible for him to do the best, you know, and he got the stick for it. On many occasions, people might've been a bit angry about it and felt that he probably could've done more. But Charlie always tried. On this occasion, he wound up in the middle like he's been so many times in the past.

And just look what happened to Eddie Richardson. He's still in prison, and I don't think he's off Cat A yet.

Tony No, he's off.

Fred Is he off? If ever a liberty was taken, it was taken with him. Five times he left the country to go on holidays abroad, and each time, they've accused him of bringing drugs back into the country, five fucking drug runs, and it was all supposition. It's like if you went down Oxford Street and went in twenty shops. It doesn't mean you brought goods out of every one. You might not have brought anything at all. And he was only convicted of one importation. One fucking bust and that was it. He got twenty-five fucking years.

Tony Bang!

Fred It's so unfair. What the fucking hell . . . how can you be convicted on similarities and circumstances? That's not evidence, it's guesswork.

Tony It's a conspiracy. It's like the torture trial, Fred. It was a liberty.

Fred Charlie [Richardson] got twenty-five years, and nobody had been killed or really badly injured.

REGGIE KRAY

In the early part of 2000, it had been stated in a couple of tabloid articles, almost off-handedly, that Reggie had been receiving treatment for stomach cancer. These were dismissed as 'false reports' by the Krays' official website, which raged that the articles were 'irresponsible', 'inaccurate', and 'very distressing', while giving reassurances that 'he is not seriously ill'.

Tony And, apparently, Reggie has got . . . the bowels.

Fred What?

Tony The Big C on the bowels. Reggie. Cancer of the bowels.

Fred He *hasn't* . . .

Tony Did you see the papers? They're saying it's stomach. It's not. It's in the bowels. Which is a bad one.

I spoke to someone, oh, whasisname, Wilf Pine, who goes and sees him and he told me that's what it is. Well, he must know. Apparently, his weight has dropped, Fred, to eight stone.

Fred Reggie?

Tony Yeah.

Fred Oh, fucking hell.

Tony He's lost so much weight, he's gaunt. Very thin, not eating.

Fred (*Sighing*) Ahhhhh. Fucking hell.

Tony See, it's one thing after the next, Fred, isn't it?

THE LAST GOODBYE

Fred When I go to funerals, I may not be emotional about the person who's dead because I think, Oh, he's had a good life, he's had a good innings. And, maybe, if it's a woman, she's reached a certain age and she's had a nice time in life, so I think of all the good things and the happy times. But when I look at the front rows of the family, and I just get a glimpse of the grandchildren, little kids crying and breaking their hearts over their grandmother or their grandfather, then it gets to me. Then I start fucking welling up.

And I suffer with this glaucoma. It's hereditary. I've got a mild case of it. My George has had it for twenty odd years, and, unfortunately, his is more serious than mine, more advanced. It's like tunnel vision. It closes in after a while until you can't see nothing. I have to take two drops every morning. And what happens is the pressure builds up behind your eye and it closes the tear ducts. But it doesn't release the tears, and they don't drain off. So as soon as you get a little bit emotional, you know, at funerals and sad occasions, you find your eyes filling up.

But you must grieve and get rid of it. That's what it's all about. When I lost my mother and father, I wasn't there, I was in prison.

Tony And the same with me. That's the worst.

Fred You never grieved and went through the emotions.

Tony You don't.

Fred Something I do and probably you do too – I wake some mornings and I think, I'll pop round and see the old man.

Tony How true.

Fred You think they're still alive, and then you realize and it hits you. You go, 'Fucking hell, they've been dead for years.' We haven't gone through that process of grieving. We haven't been to the funeral. We haven't said goodbye, or seen 'em, or given them a kiss or whatever. That's it, in a nutshell.

Tony I don't know if it happens with you and Jan, but it happens with me and Wendy. I'll be sitting there and she knows there's something not right. And I'll be looking at a photo of the old man or the old lady. I weren't even allowed out for her funeral.

Fred They rarely let you out for those things, do they? But I've been to so many fucking funerals since I've been home. You reach that time in life where all your friends have reached their sixties and seventies, and they're all going over like fucking flies. I go to a funeral and all the memories come back. Then it gets you.

Tony Yeah. Yeah. It does.

Fred I don't think you can ever get used to it. But, nah, I'm not scared of death at all. I'm a great believer in fate. When I was a little kid in the bombing, the old man used to say, 'If it's meant for us, we're gonna get it and we'll all go together,' and we all used to huddle together.

Tony 'We're gonna get it.' Yeah.

Fred 'There's nothing we can do about it.' It doesn't bother me now, the prospect of death.

Tony I'm immune to it, I think.

Fred You're worried about the people you'd leave behind.

Tony We're really lucky men in a way because we've *got* people that we can leave behind. And it always amazes me when people accuse criminals of making a big noise about a funeral. We're bound by loyalty there.

5

Making Headlines:
Dodgy Dave and Kenny Noye

Conversation in Fred's kitchen, 6 May 2000

'DODGY' DAVE COURTNEY: A ONE-OFF

Dave Courtney came to prominence in 1995 when he organized the security for Ronnie Kray's funeral. Still in his early forties, he is younger than the Sixties villains he idolized and he has become a media celebrity by individualizing his gangster persona with an audacious wit. However, in October 1999 he fell foul of 'Mad' Frankie Fraser, who launched a series of attacks on his website. 'Mad' Frankie declared that Dave was under suspicion of being a professional grass after being arrested on the M6 that summer by an elite Scotland Yard team. Dave was charged with trying to pervert the course of justice. According to 'Mad' Frankie, there were allegations that Dave had an unethical friendship with a policeman who had visited his home. While 'Mad' Frankie stopped short of condemning Dave outright, pending the hearing, Dave has vigorously protested his innocence and tells a different story about his dealings with the officer.

Tony I don't know how Dave came into the scene in the first place. I met him on a visit with Reggie.

Fred Well, the first time I laid eyes on him was at Ronnie's funeral. He did a marvellous job that day.

Tony He did, yeah. I mean, he's a character.

Fred This is like an image for the Nineties. It's not the image of when we were active.

Tony That's right. Good way of putting it.

Fred His image is flamboyant, with the dress style and the gold. We were the opposite, really. We just dressed very . . .

Tony   Elegant.

Fred   I'd say unobtrusively. Conservatively.

Tony   Can I put it another way?

Fred   *You* should've become a male model! You missed your vocation! See, I wanted to blend in with the rest of the people, melt into the background. We didn't want to stand out and be noticed. We still went to all the big events – the dinners, the boxing turn-outs and all that sort of thing, the best West End shows and premieres. I mean . . . we were still doing it, but you wasn't saying, 'Look at me!' Nobody knew who the fuck you were.

Tony   You see, what Dave's done, he's bridged a gap here, in a way, from the Fifties, Sixties, to the Nineties. It represents today. But, you see, we can't be seen to laugh about some of the things we've done. You know, when you go on TV, you can't sit there smiling about murder or whatever. Dave hasn't done that [murder], so he can say things and you can take it tongue in cheek, whatever you want to believe.

   He can glamorize it, where we couldn't do that. It's not the road to go down. There's got to be that dignity with us. I know that, and I've stayed within the rules of it. You can't sit there laughing about the sorts of things that's happened. It just wouldn't go down well. Where with Dave, he's a bit of a relief. What he's done in a way . . . he's used us as a backdrop, for his own publicity. But I don't really see nothing wrong with that, Fred, as long as it's in good taste.

Fred   He's done a great job on his image. He's built up a character and a personality that the media want – what a gangster should look like in the public's eye. They're falling over theirselves to photograph him and interview him, but it's not the way I see myself. He's a one-off. I've never met anyone like him. I don't think you will ever meet another Dave Courtney, cos he's unique in the way he handles his interviews and in the way he does these one-man shows, *An Audience With Dave*. He talks to them for two fucking hours, you know. I couldn't sit there on a stage for two hours and talk to people. I'd dry up after half an hour or so. I wouldn't know what to fucking talk about. Dave does enough talking for the lot of us put together.

Tony He feeds on it.

Fred He's a media star now, a professional. He doesn't need crime, and that's the idea of it.

Tony He's gone down the right road there. You know something – every time I see a camera or a TV crew, I think of Dave Courtney.

Fred (*Laughing*) You think Dave is gonna come out the fridge when you open it!

Tony I was at the vet's the other day, taking the dog down there for his tablets and to have him checked over, and they're doing that Rolf Harris programme down at New Cross with a camera crew. And Wendy said to me, 'Is Dave about?' You know, you expect to see him pop up every time.

Fred He's changed roads and he's done it at the right time. And if he keeps it up, I can see him getting his own weekly TV show, interviewing people. I mean, he can do it, and I wish him luck.

Tony He's a cheeky chappie.

Fred He comes over very well with the ladies. They love his old twinkling, blue eyes – well, I think they're blue. I've not looked into them lately.

Tony They love the flamboyance of it.

Fred He's very funny on a good night.

Tony And he don't talk bad about no one. I've never heard him talk bad about no one, Fred. Never.

Fred It's a shame that him and Frank [Fraser] have fell out, because he fucking idolized Frank.

Tony He did. He was very hurt.

Fred He was. It seems like something that got out of hand, and I know Dave's sick about it. Anything that's hurtful is gonna upset you, isn't it? But don't let anybody underestimate him. He's a capable man.

Tony He's capable, yeah, for sure.

Fred He can take care of himself and he never refuses a favour, but the jury's out on Dave, and we are all hoping for his sake that he comes through this trial with no doubts or questions unanswered. He's a very likeable fella and no one of us wants to see him come to any harm, either physical or reputation wise. Only time will tell. I don't know what's happening with the trial, but I really do hope that it turns out a good result for everybody concerned, including the copper. I don't wish imprisonment on any man, except rapists and child molesters. They're not men, sick or not. Animals are better. I'd shoot the bastards.

In December 2000, Dave Courtney was cleared of any wrong-doing, but he was described in court as a registered police informant. Tony and Fred decided to make no further commet.

KENNETH NOYE: THE M25 MURDER

Kenneth Noye was sentenced to life imprisonment on 14 April 2000 for stabbing to death twenty-one-year-old Stephen Cameron in the so-called 'Road Rage Murder'. Cameron had been the passenger in a van driven by his fiancée, Danielle Cable, on 19 May 1996, when the altercation occurred at the junction of the M25 and M20 near Swanley, Kent. Noye hid out in Spain afterwards. But, in August 1998, police flew Danielle there, and she identified him, in a restaurant with his family.

Kenneth Noye first came to notoriety in November 1985 when he appeared with friend Brian Reader at the Old Bailey, accused of murdering DC John Fordham in the grounds of Noye's home in West Kingsdown, Kent on 26 January that year. Fordham and his partner, dressed in camouflage gear and balaclavas, had been hiding there, staking out the house, as part of a police investigation into the whereabouts of the Brink's-Mat gold bullion. The jury accepted Noye had stabbed Fordham in self-defence and both defendants were acquitted.

In 1986 Noye was sentenced to fourteen years' imprisonment for plotting to handle the gold and evading VAT.

Tony Stephen Cameron, the kid from Swanley, was well known in the area. The fact of the matter is, it was going on for a while, this tit for tat, between Kenneth Noye and Stephen Cameron. You know what it's about, Fred, don't you?

Fred I don't. I don't know anything.

Tony I can't say too much about this, but there's two sides to every story.

Fred I assumed there must be more to it than what came out in court. I don't know why. I've just felt that.

Tony I met Kenneth once in Swanley. I was talking to him for about ten minutes, just saying hello. And I used to bump into him in Dartford.

Fred That's his manor, yeah?

Tony That's his manor. He seemed a nice bloke when he spoke to me. I mean, he never done me no harm.

Fred He's OK as far as I'm concerned. I wasn't that friendly with him, I never had any professional dealings with him at all, but I knew him as what he was and what he done. He was always a decent person, and he was a well-respected man.

It was unfortunate, what happened with the killing of the copper. What would you do if you found a man in your garden, masked up with just a couple of eyes showing? And your wife and kids are indoors – it could've been mass murderers or rapists, or someone in there to rob you. I mean, what are you gonna do? You've got a knife in your hand, there's a struggle and you stab the guy.

How can he get a fair trial in the Stephen Cameron case? Cos the jury are gonna have that in mind, about stabbing the copper.

Tony You *know* he didn't get a fair trial.

Fred Prejudged. And I don't know how they could have identified him the way they did, taking Stephen Cameron's girlfriend to Spain and getting her to point Kenneth Noye out in a restaurant. That was illegal.

Tony I've never known anything like that.

Fred That's not an identification parade. I mean, what happened? They built a case up afterwards, didn't they? And if you look at the facts of the case, you can understand what happened.

Tony Course you can.

Fred Happens all the time, road rage, doesn't it? Now, take Kenny Noye. He's only little, isn't he? Five six?

Tony Five seven.

Fred And this guy's a big, strong twenty-one-year-old, who's six foot two and a karate expert or whatever he was. And Kenneth's definitely getting battered and beaten up. It's not unusual to be beaten to death. There's plenty of people doing lives for smashing people on the chin and killing them. So, I mean, you're entitled to protect yourself.

Tony He even went back to the motor for the tool.

Fred They've had a straight fight to start with, but the geezer's beating the shit out of him. Kenneth doesn't intend to kill him. It's to stop him. Loads of people get stabbed and they don't die from the stab wound.

Tony There was no intent there.

Fred It was self-defence. You're not gonna let a young guy beat the shit out of you. It's self-preservation. I'd probably done the same thing.

Tony I'd have done the same, yeah.

Fred I would've tried not to hit a vital target. I'd have done him in the legs or something. But, like we were saying before, you can never tell, if you stab somebody, what it's gonna lead to. They can bleed to death.

But he's got a life sentence. At least he hasn't got a recommendation. And please God he gets a better result on the appeal.

Tony Seven or eight?

Fred He won't die in prison, cos this is not a premeditated murder. They won't want to be doing him any bloody favours. The case with the copper is obviously still a big influence on the police and the authorities. They always wanted to put him away for life.

I mean, look at the case when he got convicted of handling after he got acquitted of killing the copper. He got the maximum sentence, which was a fourteen. They couldn't give him a day more than fourteen years. There was only two prisoners in the whole prison system who were doing over seven years for handling money. And that was me and Kenneth Noye.

Then after he got his life sentence for Stephen Cameron, the papers started digging stuff up, as usual. There was one story that he was offering five million to anyone who would spring him from prison.

Tony   Nah. That's all paper talk.

Fred   It's bollocks. They did that same story with me.

Tony   I don't believe that other story, that he was offering money in the underworld to give evidence for him.

Fred   I wasn't offered anything.

Tony   Neither was I.

Fred   I feel sorry for everybody concerned. I feel sorry for the family who lost their son.

Tony   Oh, yes.

Fred   I really feel sorry for them. And I feel sorry for Kenneth Noye. I feel sorry for his wife. He has a lovely wife. She's been through a lot.

Tony   There's been a lot of pain, on both sides.

6

Living with the Media

Conversation in Fred's kitchen, 16 November 1999

GLAMORIZING CRIME: THE CULPRITS

Fred The big crimes of the Sixties have been glamorized because it's part of our folk history, and it's a thing that won't be repeated because of the way that the modern technology is defeating crime. Even in our active days, we had lots of failures. If we'd secured every time we pulled out on the pavement, we'd have been multi-millionaires.

Tony Who's glamorized it, at the end of the day?

Fred The press are the ones who glamorize it, really.

Tony It can't be you, cos you've been locked up. I've been locked up.

Fred There's no glamour in being locked up. Yet, we *have* become icons. That's how we were described in the exhibition [Great Train Robber Bruce Reynolds's son Nicky opened an exhibition, *Cons To Icons*, at London's Tardis Studios on 1 November 1999, showing photographs and sculptures of notorious criminals' heads, including Fred's].

In our chosen profession, the way the trials were handled at the time brought us all notoriety. I mean, the Kray trial is *your* claim to fame, innit?

Tony Yeah, yeah.

Fred Course, with the bird, you had to suffer for that.

Tony They don't see that side of it. You know, they've got a misconception of all this, the public. We never *made* the glamour. We was away when it all started, and we came out to it. I think the [David] Bailey photos [of the Krays] and all that type of stuff added a lot to it. We became high-profile criminals and we couldn't help that.

Fred We didn't wanna be, either. We just wanted a nice, quiet life, didn't we?

Tony But a lot of people respect the legend. What they respect it *for* I don't know. The glamorization of it is not really our fault. Others have done that. It's rumour gone down the road. The books that have been wrote about it, the articles, the TV programmes, that film . . . there's a hell of a lot of stuff, and it's still going on.

Fred It won't stop.

Tony By the way, what was it like getting your head sculpted, Fred?

Fred Oh, it was weird, cos when I was having it done, I had a Japanese crew filming it for a programme that went out to Tokyo. Yeah, it was quite a laugh.

Tony I bet it was! Anyway, in my opinion, the legend is out of control. People like Dave Courtney come on the scene, and they're very good for it in as much as they advertise us, but it can be a problem. Once you put the suit on, people see what they wanna see.

And I use it. I admit it. I have to use it, cos who would employ me? Who would give me a job? I've got no choice. What future did any of us have when we came out of the nick?

Fred How can you go and get a straight job?

Tony You can't. It's impossible.

Fred I'm too fucking old to get a job! But you can't avoid the fact that you chose your way of life. You're exposed to the media, and it's a way of getting a living now. It's a livelihood.

Tony Yeah.

Fred So notoriety is earning you money. It would be nice if you could earn money and still have your privacy, but you've gotta lose that. They go hand in glove, don't they? It's like if you're in show business. You're gonna be recognized wherever you go, in the supermarket or whatever. I get strange looks from people, but they don't usually come up to me. They're thinking, Now, where do I know him from?, but they can't really put a finger to it, or if they do, they won't come up, you know.

Tony They're wary of you.

Fred They are a bit, yeah.

Tony It's turned out that they see me more as the public relations man. I think I take a *bit* of blame for glamorizing it, because of my relationship with Wendy and the massive exposure we got with my book [*Inside The Firm*, published by Smith Gryphon in 1991 and in paperback by Pan]. And I think we carried up that side of it to sell it.

We've lived our lives in a criminal way, but now you've got to get on with it, whatever way you do it. Life does go on, and we're retired from crime now. Where can I go?

You live your life the best way you can. You know, you tell people what they want to hear and I think they're satisfied with that. Basically, that's what it's about. But perhaps the glamorization of it is what has kept Reggie in prison. You don't know. We'll never know that. Then there are the people who follow it. I mean, a man now called Les something, he comes out of Lewisham, and he got hold of my phone number. He rings me up and he tries to tell me every detail about my life, your life, and everyone else's life. Now, I'm supposed to sit and listen to this rubbish. We've just got this obsessive element in the following, and I don't want nothing to do with it. I've seen more than thirty people with tattoos of the twins' faces on 'em, and I've gotta answer for that. People say to me, 'Well, don't you think that's glorifying crime?' I don't want it.

Take the T-shirts, Fred. There was a really famous, best-selling T-shirt. Do you remember that?

Fred I saw one in Harrods with the Tower of London, all the Beefeaters and stuff, and there was a picture of the twins on the front of it, wasn't there?

Tony I think over the years . . . I mean, we're all a lot older now but when I look at the boys, to me they haven't changed a lot – Roy [Shaw] and Frank [Fraser] and Joe [Pyle]. And it's still a big attraction to people to see them all together in this day, cos they're known names from that period. They've all wrote their books and that.

There's not many people who don't like to see it. If there's a boxing do, everyone wants to come, for the people they might see. And they're all looking around – 'Fred's there, Charlie Richardson's there, Dave Courtney,' or whoever.

You know, I like to mix with my own people. Since I come out of prison, I'm different to what I went in, obviously, but I know I feel comfortable with someone like you around, or any of the boys from my past. I don't feel that with many people.

SOAPS AND SINGERS

Fred Loads of people from the world of entertainment want to meet us and talk to us and, a lot of the time, it's a load of crap. Don't get carried away with it, Tony. Let me tell you, it's always been this way.

Like, there's a very thin line between the police and the criminals as regards what they do for a living – they still think in common, they got drunk together in the past. And there's a very thin line between show business and criminals because we all hit the headlines now and again. Every time they write something about you, whether it's good or bad, someone else will come along and put money in your pocket, so let them write what they fucking like.

Look at Dave Courtney. No one could have as much bad publicity as him, but he is still coining it. It's the power of the media. It can make you into anything they want.

Tony That's all very well if it's the right image.

Fred Well, you're in the public eye because of your notoriety. With showbiz, it's because they do court publicity, and there's no such thing as bad press where they're concerned, as long as they spell your name right. That was the old saying in Hollywood. All them Hollywood stars got nicked for all sorts of fucking things, but it never hurt their careers at all, did it? Robert Mitchum got nicked for drugs and went to prison, but it didn't stop his career, and George Raft was a *real* gangster. We know so many showbiz people now because we do a lot of charity work, we hold fund-raising events, we get invited to functions and, as authors of books, we get on telly every now and again. You're socializing with people that you've got something in common with now, because you've been on a few shows and been invited to film premieres.

Tony Can I say something now? To know *you* at this particular time is a very 'in' thing.

Fred Oh, I don't know about that, Tony. They probably think I've still got a bit of that seven million! (*Referring to Security Express*) I wish!

Tony You think I'm building you up, but I'm not. I'm saying it as I see it and hear it.

Fred Barbara Windsor, she's a stalwart, a sweetheart.

Tony She's a good girl.

Fred Barbara's been a good girl all her life. My Jamie went to pantomime when he was a little boy and sat in the audience. He went backstage to Barbara and she looked after him. She told him what to do when he went to the Italia Conti [acting] school. She taught him about Puck in Shakespeare from *A Midsummer Night's Dream* and said, 'Do a little speech from that character,' which he learned, and that was how he got started in show business. She's been a good friend for years. She mounted the box twice at the Old Bailey to help people out of trouble. You can't ask no more than that.

Well, she was the first. We knew loads of people in the Sixties, but present-day people – I mean, the *EastEnders* cast, we know more or less all the people on that show. A lot of good ones have left, like Patsy Palmer, Gillian Taylforth, Martine McCutcheon and Marc [Gianni] Bannerman. He's a lovely kid. Gary Oldman's a good friend of Jamie's and mine. There's so many actors, you can't name them all. And then we meet loads of pop stars, like Roger Daltrey, and entertainers.

Tony Yeah, all the time.

Fred You know Shane Richie, don't you?

Tony Good man, yeah. And Michael Flaherty.

Fred Did he teach you a few steps?

Tony   (*Laughter*)

Fred   And Dale Winton is a nice guy.

Tony   Very nice man. I like Dale. You know, I met Cliff Richard, and he invited me to see his show, *Heathcliff*.

Fred   Well, this is the funny thing with Cliff Richard, cos you took him my book as a present, and he signed it and sent it back to me!

Tony   I met the Fun Lovin' Criminals recently, and, oh, Mark Morrison, and Brian Harvey.

Fred   Have you heard the single that Suggs [of Madness] done with Ian Dury just before he died? It's called 'Drip Fed Fred'.

Tony   It must be about you.

Fred   I don't know about that.

Tony   They're using your name.

Fred   I know Suggsy. He came to my book launch [for *Respect*, published by Random House in 1996] at the Café Royal.

Tony   Fred, it's gotta be a compliment.

Fred   It's a compliment if it was referring to me, but it's just a fun record.

Tony   I know Chris Evans very well. The first time I met him was at Nicky Campbell's engagement party to Tina at a club in Frith Street. Funny thing, I used to look after it when it was a clip joint! And Tina introduced me to Chris Evans. I found him a very pleasant guy, I must say. I found him down to earth. He was very interested in all of us. Cos, as you know, he's behind the series *Lock, Stock & Two Smoking Barrels*. His company, Ginger Productions, is doing it. He'd read books about us. I found him a very, very interesting man. He was polite to me, and he seemed to know what he was on about.

Like Rod Stewart. About six months ago, he wanted to come over to drink in the East End. He's very into the Krays.

Fred   Is he?

Tony   Didn't you know that?

Fred   No.

Tony   I was approached through a DJ to take Rod Stewart drinking round the East End, but at the time, Frankie Fraser was doing his tour, he's still doing it now, and I didn't want to tread on his toes. But Rod was very disappointed.

Fred   You should have put him on Frank's tour.

Tony   I met Mickey Rourke at Browns in the West End. Frankie Fraser took him out one night, him and Marilyn. And two days later, I met him at Browns again. Then we done that thing with Brad Pitt [filming for Guy Ritchie's movie *Snatch* in London].

Fred   Well, we went over to do it and we was used as fucking unpaid extras.

Tony   We *was* used there. There was a fuck-up. The man who arranged it all got it wrong.

Fred   We was there when he [Brad Pitt] was shooting the fight scene, but we never got introduced to him. And I fucked off round the pub. I said, 'We're sitting here as unpaid extras. Fuck this. I'm going for a drink over the road.' And we met Jack Halloran, who was Jaws in the Bond film.

Tony   He was there, that's right.

Fred   And he was a lovely man – a big, powerful man and a great character. We got on very well together.

Tony   I must tell you a story. I had my play [adapted from *Inside The Firm*] running at the Edinburgh Festival, and me and Charlie Kray flies up to do promotion. Steve Ovett, the runner, is on the plane. So when we arrive in Edinburgh and we get off the plane, they've got all the press there. Charlie said to me, 'Someone famous must be getting off the plane, here.' And we thought the reception committee was for Steve Ovett, but it wasn't. It was for me and Charlie.

Fred   (*Laughter*)

Tony   Steve Ovett was gutted. He thought the press was there for him. Anyway, when we get to the theatre, who's waiting for us is Michael Ball, a pal of Charlie's, and Eartha Kitt, and all of a sudden, this woman came over and she went to Charlie Kray, 'I know you from somewhere.' Now Charlie was one for the ladies . . .

Janice   (*Happening into the room*) Now, get it right – the ladies was one for Charlie!

Tony   *You* know, Jan. You know.

Fred   The ladies chatted him up.

Tony   He was a character, Fred. He was so innocent. And the first thing he did, he always pulled out the shirt cuffs to show the bit of gold! Anyway, this bird is all over Charlie, ignoring Michael Ball standing there, and Eartha Kitt. Michael Ball tried to give her the nudge – 'I'm Michael Ball.' She went, 'I don't know you, who are you? But that's Charlie Kray.' That was the difference.

Janice   What's Eartha Kitt like?

Tony   (*Laughing*) Well, what she done to Charlie, Jan . . . she had hold of Charlie's neck and she had her leg round his waist. She's getting on now, but she is amazing. And she fancied Charlie.

Janice   Women were attracted by him. There was a magnetism there.

Fred   He was charming.

Janice   We could never leave Fred and Charlie on their own. Us girls, we could never go to the toilets because by the time we came out, you had to actually fight your way back to your men. And Charlie would go, or Fred would go, (*Stammering*) 'We, we, we never had nothing to do with it.'

Tony   (*Uproarious laughter*)

Janice   And we'd be, (*Mock incredulity*) 'Reeeeally?'

Fred   I'll tell you who was a real gentleman, and that was George Best. I met him when I was in Spain. He came over there and played with the International Eleven in the football stadium, all for charity. He couldn't move too well then, cos he was out of condition. He would just stand on the side and have a drink of water – well, it looked like water anyway – while the game's going on, and he'd talk to the crowd. Then they'd give him the ball and he'd do a bit of magic – run past three or four players and bang, score a goal, you know. And then he'd walk back and get another drink. Every time he got the ball, he *did* something with it. If you give him a ball, he's up for it, he's class. He'd run and run with it, and go through a few players. That was his job. You get forwards today and they're looking round to pass it to someone rather than turn on it and do something with it.

We met at different barbecues, and he was a lovely man. I'm sorry that he's been ill lately, but perhaps if he could give his body a rest, give his old liver and kidneys a bit of a chance, he can recover, can't he? He can get his health back, cos he's still a young man. Please God he can keep off the booze.

Tony   Do you remember me telling you about that time with Gazza's mum? We go to this benefit. So there's Gazza ['bad boy' footballer Paul Gascoigne], the mother, the aunt, the sister, a cousin and 'Five Bellies' [Gazza's best friend, Jimmy Gardner].

Fred   Up in Newcastle, are we?

Tony   Oh, yeah.

Fred   What year you talking about?

Tony   Nineteen ninety-three.

Fred   I was still in the nick.

Tony   I kept looking at Gazza's mother and she's got exactly the same chin as him. So Charlie [Kray] arrives to a big fanfare, Fred. They loved him. And after a couple of Scotches, Charlie starts to loosen up.

Fred   We all loosen up with a few drinks.

Tony   So the mother's looking at Charlie and she says to me, 'He's a nice man, isn't he?' He looked immaculate. 'Is he married?' 'Not really.' 'Well, he's available then.' Could you imagine Gazza calling Charlie Kray 'Dad'? Oh yeah, Charlie. He played it up to the hilt. That was Charlie. I loved him for that.

Fred   He could chat a bird up.

Tony   *Cor!* Could he charm the ladies, Fred. They could be one or ninety-one, it didn't matter. He just loved the ladies.

THE PROBLEMS

Tony Me and Wendy sat there and tried to count last night how many books have been wrote on all of us. We got to sixty-nine. Who are these people that have come into our lives, giving an opinion on you or me? They've no right. Like some of these television people. What right have they got to set us up, or to edit things that we've said to suit themselves? The last straw was the way they treated you on that documentary [Carlton's two-parter *The Krays*, screened across ITV on 10 and 12 January 2000], Fred. I didn't fucking like it.

When I started doing TV appearances, I didn't know what they were getting at. I thought I was gonna go on there and talk about my life as I saw it. But a lot of the time it wasn't like that. They edit it so that it turns into something untrue. They done it with you, Fred. There's a prime example. But they done it too well, because it didn't wash. It was so anti-you, it was *too* anti-you.

Fred Some of the narration by Dennis Waterman was exactly the opposite of what I'd told them.

Tony Fred, did you know that Waterman was going to do the narrating?

Fred I never knew that. It didn't matter. But I was supposed to get programme approval, and they never gave me that. They just put the programme out without me seeing it beforehand. I did about four hours' work one afternoon – and it turned into a two-hour TV programme with seven million viewers.

I didn't know what they were gonna do with that end scene, going up and down the escalator in the underground.

They put their footage together to make it look as though Albert Donoghue was going up the escalator at the same time as I was going down. It looked like I was glaring at him. It's surprising the amount of people who believed that happened. Now, they're saying, 'How did Fred stand for that?' cos they thought that we both had to be there, working together, to get the scene. But instead of that, all I was looking at was a cameraman and his two assistants. And I went up and down there four fucking times.

I said, 'How many times have I gotta do this? What are you looking for?'

Tony You don't know what it's for, Fred.

Fred He said, 'Just look at the camera, angry.' I said, 'I am fucking angry now, going up and down there four times. I thought you got it in the first take. What do you want to do it again for?' I said, 'This is the last time I'm gonna do this, so you'd better get it right.' They wanted me to be angry, but they didn't tell me that they was gonna have Donoghue going up the other side when they edited it together.

Tony Cos you wouldn't have done it.

Fred I wouldn't have agreed. That's why they wouldn't allow me to see the finished article. Carlton Television were saying, 'Don't tell Fred what we're doing.'

Tony I bet they were. I can't get over that. Let's get down to some nitty-gritty here. What fucking right do people have to twist it around to make it look like something else? On the second night of the programme, they were trying to say that you was over-friendly [i.e. in cahoots] with a copper. That was a bad lie.

Fred Oh, I mean, Frank Williams was a straight copper and he did his duty. They called him as a prosecution witness *against* me in the Mitchell trial.

Tony And they twist it and turn it and knife you.

Fred I was friendly with him all right. I liked the man. He did his job and he didn't take no money off anyone. He never tipped me off about nothing. But he wouldn't fit you up and verbal you up. We knew each other in Kennington back in 1958 when I had the club, the Walk Inn in Lambeth Walk, with my brother George and Buster Edwards. He used to come over. And he took our fucking licence away for drinking after hours. But the relationship I struck up with him lasted for about fifteen years.

What I liked about him . . . I got talking to him one day and he said to me about all my brothers being in the war and seeing a lot of action. He was at the battle of Anzio in Italy, and there's a famous photograph of him climbing up the hillside taking the surrender, carrying the British flag, with all the troops behind him. That's when they finally took the Italian monastery, which was occupied by the German army. It held up the British advance for fucking months because it had thick walls. They was bombarding it and they couldn't get the Germans out. So we had that little bit in common because I was very interested in the war years.

Tony I've learned my lesson about TV programmes. I'm sorry, I'm not having it no more. It takes a long time for it to sink into me. What they tried to do to you was wrong, bad. The attitude was, 'Reggie wasn't such a bad fella, he was tolerable, but in the background was lurking this fucking monster who is Freddie Foreman.'

Fred Eh?

Tony This is how it came over, Fred.

Fred Did it? I didn't believe any of it, myself. The TV people set *you* up on a couple of programmes, didn't they?

Tony They set me up on two instances, with Micky Duff and [former petty crook] Lenny Hamilton. They never told me they would be there. Do you think I would've gone on with them? I've ripped into [Dave] Courtney, because when I done the programme with him on it, Micky Duff [world-famous boxing promoter and matchmaker], I see them all shaking hands with him, and the only one who backed me was Marilyn Wisbey. She walked over and fucking spat on him. And when I saw him there I said, 'What the fuck? What's this? What's he doing here?' Cos he made comments about us to the newspapers after the trial. He said we were going to do him. He told a pack of lies.

Fred He said we was all scum.

Tony Scum! I was nearly going to do something stupid, like chinning him on TV. I'm on a life licence, Fred, so it's just as well I didn't. People said to me the next day, 'Why didn't you up Micky Duff?'

Fred He's wrote his book, you know.

Tony He mentions me and Chris in it. He's had a right pop at me and the twins.

Fred He's had a pop at all of us. He was the one who used to run about with [Fifties gang leader] Jack Spot when he was a kid, and fucking run errands for him. So they had him there for you, and they had someone for Marilyn. They set her right up there with a woman who had had a little kid murdered by two youngsters at a school. Now, what's that got to do with Marilyn or the under-world?

Tony What's it got to do with us? These fucking toerags, they set people up and they stab you in the back.

Now, Lenny Hamilton, he was on the same programme. I've never met this man before in my life. He's sitting there telling me about Ronnie Kray blinding him in one eye in the Grave Maurice pub or a club or some spieler or something. I said to him on TV, 'I don't know nothing about this. I wasn't there. What's it got to do with me? Don't ask *me* about it.' Apparently Ronnie stuck a red-hot poker in his eye, which I find hard to believe. In a pub? He gets a poker and sticks it in his eye? No, I'm not having that.

Fred Did he have a glass eye? I didn't see nothing wrong with him.

Tony They were asking me questions about other people, and that's when it starts to go wrong. I can't answer for you, or Joey Pyle, or anybody else. It's not for me to do that. I say, 'Ask *them*.' That's my way out of it. And then I was set up with Lenny Hamilton again on a programme in Birmingham. Funny enough, it was the same researcher . . .

They're jumping on bandwagons, all these TV people. They want you on their programmes. They're the ones that are ringing *us*. We're not phoning them. Then if you ask to be paid your expenses, they don't fucking like it, so you're no good. But if you do it for nothing, oh, you're a lovely man. And you've got no recourse on what they broadcast. That's what annoys me. It upsets me. No matter what they put out you can't say anything back.

So, I've learned two lessons recently. I've had two warnings. Charlie was one, getting twelve years for nothing, just cos he couldn't handle the fans. He was nice to everybody, he took everybody at their word, and look where it got him. And the other lesson is what they done to you, Fred. So we must all learn from it. We've gotta be careful about these programmes.

Fred Cos tapes can be doctored to make your meaning completely different. The lesson is that you've got to elaborate so they can't fuck about with what you say.

Tony I don't complain about it if they stick to the facts. I've never, ever had regrets about my life because what's done is done. Do you have any regrets, Fred?

Fred I fucking do.

Tony You have 'em, Fred. You've got 'em.

Fred I wish I'd never picked Jack [McVitie] up that night and done what I did. If I hadn't, the police would've found him and they all would've been arrested within a week instead of two years later.

Tony It would have nothing to do with you.

Fred And it would have turned out to the twins' advantage, in a way. Because it would've turned out that it was a row at a party that got out of hand, and it would've been a charge of manslaughter rather than premeditated murder. The injuries on Jack, the witnesses there that night, would have proved manslaughter without a doubt.

Tony I've got to accept that.

Fred In a sense, I gave them two years' breathing space.

Tony You did.

Fred It's only people's own fucking talking, their own mouths, that got them nicked.

Tony It fucking wasn't me.

Fred I cleared it up, so no one need've got nicked. But I did what I thought was the right thing at the time. At the end of the day, you're judged by your fellow man, aren't you? It's like what's in the Bible – as you sow, so you reap, in your life. I like to think that the people I haven't seen for forty years, they could never say anything bad about me. I could go anywhere in England, hold my head up, not be afraid of walking anywhere and know that I'll be treated with respect. They can't point a finger at me and say, 'You should be ashamed of what you did.' I like to be able to treat people equally, as I wanna be treated myself. I just want to be treated with respect.

CLOSE ENCOUNTERS

Tony I met a lunatic, Fred, and I went out with her. This was about six months after I came out of the nick. She was a journalist, and she'd written a book. She was a clever girl, well educated. She lived at the Borough. You do meet them at the Borough!

Her father owned a property in a village in the country. She had long black hair and she spoke very well, right la-di-da.

She'd heard about me and she approached me about a book, Fred. I didn't know how to write a book, where to start, who to approach. She must have saw a potential, so we sit down and do a synopsis. And then I decide to take her to see Ronnie Kray without telling her who he is.

Fred Oh, yeah! That must've been fun!

Tony She didn't know who she was going to visit. She never had an inkling. I only told her that we were going to see a patient in hospital. So we arrive at Broadmoor.

Fred A shock to the system.

Tony Not much!

Fred (*Laughing*) It's all coming out now. Was that the little bit of foreplay, taking her there?

Tony Ronnie says to her, very politely, 'What do you do for a living?' She went, 'Actually, I'm a journalist.' He went, 'Well, you could do me a favour. If you wanna do a story in the *Sun*, I'll give you the number to ring. And if I tell you what to say, they'll want to do a story on it, and we'll have a nice little drink.' You know how Ronnie thought, don't you?

So she wrote a few notes down but Ronnie was just having a laugh with her. I broke up. I couldn't keep a straight face. He kept telling her all these naughty stories and she'd say, 'I really can't write that, Mr Kray.'

Fred (*Laughing*) That's terrible, that is.

Tony He started on Boothby – 'I'll tell you about Lord Boothby, shall I?' I'll tell you what, Fred, he had a sense of humour second to none, Ronnie Kray did.

Fred Did she want to go back and see him again?

Tony Oh, it was funny. He was telling her a story about the snakes. He had two snakes, Fred.

Fred Yeah, I know – Read and Gerrard [named after the police officers Nipper Read and Fred Gerrard, who were investigating the twins at the time]. They used to roam around the flat and they used to get lost. You'd be sitting on the settee and they'd come up between your legs.

Tony Ronnie was telling the journalist girl that he wanted to use Checker Berry's little pug dog as bait for one of the snakes because the dog was ugly. So she starts saying, 'Well, it's a nice dog, Mr Kray.' 'No it weren't,' said Ronnie. 'It was ugly.' The whole visit went on like that. He was winding her up.

So, we had a little affair going, me and this woman, which suited me at the time. Because she lived near me, I used to go up and stay there the night, and she cooked dinners for me.

Well, this beautiful house they had in the country was like a farm, and I get invited up to stay as a potential suitor for this girl.

Fred (*Amused*) Potential suitor! Fucking hell! Didn't they know the truth about you, then?

Tony (*Hearty laughter*) Well, they soon did, Fred! I'll tell you what happened. I arrive at this village, this lovely property, and all the byres and the outhouses were turned into, like, suites. There was the father, who was a well-to-do man, and the mother. She was the director of a packaging company. I get the master bedroom – potential suitor for the daughter, right, so I'm being looked after. But the first sign that things were going wrong was when . . .

Fred (*Laughing*) You started slopping out in the morning!

Tony (*Also laughing*) You got it! You got it! But, no, I woke up the next day and the local bobby had made a phone call to her father, telling him to come down the little police station to have a word with him.

Now, during the night, I got up to go to the toilet and I fell down this little flight of three stairs. Well, the language was shocking, Fred. Just come out of the nick and all that – you get bad habits.

Fred Yeah.

Tony Not only that, but when I went to bed, I fell asleep with a joint in my hand and I burnt the bed.

Anyway, her father goes down to the village to see the local bobby. When he comes back, my belongings are moved out to a caravan and into a field at the back. Out of the house, Fred.

Both (*Uproarious laughter*)

Tony I heard the father go, 'My God, she's got a thug, a gangster and a drug addict in the house. We want him out.'

Fred Well, you made your usual good impression! And that was the end of your relationship, was it?

Tony No! But the next day, Charlie Kray's gonna turn up, isn't he?

Fred Oh, Charlie! I forgot you'd invited him.

Tony (*Hearty laughter*) We've invited Charlie up for Sunday lunch! So Charlie turns up with a grey suit on, all the jewellery and, you know, that smile, and I'm out in the caravan now, after one night. Charlie was invited in to lunch, and all the rest of 'em all sitting down . . . The father was like that, Fred (*hands shaking*). Then the police turn up at the house.

Fred Wanting to know what you was both doing there?

Tony Well, Charlie Kray stands out like a sore thumb. I mean, they've never seen anything bigger than the local burglar, if that, and Charlie, then, was very recognizable. So he got aimed out, too.

Fred Daddy didn't want him there.

Tony They were lovely people, but to have me turn up on the scene, and Charlie Kray for Sunday lunch, weren't exactly a bright idea of mine. They obviously thought I wasn't good enough for their daughter.

And when we arrive back in London, course there's been a fall-out, now. I wanted to get rid of her by then, because I knew there was something wrong with her. She was a hypochondriac. She was always sick. Well, I thought nothing of it at first. But then every time I said something about an illness, she had the same illness. If I had a headache, five minutes after that, she had a headache. If I had stomach problems, she had stomach problems.

I didn't know I had an ulcer. I've never had pain like that in my life. They say it puts a big man down, Fred. Believe it. Anyway, one day I've got these terrible cramps. I've been driving along with this journalist woman, going round to different publishers with her. And the pain, Fred – I had to get out the car and sit on the pavement, it was that bad. Later, when I went to the toilet, it was black, like tar, from the blood coming through me.

Fred Well, it burst, didn't it?

Tony There was two – a duodenal and a peptic. I had one of each.

Fred Oh, a full house there! You're not satisfied with one, you greedy bastard!

Tony Ohhh, no mucking about. But I'd been taking that kaolin and morphine in the brown bottle. You buy it in the chemist – ugh, terrible stuff. I thought it was just bad indigestion. That's what people kept telling me. Anyway, she's listening to this, so she's complaining about her stomach too.

I run her up to Guy's Hospital with Lenny, the mechanic who worked for me. I had a little garage. We drop her in, come back, sit and have a drink . . . phone goes. It's the doctor. 'Ah, listen, would you come to the hospital immediately?' I said, 'Yeah, everything all right?' He said, 'There's a slight problem.'

So when we go up there, she's in a recovery room. He said to me, 'There's nothing wrong with her.' 'What do you mean?' 'Well, to be truthful,' he said, 'you've got a raving hypochondriac. Every hospital in the south-east has heard of her.' That's a disease, innit?

So then she's saying, 'He dunnit! Him!' That's me! 'He made

me ill! And I'm gonna report him to every authority.' This is how bad it got. And she goes to my probation officer, Keith Norton, at Camberwell. She said I was driving her mad.

Unbeknown to me, she'd become very friendly with this Keith Norton. Cos I was reporting, I had to declare everything I did, Fred. You've got to tell them who you're going out with. I'm telling you, they'd look up a ferret's arse. Which gave her, in a way, a bit of power over me, and she used it. But I did get rid of her then, and I got my book off the ground without her. Also, I met Wendy. We bumped into this mad woman together a couple of times, because she still lived in the Borough, and Wendy wasn't that happy to see her. There was definitely a growl going on there!

7

Notoriety:
When It's a Nuisance

Conversation in Fred's kitchen, 8 March 2000

Tony Fred, since you've been out of prison, how many people have approached you to do something about someone? You know, you can't. You just don't get involved. If you took it serious, you'd drive yourself mad. You get it all day long. It's not your business.

Fred It come to the stage where people used to say to me, 'I've had my car nicked last night,' and expect you to fucking know who nicked it. 'Could you get it back for me?' It still happens.

Tony Quite a lot.

Fred I mean, how the fucking hell can we do this? As soon as something happens, they think you can just wave a magic wand and put it all right again, get their goods back.

Tony And then there's the other sort, that try and make themselves look big by having a go at you in company. I was in a pub in Mile End one New Year's Eve and someone made a remark about [Jack 'The Hat'] McVitie. I smashed the pub up. I don't know what made me do it. I just picked up a chair and threw it at him, across the bar. Of course, the police were called. They carted me off, Fred, to Leman Street. And I'm sitting there with a problem, now. Because with a life licence, they've only gotta look through the computer and I'm in breach, showing violence, see.

Fred Yeah.

Tony Then an inspector came round, and he went to me, 'What was it all about?' He said if I signed a bit of paper saying I wouldn't drink in the area for, I think it was three months, I could go. Otherwise I would go to court. And that got me out of it. I thought he was kidding me.

Fred He done you a favour. You know, people do get over-familiar. I was at a boxing show in York Hall, and there were about six guys in the bar who were a bit drunk. I had to push through. One of them said, 'Hi, Fred, have you killed anyone lately?' I stopped and I just looked at him. I said, 'The night's not over yet.' He started laughing and said, 'I didn't mean anything, Fred,' and wanted to shake my hand. They all wanted to be friendly, so I let it go.

I mean, you do get people wanting to have a pop at you so they can go off and tell their mates what they fucking said – 'I said this to Freddie Foreman, and I said that.' They might finish up in intensive care afterwards.

Tony Yeah. That could happen.

Fred And I don't want that. If I kick off with somebody . . .

Tony You know what's gonna happen.

Fred There's always other people waiting to jump on 'em. And they do the damage that you can't fucking stop. I've had this happen in the past plenty of times. You know, I've hit people on the chin and they're on the floor. Then you get somebody wanting to fucking jump over their heads and start stabbing them. That's the danger.

Tony The minute you throw a right-hander, six people are gonna jump in and do it for you.

Fred If they're there. It don't make a difference if they're there or not – I'm still gonna do it. I still find myself very quick-tempered. I'll turn on a fucking sixpence if someone says the wrong things.

Tony You have a way of doing that.

Fred I do. It's just my nature. I get a little rush of blood to my head. But the thing that I don't like is when you do it and then other people step in and start stabbing 'em. And then who's had the row? You've had the row, somebody else has finished it, the person's fucking brown bread in the mortuary and who's up on trial in the Old Bailey? Me. And all I've done is give a geezer a right-hander. It's happened to me on a couple of occasions.

Tony I remember you telling me about this, Fred.

Fred On one occasion I give a geezer a thump, and next thing I know, someone's slipped round the side and stabbed him nearly in the heart. And there's my fucking motor car there, they know I've dragged the geezer out the club and battered him ... I mean, a right-hander don't hurt nobody, a couple of digs or whatever, but someone comes up and stabs him – that's clever when you're fucking unconscious, do you know what I mean?

Tony It's not on.

Fred And they say, 'I've just done that.' You know, you say, 'Oh, thanks very much. You've just fucking stabbed a geezer and I'll be on a fucking murder charge.' This is the trouble.

Tony Even in small ways, people do cause us a lot of problems. I don't like anyone using our names without asking. Last week, an example. Somebody, and I know who it was, went to the Titanic club in the West End and stuck my name up, yours and Joey Pyle's, to try to get in. Now, the manageress was so wary of it she phoned up Frank the doorman to get hold of me or you or someone. I've only ever been in there twice, and they've always been kind and made me welcome. If somebody goes there and sticks our names up, it ain't right, but there's nothing you can do about it.

Fred It's OK if they're family or close friends, cos you're confident that they'll conduct themselves in a proper manner.

Tony We help our own people. That's what I like doing. But, yes, I think a lot of others do try to use us. Organizers of events phone me up and say, 'Get Freddie there, and then a lot of people are gonna turn up.'

Fred Well, there's certain people you wanna help and certain others you don't.

Tony Yeah, that's right. There's not a day goes by ... one man recently, a boxing trainer, came into the Monday Club [a regular gathering of Sixties 'faces' in a pub off the Old Kent Road]. He was there cos he heard you and George drank in there, and he came up to see if you were about. He knew me cos he'd seen me with you. Then he came down again. This is twice I've seen him, and I said, 'No, Fred's not here, he's a bit busy at the moment.' But then he upset someone in there.

Fred Did he?

Tony Yeah. This geezer, grey hair with glasses. Someone you know well – I can't think of his name. There was a bit of an argument. I don't know what was going on. And one of them went, 'I'll see Fred about this.' Right away, your name came into it.

Fred Yeah, yeah. See what I mean?!

Tony You know nothing about it.

Fred Put in the fucking middle.

Tony Your name is always cropping up. I was sitting in a pub in Blackfriars earlier tonight, and a woman came over. She went, 'You're Tony Lambrianou.' Then she said, 'Oh, I seen Freddie Foreman on TV a couple of weeks ago. I know all you.' And I'd never seen the woman before in my life!

We've gotta be careful, and that's the warning again from what happened to Charlie Kray. I get approached by strangers, hangers-on, all the time. I get phone calls from them. The lesson is, don't do it. Just keep away.

Fred I don't get mixed up with them. Nah.

Tony They'd love to get hold of you. I mean, they try. I've seen it at functions, book signings and that. And you feel obliged to give 'em a few minutes of your time because they've bought your book. That doesn't mean to say they can impose on your life. That shouldn't happen. They want your home phone number, they want to pal you up. I get it all the time. But you can't live with that. I don't even answer the phone unless it's someone I want to talk to. I'm known for that.

Fred You wait and see what number comes up, don't you?

Tony Yeah. You've gotta have a bit of private life.

Fred But they still fucking recognize you.

Tony Yeah. I have sometimes ten people a day asking me, 'When's he getting out?' You must get that, Fred. I get sick of answering that one.

Fred 'When's Reggie getting out?'

Tony I get journalists ringing me up for your number. 'Can you ask Fred this, can you ask Fred that?' It's not for me to do that. You don't really want to know.

Fred Too right.

Tony But we attract so many hangers-on. I've seen you wanna get away from people. I've seen that with my own eyes.

Fred Well, you know, you be nice, you be polite, have a bit of general conversation with them, but you don't wanna tell them your life story, do you? Let them buy your book and read it.

Tony Well, it seems to me, they want it from you.

Fred But you don't know who you're talking to anyway.

Tony That's right.

Fred They could be a fucking freelance reporter. Next thing, everything you say is in all the papers.

Tony You just never know who people are. We was in a pub last week that we use in Blackfriars, and I never knew until then, when someone pulled the guvnor, that he used to be on the Flying Squad.

Fred Yeah. Well, it's nice to know, but it's not that unusual. Coppers years ago always retired to run a pub. I could name loads of them. I never made them my local, but I was never afraid to have a drink in them. We don't do nothing wrong, so these coppers aren't any threat to us. They could've been, years ago . . .

If I was an active person now, I wouldn't be fucking writing books for a start. I wouldn't be putting myself in the spotlight, cos all the years I was active, I was trying to be low-key, a shadowy figure in the background, only seen as a businessman.

Tony I think, in your case, you had no choice. But it's a thing we should know.

Fred Then it's all right. It don't come as a shock. I could go into any pub and say, 'I'm an ex fucking robber, I'm an ex-criminal, and I did some nasty things years ago.' I'm an open book to people now. They know I'm not hiding, and if they come over and talk to me, they talk to me openly. There's no fucking surprises up my sleeve. They're not putting themselves in any danger by talking to me. If they don't want to come and talk to me, that's OK. It's up to them.

Tony We are an open book, Fred. Some of the followers know more about our lives than we'll ever know. Do you know, people that we don't know turn up at our house just to look at it – even criminals. They'll say, 'Oh, so and so sent me round.'

If you're in the public eye, you've gotta expect that. You just wonder what they want to see. My life indoors is totally different to outside. I've said it before – once you put a suit on, you're there to be what they want, and you learn to live with it.

Were you around for them two brothers, the Fraynes [Leslie and Leighton]?

Fred No, no. From Wales, were they?

Tony Yeah. Fred, this was something I could not believe I saw. I walk in The Florist, a pub in the East End, one night and there's Kevin Kray, the twins' nephew, there, all the meat market boys, and this Welsh firm had come down. Talk about how we could influence people, Fred. It was shocking. They had reproduced us to a T. They were a reincarnation of the twins – the suits, the hairstyles . . . I mean, I had to look twice. In the end, they got nicked [in 1992] for robbery and conspiracy, with another nice piece, a Scot, who Reggie introduced me to.

He knocked on my door once with a geezer called Bernie, and I wasn't in. Wendy says to them, 'Call back.' A few words was said to Wendy, and she's a bit upset now. So I get back and I look at Wendy and I say, 'What's the matter?' She says, 'There's been an argument.'

This Scottish geezer, I got his number, phoned him up. I said, 'Have you been round my house?' He said, 'Yeah.' I said, 'Come round. I want to see you.' I've got my mate Andy with me and I had a fucking hammer, Fred. Soon as they walked in, I said, 'You come back round my house again and I'll smash this right through your head. I'll kill you.'

Fred People don't seem to know where I live, really. That's why I don't live in south London. I live over north London now. Cos I get a bit more freedom, peace of movement. You're anonymous. I can walk down the shops and get a newspaper, and nobody knows who I am.

Tony You're lucky. There are people out there that you don't want to get mixed up with. Here's a funny one. Do you remember Carol Thompson, a slim girl with long, ginger hair that Reggie used to go out with?

Fred Yeah, I remember her. Nice girl, nice face.

Tony Yeah, a quiet girl. I think she visited him for a while after he went down and then she went off the scene, disappeared. I understand she's married.

Anyway, two or three years ago, the east London local paper rang me up. Do I know a Carol Thompson? I says, 'Yeah. I know Carol Thompson.' 'Would you recognize her if you saw her?' So, I thought, It's been over thirty years since I seen her, but I'd know her. They asked me, 'Are you sure?' I said, 'Yeah.' So down me and Wendy go to the *East London Advertiser*.

When I get there, there's a photographer and two reporters, and there's a woman sitting there, a fattish woman with curly hair, Fred. And as soon as I walked through the doors, they were all looking at me. Now, I could sense something wasn't right, that this woman was something to do with it. This is supposed to be Carol Thompson but it definitely wasn't the Carol Thompson I knew.

Fred Did she recognize you?

Tony Yeah. She'd obviously seen photos of me. Now it turns out, this woman has been saying she's got a son by Reggie.

Fred That's what she's claiming.

Tony Have you heard about her, Fred?

Fred I have, yeah.

Tony She was saying nutty things, Fred, about Jack The Hat, talking about being there that night. I said, 'I've never seen this woman before.' If it was Carol Thompson, Fred, I'd have known her. She'd have come over and said hello.

Fred Yeah. She wouldn't have changed *that* much.

Tony But she was adamant she was Carol Thompson. And she wasn't the same one. She popped up again recently. She was outside a nick where Charlie was, Belmarsh, screaming blue murder.

Fred What, on his last trial?

Tony Yeah. People never stop surprising me. I went down the records office to get a copy of my birth certificate for a passport, and they've replaced it nine times.

Fred Yeah?

Tony I wonder how many times they've replaced yours? Do a check on it, Fred. This is the followers again. I met one fan, a girl, in Newcastle. She gave me a silver dollar as a lucky charm, and she used to pray for me. (*Laughing*) She can pray all she wants, it's still not gonna do me any good, is it?

I've got a woman now who's very friendly with me, and she's an embalmer. The other night, she said to me on the phone, 'Look, if any of your friends are going, I'll do it for nothing.'

Fred She must've watched *The Godfather*! You'd better give me her address!

Tony (*Hearty laughter*) If you know of anybody that wants any embalming, let me know!

Fred She could make you better-looking. She should get to work on you now, not fucking wait till you're dead. *I* could do with a drop of that embalming fluid . . .

Both (*Uproarious laughter*)

Tony Do you know what it comes to to embalm a body? You pay for what you get. Those fluids come to a fortune.

Fred Oh, course they do, yeah. (*Laughing*) They're so expensive, they drain 'em out before they screw you down and use 'em on someone else.

Tony Why she approached me with all that, I don't know. But another thing she does is catering for functions, sandwiches and that.

Fred I've had some of her grub!

Both (*Hearty laughter*)

Fred I wish you'd told me she was an embalmer before I ate it! No, just as well you never . . .

Tony   Well, she was catering for a big do the other week, and she had to get up early to sort out two bodies in the morning. I might go round there to see how it's done, Fred. It interests me, that. I've seen an autopsy.

Fred   Oh, yeah?

Tony   When I was in the hostel. Anybody who works on a hospital, they ask if you are prepared to see an autopsy. Did you know that? I find it very interesting. Very interesting.

Fred   Well, I've seen enough dead bodies . . .

Tony   Talking of dead bodies, Fred, they thought they'd found mine a few years ago, when I was living in the Borough! There's a copper there, they nicknamed him Beardy. He was on the heavy squad, used to travel around in a van.
    One day he pulled Wendy at the Elephant and he said, 'Wendy, they've found a headless body in Sussex.' And for some reason, they thought it was me.

Fred   (*Laughter*)

Tony   God knows why. And then the rumours started to circulate! But the same sort of thing happened with you as well, when it said in that book that you'd been murdered.

Fred   All you do is laugh at it.

Tony   It don't upset you. You listen to every rumour, it would drive you mad. Rumours galore. That's what it's about.
    Did I ever tell you about the other time they got me mixed up with someone else?

Fred   What was that about?

Tony   One day me and Wendy went out with the dog. Then I go for a walk and when I come back, Wendy came running round the corner, saying 'Don't go near the flat.' They've hit the flat while I was out, fifteen coppers off Tower Bridge. What had happened, a kid who lived on the estate had murdered a bird out of Epping, and because of my record, they got the wrong address.

Fred   Hit your house by mistake.

Tony Yeah. So I phone up the solicitor and go round to Tower Bridge. They've got a cop on the desk there, and I send Wendy in first – 'Do you want to see Tony Lambrianou?' He said, 'Wait there a minute.' Went away, came back ten minutes later with a smile on his face. 'Don't know what you're talking about.' They nicked the kid, apparently. He was a right nutter as well. Stabbed the girl to death. But this is how our past keeps bringing us problems, when we haven't done nothing. Last night on the news, it said that a man had given evidence against a crime family out of south London. Did you see that?

Fred Yeah, yeah.

Tony Well, you know who he was referring to, and it ain't south London.

Fred Course it ain't.

Tony It's north London.

Fred The Adams family, yeah. Well, the Adams family are going to get the blame for everything. If someone's dog gets run over or their budgie dies, they'll get the blame.

Tony Do you know, I had four phone calls – 'Is that Freddie Foreman they were talking about?' That is how things can be turned round. Because they mentioned south London, right away people assume, 'Freddie Foreman'. You know, when I'm out with you, I'm wary of the people that are approaching you. I'm always watching. And I'll say to a few of the boys, 'Do me a favour. Keep an eye on Fred and who goes near him.' Cos sometimes people can get a bit overbearing.

They come up to me and say, 'What's he like, Freddie Foreman? Is he approachable? Can you introduce me to him?' I ask myself, 'Does Fred really want to meet this person?' I know roughly who you'd wanna meet and who you wouldn't.

Fred You suss 'em out first. You keep them at arm's length until you know who they are and what they're like.

Tony I am good at weighing people up. And when Wendy and Janice are there, I have got to be ultra-careful who comes into the company.

Fred You wanna know the strength of them.

Tony Yeah, I wanna know.

Fred It's like any businessman – you've gotta get past the secretary, ain't you?

Tony That's right. Yeah, yeah.

Fred If you see they're gonna give aggravation, they ain't gonna get in the door, are they?

Tony That's right. If I introduce someone, then I've gotta watch that person. I get people asking, 'Can I talk to Fred about this or that?' If it's something I know you don't wanna listen to . . .
    Then again, if I think they're OK, I'll come over and introduce them. But never a nuisance.

Fred People like that can spoil the whole fucking night, can't they?

Tony Upset the whole evening. But sometimes they slip through the net, Fred, unfortunately.

Fred They do.

Tony They do slip through the net. If people want to make themselves busy there, or if they're getting loud, then I've gotta say, (*Quietly*) 'Can I see you a minute?' I'll always do it discreetly, though. I've said it to one or two or them – 'Don't fuck about. Now leave it at that.'

Fred Yeah, you've gotta do it. I was at a restaurant party the other night, and there was a little row happened. This guy, he was only a young fella, but he was asking for it all fucking night. There were a couple of old people there, and he said to 'em, 'I'll fucking stab you,' and all this sort of thing. Before the night was out, he'd got served up.

Tony Didn't no one see it to stop it, before it got to that stage, Fred?

Fred Well, all these people come and tell you afterwards, he should have been spoken to earlier. This guy's father was a face, so he thinks he's got a licence to get away with it and say what he likes. But you've gotta observe the rules. I remember the kid when he was in Spain. I helped him out a little bit. Now, all of a sudden . . .

I mean, there was one geezer down that Tardis when we had the [Nicky Reynolds] exhibition on. A young guy, I don't know who he was, came up to me, he started name-dropping and he said, 'Do you think it's right doing this and doing that?' He said a few nasty things. He was down there to make snide remarks, to cast aspersions on the exhibition. My Jamie was standing there by the side of me, and he said he was gonna give him a fucking dig as well. The guy came very, very close to getting a right-hander.

Tony I had a guy phoned me today, and he said, 'I think I'll give Fred a ring.' I went, 'Hang on a minute.' He had your number once for a genuine reason, but it doesn't give him the right to phone every day. He might have an audience there, cos you get that. I have people phone me up and they're with people that they're trying to impress. Well, you don't want that. Our names come up and they get used. You've gotta be very careful, Fred.

Fred We don't know half of what gets said in our names.

Tony No, we don't. All we can do is try to keep the hassle to a minimum. Remember what I said to you once – I never drink where I live. Familiarity breeds contempt.

Fred Yeah, yeah.

Tony There's a pub fifty yards away. I've never been in there. And the guvnor says to me, 'Why don't you ever come in?' No. Cos of the familiarity. I always give the local papers a little story when I move into a new area. It stops any pressure later on, keeps them off your back. I tell them, 'It's nice here, I like the gardening side of it, I like the country.' What they wanna hear.

But there are certain people I like to know in my area. I've lived in three different places since I came out of the nick – the flat in the Borough, and two houses in Kent, and I've always got to know the local tearaway.

Recently, when I moved to Swanscombe, I went round the betting shop in the high street. Now, a tall fella with glasses was standing there, looking at me.

He was very friendly with someone I knew, and a few days later, he 'just happened' to be driving by my house, which I don't believe for one minute. He came in, we had a cup of tea in the garden, and he went to me, 'Oh, by the way, Tony, if you ever get anything missing out your house, anybody ever breaks in, let me know and I'll sort it out for you.'

I went, 'What? Let me tell you something now. If anything happens at my house, you're the first one I'm coming for. *You*. Now it's down to you.' And I've seen him around, but I've never spoke to the man since. Cos he was behind the burglaries in the area. I knew he was because he told me that. By saying that 'I'll make sure it's put right,' he was admitting that he was controlling the break-ins and burglaries around there. My pal who knows him confirmed that to me.

He thought he was doing me a favour – 'You don't get touched, but if a mistake happens, just let me know.'

You don't break into people's homes. You don't housebreak. That goes down bad. It's a no-go area, that. You can't hurt working people.

'You're the one I'm coming for.' He knew what I meant.

8

Modern Crime Is Rubbish!

Conversation in Fred's kitchen, 8 March 2000

Fred I was known as a latchkey kid when I was a boy. You came home from school, you put your hand in the letterbox, you pulled your key out on a piece of string and you went in. You got the tea ready for your mum, if she was working, and lit the fire in the winter, put the coal and the wood in the old iron stove with the oven at the side. That's what I used to do. I laid the table and had everything ready, put the kettle on, so that when your mother came in, she'd have a cup of tea waiting. My dad was working – he was a cab driver. I was the first one in before my brothers came home from work, and that was my little job of a night.

But could you leave your street-door key on a fucking bit of string in your letterbox today? Eh? Could you? Fucking hell! People was poor then, but they didn't go robbing one another's homes. They didn't rob their own people.

Tony This is the morality of it. There's certain rules, and you abide by them.

Fred See, I was reading this big article in the *Daily Mail* two days ago, the day after my birthday. It was 'Are We Now A Nation Of Strangers?' by Dr Anthony Daniels. He was talking about, you know, people not speaking to anybody like they did years ago. You don't know who your next-door neighbours are. But this one thing he seems to have overlooked is when people are in trouble – there was the old thing, they'd come in and help the mother if she'd had a baby, or if she had three or four kids, they'd give her a bit of a break, take them off her hands and look after them, cook 'em a nice pot of stew. Oh, the old pots of stew was always on, weren't they?

Tony Barley, Fred.

Fred I mean, they may have been nosy, but they was helpful neighbours because it was a little community where everybody knew everyone else's business. I've been here for three or four years now, but I don't know the names of the people on either side of me.

Tony I don't know my neighbours at all.

Fred And this is what's happened all over London, you know, where people don't really talk to each other any more. And then, of course, you get the crackheads and the druggies and the people who are lonely, putting their music on fucking full blast.

Tony Yeah, and we've all had that.

Fred Causing all these rows and troubles.

Tony Do you remember the early to middle Sixties? You could walk through any street on a Sunday morning, Fred, and you'd see the washed steps, red or white, polished highly. Everyone was dressed in their best suit, going to their Sunday lunch.

Fred You wore it once a week, yeah.

Tony That's how life was lived. And then things started to change. But that's the environment we was all brought up in. That's what I remember. That's what I miss. But, like I said before, I can't afford to get too friendly with people these days. And that's a shame.

THE OPPORTUNIST THIEF

Tony Well, that's the way of the world now.

Fred They're the lowlifes, the smackheads who are robbing just to get a tenner for a fix. They'd nick anything. They don't spend five or six months planning a robbery.

Tony They're not criminals.

Fred They're opportunists. They see something in a car and break into it, or they see the street door or window open and they climb in. That's the difference between the professional robber and the lowlife robber, stealing off anybody just to satisfy his fucking craving for drugs. Recently, a planned robbery at Vauxhall went wrong.

Tony Went badly wrong.

Fred And that, obviously, was professional people trying to do a professional job.

Tony They're few and far between now, Fred. They were trying to do a security van with a lot of money on it, and it came unstuck.

Fred Cos they couldn't get into the van. They've got a goods depot there, at Vauxhall.

Tony It was all over the news.

Fred Two cars were set alight, and that's how they got away, on foot. They went down on the river and got away on a speedboat. In my opinion, good luck to 'em.

Tony Good luck to 'em, yeah.

Fred It's a shame they never got the money. That was the first really planned robbery I've seen in a long time. That and the one down in Walworth Road.

Tony They done another one near me. I lived near where they pulled the van in, Fred. I mean, I'm sitting indoors, what did I know about it? But it was in the papers that I lived 200 yards away. I said, 'Well, good luck. No one was hurt. I wish it was me.'

But good robberies today are very rare because most money is done through cheques or giros or whatever. So you haven't got the money-loads of the Sixties, Seventies or Eighties. They ain't carrying that type of cash about. Professional robbers are a dying breed.

Fred They are. In my time, there was robberies being committed every week. You'd pick the paper up, there was a robbery. The new breed are not robbers, they're just petty thieves.

Tony Mugging – I mean, we know what it's about. Heroin, and all that carry-on.

Fred It's a very old crime. In my father's time, in certain roads or areas, the toffs might get mugged every now and again. They used to hit them, or put 'em in the horse trough, and nick their fucking gold watch off their waistcoat. That's one of the oldest crimes in the book. But it's much more prevalent now. And you've gotta face it – I know it's politically incorrect to say so, but it's mostly a black crime. That's the finding from the surveys that have been done.

Tony Yeah. I mean, I've never seen a mugging, and I probably go to some of the toughest parts of London, like you do. To me, it's an alien way of thinking. It didn't happen when we was around. And perhaps it's people like you and the Krays that did probably stop it happening. When youse was out, this didn't happen. You've heard it many, many times, Fred. People are always bringing it up, but that don't mean it's not true. Angela Rippon got done, you know that, Fred?

Fred I know, she's in the papers. She got mugged in Notting Hill.

Tony It shook her badly.

Fred It's shock.

Tony Then there's car crime. Have you ever heard of the 'doggy run', Fred? You probably have. Most car crime is committed between nine o'clock and eleven o'clock in the morning and between three and four-thirty. Why? Mothers are taking their kids to and from school and they leave their bag in the car. What woman doesn't, Fred? They always put their bag under the seat. They don't think about locking the car. So those are prime times for car crimes. They call it the doggy run. That is a fact.

THE SERIAL KILLER

Tony There was a problem, there, when we was on remand. A man called Silver murdered some children, didn't he, Fred, remember that?

Fred Yeah, yeah, the sick bastard.

Tony A big, tall fella in Brixton. Said hello to you, and you wouldn't talk to him. Killed four, five was it?

Fred Four kids, I think it was.

Tony   On the Sussex Downs he done it. They'd released him from a mental hospital, he took the kids on a picnic and done all four of them.

Fred   There's always been serial killers.

Tony   The film *Silence of the Lambs* brought them more to attention.

Fred   Oh, they're just sick bastards, aren't they? They're mentally ill. I mean, in the criminal world that we know, a murder's only committed if there's a reason for it – if a man's done something wrong, and you judge the seriousness of its effect. Like the judge sits up in the court of law and he puts the black cap on, or he used to, and sentenced a man to death. Well, that can be done in the criminal world without any court of law, but they still have to have a certain judgement. There still has to be correctness in it happening, otherwise it's looked on as a liberty, as though the person took it too far – he overreacted.

So there's gotta be a real reason for a man to go and shoot somebody else And then it only applies to that person. It don't apply to his wife and kids, his grandmother and grandfather, the budgie and the fucking cat and the dog. You know, it's only the man himself who gets done. Again, this is the morality of the way we lived.

Tony   It *is* morality.

Fred   Well, we wouldn't have nothing to do with a serial killer in prison. He would be a nothing. He's one sick bastard and he deserves to be locked up for the rest of his fucking life.

THE PAEDOPHILE

Fred   If a man's a robber. he comes to a stage in life where he can't commit those crimes any longer. He's too old to do it. And he loses the thrill or the need to go out and get money, so he stops. He says, 'Fuck that, I'm not risking my liberty any more.' He's not sick in that respect, like a paedophile is. A paedophile can still be a paedophile when he's eighty-nine years of age. If you took your grandkids round there, he would still want to interfere with 'em, molest 'em. He cannot be cured. He don't have to be dangerous to any adult, but as old as he is, he can still be dangerous to children.

And serial killers will kill because they get a thrill from killing people. I mean, in the underworld, people are only killed because it's gotta be done. There's a reason for it. It could be a drunken fight that's ended in death, or a revenge, or a rip-off over money. It could be an eye-for-an-eye situation. Or it's, 'Get him before he gets me.' Or he's done a terrible thing and put people away for fucking twenty and thirty years. Then you're perfectly justified to take your revenge. But in the underworld, they don't go out killing complete strangers at the drop of a hat. They don't walk down the street, see an innocent kid and say, 'I'm gonna kill him or her,' and jump on them at that moment, just to satisfy their own sick lust.

I went in the shop to get this book today – *The Long Firm* by Jake Arnott. Everyone's saying what a good read it is. I'm going to get into this, so I'll let you know when I've finished reading it. It's all about us. He [Arnott] is using a lot of true-life stories, and he goes into each character as though he is the character talking.

It so happens that one story in here is about a young kid from north London. He was a bit slow, not retarded, but they reckon some paedophiles got hold of him. It says in here that he was a rent boy, but he wasn't. He was just a poor little kid who used to get up onstage in the youth clubs and sing, things like that, you know.

He was a pal of the son of a very dear friend of mine. Anyway, they found this little boy's body in a suitcase. Them paedophiles had been at him. It is true.

I mean, if you knew someone was a paedophile, you'd hope the authorities would've dealt with him. But you just couldn't phone up the police and tell them. You'd probably sort him out yourself, if you knew what he was like.

There's many a liberty-taker used to get seen to – the local thief breaking into old people's homes, people who were mugging, or beating up their wives. We used to give 'em a clump or something like that. You feel it's your duty to try and do that. In the case of a paedophile or a rapist or a mugger, all you can do is batter the bastard and threaten him, and maybe you'll prevent him from doing it again to any other little kid, or any woman or old person.

Tony We come back to this thing we was talking about, the morality of the underworld. It's not a written document. You can't write rules into it. It's just the way it happens.

Fred You can't fucking offer him up to the police. It's right against your moral judgement. And you have to remember that whatever you do to the offender, you're the one who's gonna wind up in the nick and be punished for it. You seem to read more about these sorts of crime these days, but I think it was just more hidden before. I think they've got away with it all these years.

THE STALKER

Fred Aw, well, they're another sick sort, aren't they?

Tony They've always been around too.

Fred But they wasn't brought to your attention. I mean, there was girls, sisters and girlfriends, saying, 'He follows me about, that guy, he's very creepy, getting on and off buses when I leave work.' But these girls would always have someone like ourselves to stand there and say, 'Oi, you, what do you fucking want? What are you after?' And then you pin him up against the wall and say, 'Are you following this girl?' You'd prevent it from that angle. But not everyone has that sort of help, have they?

Tony Now it's highlighted, so there's a difference.

Fred We never had the television then. We had the radio. But now people watch celebrities on television and they get obsessed with their looks, so it's the media, I suppose, that's brought about the modern stalker.

Tony And also, a lot of celebrities bring it upon themselves. Having said that, I've had stalkers. I've had one recently, round the corner, where I live.

Fred (*Laughing*) Was she a good sort?

Tony (*Also laughing*) Nah, terrible, Fred. Terrible. Drove me mad. She used to follow me everywhere I went.

Fred Yeah? She wasn't posting her knickers to you, was she?

Tony I'll tell you a story about Ronnie Kray. One day he says to me, 'I want you to go and see this girl in Southampton to get a book for me,' some book he wanted. She had a boat. She was well-to-do, well educated, and her house was, like, two cottages knocked into one, right by the docks. It was a nice area. And the first thing that hit me, Fred, as I walked in was this great big photo of Ronnie.

Fred A shrine. (*Laughing*) Was she a plaster-caster?

Tony *Cor!* This was a nutter. Around the rooms, she had more stuff about us lot . . . and she had two or three guns. She was in a gun club. Later that night, I put my hand under the pillow. There's a .38 pistol there. 'Why you got that?' She went, 'Well, I always keep one about,' just like it was nothing. I went back to London and I got loads of phone calls from her.

Fred (*Laughing*) She couldn't have been very impressed with your lovemaking, could she? She just stalked you on the phone . . .

Tony And Ronnie Kray, the next time I went to see him, said, 'What was she like?' I said, 'A nutter.' And he said, 'I knew that.' I've still got her address.

Fred (*Still laughing*) Oh, *I'll* have that . . .

Tony I'll tell you what. I've got a girl, she's in a motorized wheelchair, and she goes to my dad's grave in north London, looks after it and puts flowers on it regular, every fortnight. I don't ask her to do that, Fred. I got a letter from her the other day. And I never speak to her. Yet it's her *life*. She goes to Violet Kray's grave, too.

Fred If I get any stalkers, I'll send my Janice out! She's like a Rottweiler. She'll go out there and sort 'em out.

Janice (*Coming in, right on cue*) Huge teeth. Paid a lot of money for these teeth.

Fred He's got a stalker in a wheelchair, Jan. What's that shopping centre – Bluewater? Tails him all around there.

Tony You get it. You've gotta expect it.

Fred She puts flowers on his father's grave. Perhaps she was one of his old girlfriends.

Tony Flowers on the grave every fortnight. What can you do?

Both (*Laughter*)

Janice It's not funny. You don't want to be laughing.

Tony If they wanna do it, it's up to them.

THE FRAUDSTER

Fred It's usually the high-class people, the toffs, that are involved in fraud or conning people. And, I mean, they've had every opportunity, they've had the education, and they've never been short of a bit of food in their mouth. They've had it easy all their lives and yet they turn to crime. But it's never the sort of crime that we did, armed robberies and stuff like that. We went out and took our chances.

They can only get away with these offences, fraudsters and conmen, on the basis of a friendship with somebody. They can get into the confidence of that person and persuade them to part with their money. They're fleecing them, stealing their money through the good nature of the person. They're taking advantage.

I've got no time for them people, those conmen who rob off their own. They've got that plausible way of conning somebody into parting with cash with the intention of stealing it or not paying it back. They get them to invest in fraudulent deals and scams and just run off. When it comes to the cut-up at the end of it, they tail it into the long grass with the money.

ROAD RAGE

Fred It's getting more and more common. We saw a right fight only the other day, Jan, didn't we?

Janice Yes, we did.

Fred That was going over Waterloo Bridge. The guy behind us stopped and he's got out the car. He's run back to the car behind him . . .

Janice Opened the door . . .

Fred   And the geezer's tried to get out, and he's pulled his coat right off, hasn't he? And then he's punched him in the mouth . . .

Janice   And kicked him . . .

Fred   And the car's running away. The brake was off.

Janice   He's not in control of his car, and it's now going to crash into the car of the guy who's punched him, which I thought was hysterical.

Fred   This is road rage. Years ago, I hit a geezer on the chin who I had a road rage with in Chancery Lane. His foot got caught in the accelerator. The car took off, went up the pavement, went round in a complete circle and smashed into a road sign – you know one of the old things for crossing, where you stand in the middle of the road with the sign.

It happened only because I was over the white line. I stopped to let him go, but he don't wanna go. He just sits there and he wants to give me a bollocking, because I'm a little bit over that white line. Of course, I said, 'If I get out of this car, you'll be in trouble. Now keep going, get on.' But he still don't want to move away. He still wants to be the big-time Charlie.

Janice   It always amazes me, the pettiness of people.

Fred   It *was* petty. I got out and I said, 'I told you . . .', and I just hit him on the chin. He went spark out. That's when his foot got caught on the accelerator. There were people running and jumping everywhere out of the way, cos he wasn't in control of the car.

I think the reason road rage is more prevalent is because there's too many cars on the road. It's like, you put six rats in a cage, they'll run around and find their own passageway. They're not obstructing each other. You put another five rats in there and they're tearing one another to pieces. It's a matter of space. You're invading other people's space on the roads. It never used to be that way.

Janice   But the government are forcing this situation to happen. They are causing it. There are less car spaces, to force you into public transport – which is never gonna happen because the public transport is so diabolical.

Fred Some people say road rage is just an excuse, or a cover-up for other things, but I don't think so, no.

Janice Well, it could be. I mean, if you've had a bad day at the office or you've had a row with your husband or your wife and you've got in the car, it's so easy to snap at everybody else. It's not road rage exactly. It's just because you're in a bad mood and your temper is short, so if they do the most minor little thing, you're off, aren't you?

Fred There was one girl put it down to road rage when she murdered her husband or boyfriend. She said he'd been attacked in a road rage incident. But she got found out, didn't she?

Tony I sometimes suffer from road rage if I'm sitting in a traffic jam or if I get cut up. We all do. It happened tonight, coming here. Four people cut me up coming round King's Cross. You're cursing every driver in your way. I'll tell you about another one today. Wendy was on a bus and two blokes got on the bus and beat the driver up. Tried to drag him out the bus.

Fred He's probably cut them up. I did that once myself. I got that uptight, I chinned a bus driver. He cut us up. He nearly fucking killed us.

And there was a coach driver that deliberately ran me up a big, high pavement in a motor I'd hired out. It fucking ripped the side of the motor right off. And I've got a deposit on it. I've gotta take it back. But I caught him up at the Elephant, in the traffic. I've come round the side of him and I pulled the door open. I've got up in his cab and, you know . . .

THE GANGS

Tony They talk about things now, like the Russian Mafia and the Yardie gangs and this, that and the other. Really, how did this all come about? You know, it's easy to talk about 'gangsters' and 'the underworld' and all this carry-on. It's just a title put there, but you are stuck with it. What are we on about now, the Russian Mafia? I know nothing about it.

Fred Well, we ain't come in touch with it.

Tony I've never met a Yardie. What's a Yardie?

Fred They don't come near us.

WHO'S GUILTY?

Tony A week or two ago, Esther Rantzen done a programme on entrapment. Did you see it, Fred?

Fred No.

Tony They had a solicitor there, who spoke very well about entrapment, and a reporter. They said, 'Look, if you want to get a gun, for example, and you approach a criminal, then you are setting up a crime by asking for it.' The minute you approach someone with a criminal record to go and get something for you, then you're just as guilty as the person you've set up. Nine times out of ten, these days, it's reporters who do it, Fred. They ask a known criminal to get them drugs or whatever, knowing there's a weakness in him. If he goes ahead with it and he gets arrested, why ain't the people who set it up nicked? It's newspapers and police who are doing it. They're behind a lot of it.

Fred They create their own stories. There was a television programme the other night about the Customs & Excise. They financed a fucking boat that went all the way to the Morocco coast to buy drugs from the Moroccans. They got the drugs on board the ship and then they run into trouble. They got arrested by the Moroccan coastguard and it turns out that they were all customs officers on board the ship.

They had a hundred grand in customs money to bring back drugs to this country so they could find someone to buy them and then arrest them. Now, what do you think of that?

Tony It wouldn't surprise me if half the drugs on the streets of London are brought in legally by Customs & Excise, because they do these deals, Fred.

Fred They're encouraging crime, not fucking preventing it.

Tony What they're actually doing is spreading the stuff about.

Fred And what about Roger Cook?

Tony You're right. You're right.

Fred He did a programme on Ronnie Knight. It looked like he was up in the helicopter, filming from the mountainside around Ronnie Knight's. I watched this programme on television, and there was footage of Ronnie round the bloody barbecue, cooking their bits of sausages and burgers or whatever. But it was later alleged that this had been filmed earlier by another production team. And what makes me laugh is when Ronnie Knight has cups of tea with Roger Cook and treats him like a friend afterwards, all jolly, pally stuff, you know.

THE HITMAN

Tony Professional hitmen don't exist, in my eyes. I done a programme about someone up north who hired a hitman – and he turned out to be an undercover copper.

Fred Yeah, yeah.

Tony Same old scenario, Fred.

Fred People going out to hire someone to do somebody else. I mean, you can't do that. You're gonna wind up meeting a copper.

Tony Hitmen don't advertise their wares. It's word of mouth, if anything, but I don't believe there's any about. Do you know a hitman, Fred?

Fred Naaah. How could you ask a complete stranger to shoot someone? You'd have to do them right afterwards, just to keep their mouths shut!

Tony You know that and I know that. I don't know anyone I could go to and say, 'I want someone shot, here's ten grand.' Cos you can get hold of a nutter now, a junkie, who will go and do it for you for nothing. Am I right, Fred?

Fred Yeah, I suppose so, but it's the same thing. You would have to shoot him afterwards.

Tony   It's been put to me many times. I'm sure it's been put to you. But you take it with a pinch of salt. You learn to say, 'It's all right.'

Fred   Ah, it's all forgotten, it's all in the past.

Tony   Yeah, it's all in the past, but people believe in that life. I mean, they had this hitman theory about Jill Dando. I always thought it was a crazy fan, someone who just took a liking to her.

Fred   Yeah, yeah. There's some real nut-nuts about. You have to be careful with your fan club, Tony!

Tony   But when they talk about professional hitmen – I couldn't name one.

Fred   And I was talking to a pal of mine only today. He told me about a guy living just outside London who's gone up to a mother and a two-year-old baby and thrown acid over them. And the police said that they've been looking for this fella for two fucking years. He's done things like this on several occasions, but they can't find him. They will do eventually, obviously. But, I mean, these are the sort of people walking around in the general public. Jill Dando's killer probably got an obsession for her. He'll turn out to be a complete fucking crank.

9

Ghosts from the Past

Conversation in Fred's kitchen, 7 February 2000

Tony and Fred have just read Martin Fido's The Krays: Unfinished Business, *giving rise to this emotionally charged conversation. In his book, Fido reveals that before the Old Bailey trials, Chris Lambrianou had handwritten a statement which 'told the essence' of what happened at Evering Road, and implicated the Krays. This statement, said Chris, was read by Ralph Haeems, who reported it to the twins. Ronnie, in particular, was 'livid'. The statement was amended and Chris was then told what to say.*

Under the thirty-year rule, Fido also publishes for the first time statements made to solicitors by Tony and Chris Lambrianou and Ronnie Bender after the convictions, as appeal bids. All three claimed to have been afraid to tell the truth at the Old Bailey. They now acknowledged and described the murder of Jack 'The Hat' McVitie. Both Tony and Chris sought to call as appeal witnesses Trevor and Terry, the two boys dancing at the party, who had not been brought to court despite the fact that Trevor, at least, had made a statement to the police, also published in the book. The appeals were rejected.

Fido suggests that the very existence of Tony's statement makes a mockery of his previous assertion that he had 'held his silence', in keeping with the gangland code, until after Reggie Kray confessed to the murder. He also quotes from Ronnie's 1993 book My Story, *in which Kray condemns Tony as a 'lackey and a grass', having somehow heard about the appeal statement.*

RONNIE: MAKING IT RIGHT

Tony Ronnie might have said some of the things in the book in a fit of rage, he was down at the time or he didn't have his injection, and then felt sorry about it later. Or he might not have said them at all. It didn't bother me a lot, him having a go at me in the book, because I knew Ronnie. He said things he never meant. I can't hold it against him – the man had done twenty-five fucking years in captivity by then. I know what he went through. I was still on good terms with him. My last visit to him was in 1993, two years before he died. I've got letters from him wanting me to come and see him.

Then Kate Kray [Ronnie's wife] writes another book, *Ronnie Kray: Sorted* [published in 1998], and there's a piece on me.

This is what it says, Fred: (*Reading from book*) 'Tony Lambrianou . . . stood in the dock, side by side with Ron. He did 15 years for his part in disposing of Jack The Hat's body. He didn't grass. When he got life, he was 25 years old. He didn't complain, not once. I met Tony on a visit with Ron. He is a big, imposing man with silver grey hair, looking every bit the gangster. The first thing that strikes you about Tony is his distinctive voice. It is deep and demanding. If he said, 'Sit!' everyone would obey, not just the dog. He has a menacing look with eyes that hold you, and you would be a fool to cross him . . .'

Rubbish, that is. It goes on, 'He spent 15 years in some of the toughest prisons in Britain and he never betrayed Ron. Ron told me that I could always trust Tony, that he was a loyal friend . . . He deserves every success.'

SINKING WITH THE TITANIC

Tony What it felt like coming up to the trial . . . I was on the *Titanic* in the middle of the Atlantic Ocean, but I didn't by chance hit an iceberg, I hit a fucking thousand, and it was rudderless.

At the time of the trial, my future rested solely and truly on what happened to the Kray twins. I never put a witness up, I just denied everything. What chance did I have?

Fred None. You were twenty-five years of age, only a young kid. It's a lot to contend with, I know. A fifteen-year recommendation is a nasty fucking sentence when you've done fuck all, really. You've been lured to a party and now you're doing fifteen years.

Tony Fred, I'll take it a step further. We employ a man called Brian Gammon to do our appeals, and Ronnie Bender and my brother and I said, 'Right, we'll ask them [the twins] for a bit of help,' which they was entitled to give us. An approach is made through Ralph Haeems, who immediately went back to the twins and reported that we'd changed briefs.

Fred You sent a message to the twins to give you some help to get you out on appeal?

Tony Yes. I appealed against conviction. We approached them to give us a bit of help on the appeals, the twins, and we got a deathly silence from them. We never, ever heard a thing about it. The twins were gone, they were lifed off. We all knew that, but they could have helped us – 'Give me a crumb from the cake, at least give me that.' I'm not asking for a slice of the cake, I'm asking for a crumb. And bearing in mind that we couldn't defend ourselves at the trial – well, excuse me, but they was entitled to give me a crumb. After all, it was nothing to do with me, what happened, but I'm involved up to the hilt. Give me a fucking break, here. Am I asking for the world? I'm asking for someone to help me.

Fred Would their word have counted for anything, given that they were convicted? What could they have done? What could they have said? I suppose they could've said they had no knowledge of what was gonna happen, something to that effect.

Tony They could've done that, Fred.

Fred Would they have been accepted by the Appeal Court?

Tony Did it matter, Fred? Didn't I give *them* a chance in the beginning?

Fred You kept schtum, we all kept schtum. The most damaging thing was the fact that you had the same solicitors. That wasn't helping at all.

Tony That was stupid. I had no defence.

Fred Just saying it never happened and that you wasn't there.

Tony It's always bothered me, about my brother.

Fred He accused you of setting him up. Cos it's in the deps [depositions].

Tony That is the scene, thank you, Fred. It caused problems between us. But I feel guilty, because he fucking looks at me and he's thinking, Yeah, I'm your brother. You didn't fucking help me, but you helped them two. And I've got no answer there, Fred. I haven't got an answer.

He done the right things that night. I never knew he was gonna be involved in anything like it. I always felt guilty about that. I felt terrible about Charlie Kray being involved in it. How you became involved, Fred – I was never even aware of any part you played in it until I saw you in court. But Chris . . . fifteen years for something he never done. It's a hard one. It's a fucking hard one, Fred.

Fred It is, yeah. Oh yeah.

Tony And it's caused . . .

Fred Bad feeling in the family, yeah?

Tony Bad feeling. The whole thing, it wrecked my family. I lost my marriage, my kids, I lost everything. Never once have I ever complained about what happened to me. Never. I've accepted it. So that makes me angry (*pointing at Martin Fido's book, on the table*), trying to say that we might've damaged them [the twins] in any way.

Fred The damage was already done.

Tony The damage was done to us. Because I stood loyal to them to the day they died, and I died with them. Like I said, it was like being on the fucking *Titanic*, in the middle of the north Atlantic with icebergs all around me and no steering. That's the position I found myself in. I never got the loyalty back. It hurt me.

Fred You've always spoke up for the twins and defended them all the way through.

Tony I do feel betrayed by them. Yeah, I do. I do. But I'm entitled to have an opinion. Look, at the end of the day, if people could have been got out of it, then that should have been done. That's what I want to say. I can look in that mirror. I could've jumped on the bandwagon, but I didn't. No way. But I was entitled to that crumb of cake afterwards. We felt them out about it, but no response.

He felt it, Ronnie. I know he did. I believe he regretted that me and Chris went down, and I could never go against him.

Fred Oh yeah, course. Ronnie was a good man at heart and with hindsight, when he looks back over the years – and don't forget, he was having all that fucking jollop and drugs – the old mind opens up and he lays in the bed, he thinks things over and it becomes perfectly clear. With them hallucinatory drugs or whatever they have in there, they go on fucking mental trips, and it's probably become obvious that his actions have resulted in other people suffering.

Tony He didn't like it, I know he didn't. It did hurt him, Fred, I know that to be true.

Fred That was just the madness of the time and the fucking way things were.

Tony He didn't like everyone going down and I could never say a bad word about him. But a man's entitled to say, when my father died, no one remembered him, or my family. It fucking hurt me, Fred (*breaks down in tears*).

Fred Yeah, I know it did, Tone. It fucking brings it all back this, don't it?

Tony Fucking hurt me.

Fred Brings it all back, mate. We've got to face up to all this stuff, haven't we? You done fucking fifteen, sixteen years . . .

Tony Fucking half of it down the block.

Fred Twenty-five fucking years of age, and it's not nice, is it, when you're fucking just keeping your mouth shut, nobody to represent you and get up there and give you a fighting chance?

Tony Fucking hurt me, Fred. Fucking stood with 'em. For thirty-five years I've fucking defended them.

Fred You needed a little squeeze, there, after the sentence. And you've stood by 'em all this time.

Tony Because it was the right thing to do, keep the legend going.

THE KEEPER OF THE LEGEND

Tony Afterwards, I went along with it. That's all I ever did, was keep the legend going. What I said was what would keep the legend going, not my true feelings.

I ain't gonna talk bad about the twins, I can't do that. But Reggie's gotta understand one thing, to say 'thank you' to people. I've never heard him talk good about no one. You know, that hurts me, Fred. I've never heard it. All I was asking for was for them, the twins, to turn around and say these words, 'We owed Tony that.' The man [Reggie] stands up and looks at his life, he's sixty . . . how old is he now, Fred?

Fred Sixty-six, ain't he?

Tony At least you got up there and said about [Frank] Mitchell – and I admire you for this – 'I apologize to the family.' You said it publicly, on television. I couldn't apologize, I didn't want to, because I didn't want to wreck the legend. I've been a prisoner to the legend all this time. So now we've got this [Fido's] book. Well, it can try and make you a look a lot of things . . .

Fred He's accusing me of committing seven fucking murders in this book. Well, Nipper Read is saying that.

Tony What recourse have you got on it?

Fred They can say what they fucking like. There's one book, *The Scotland Yard Files* by Paul Begg and Keith Skinner, and they said, '. . . Following Foreman's murder in 1990 . . .'

Tony (*Managing a laugh*) Where did they get that from, Fred?

Fred Oh, fuck knows. It's gotta be wishful thinking on their part, hasn't it?

Tony When I came out of prison, I was lucky enough to meet Wendy, the film *Goodfellas* was released and *The Krays* was coming out. It all fell right in my lap, and I didn't want to break the legend of what it was all about. It had gone too far for me to break it anyway, because no matter what I said, and no matter what *you* say, right or wrong, the public are gonna believe one thing. Whatever you tell them, it doesn't make the fucking slightest bit of difference, so you go along with it. You're locked into it but you've got to sort out fact from fiction somewhere along the line here.

Take the film *The Krays*, for example. I understand what they've done. They've played on the one part of it that the public want to know about.

That's the biggest-selling thing we've got. Look, we're all getting on now. I was lucky, I was the youngest. I'm fifty-eight now. What right do I have to break the legend? But do I want this legend? I ask that question, and I don't know any more. I'm fed up with it. Yeah, I am, in a way. I've had enough.

Fred   Had enough of it, yeah.

Tony   Cos I see people jumping on it that I don't even know. Why should I have to answer to fucking idiots who think they've got the right to ask me about my trial or your life or anyone else's life? I used to be patient with everybody, but I'm meeting people all the time who want to get involved with us, hangers-on, Johnny-come-lately types who don't know what they're talking about.

We went down a certain road but there was only a few people on it. What fucking right do people have to come and give their comments on it, these people I don't even know, who was nothing to do with it, who've jumped on the bandwagon? Get on the bus, ring the bell. We started off with a few, now we've got a full bus with standing room along the way.

I've seen so many documentaries, there's the film, books, newspapers, and a lot of it is the biggest load of shit I've ever read, but you can't tell people that. Only the people that were there know the real truth.

I don't wanna break the legend, and I say that with all respect for it, but I'll break it on one point – that they talk about it as it was, as it really happened. Did Reggie Kray owe me that? Yes, he did. There's a fucking cake been baked. Give me a crumb. Yeah, I am addressing Reggie. Not Ronnie Kray.

Do the Kray twins measure up to the legend? What say did they have in it? Ronnie's dead. What say does Reggie have now? I think what's happened is, it's swallowed us all up.

Fred   Reggie's earning, he's getting a living out of his days in the nick.

Tony   Let him get a living. Good luck to him, yeah.

Fred Let him get some money out of it.

Tony I'm all for it. So I go along with it.

Fred It's not a hollow legend. You can't get away from the fact that these things happened, and it's something that should be told because it's folklore now.

Tony I done over the recommended fifteen years and the legend was there when I came out. So it couldn't have been me who created the legend. It was just there. Was it a glamorous life? What was fucking glamorous?

Fred It wasn't glamorous. They're stories that should be told in a factual way. Well, when you look at Elliot Ness, he never, ever fucking saw Al Capone.

Tony That's right, yes.

Fred The taxman done Al Capone, they never came in contact, but look at the films they've made about Elliot Ness and Al Capone.
As kids, the gangster films with Jimmy Cagney and all those, we loved them. Hollywood has earned billions of dollars out of making these films – why not let the British film industry earn money the same way?

BRING ON THE DANCING BOYS

Tony Trevor and Terry, the two young boys who were dancing at the party that night, are the crucial part of the puzzle.

Fred Because they wasn't part of the firm. They was just two young kids. One was a croupier and one was his friend. And they went and made statements to the police. One of their statements, Trevor's, is here [in Fido's book].

Tony And if they had've brought them to court, they would have come out with the facts, and that's not what the prosecution wanted. These boys are gonna make the case a bit different now. It's not gonna be the premeditated murder that they found it was.

Fred That's why they never used them, cos they were honest witnesses. They told the fucking truth. One of them actually joined in the fight, when Jack was having the row.

Tony There were a few people bashing him up before the murder.

Fred The kids thought it was just a fucking punch-up. Then they realize it's more than that, it's becoming nasty, and that's when they want to get out of the room.

Tony Bringing those two boys into it, see, that's I wanted to do on the appeal. What was wrong with that? Make it a different ball game. There might've been a possibility the case could reopen.

Fred It would've reopened. There would've had to be a retrial.

Tony But they [the authorities] don't want that to happen. This is the dangerous side of the legal system in those days. Don't you see what was done here?

Fred This statement by Trevor that I'm reading here in this book – no way would the judiciary have allowed this to be heard, or the judges on the appeal court. They wouldn't send it up for appeal. They knocked it back.

You see, they had enough statements, and they only wanted the ones that was good for the prosecution. These two kids would've thrown a different light on it. When Jack The Hat was killed, their statements were withheld. They should've been offered to the fucking defence. In today's court, they've got to produce every statement.

Tony That could've changed the whole outcome.

Fred Yeah. It would've done.

Tony This was not a premeditated murder, and the boys confirm that. This is the first time I've heard Trevor's statement.

Fred It would've helped the twins and everybody else. Cos it would've made the case a manslaughter.

THE CRIMINAL CODE: TONY'S STATEMENT

Fred You can't get away from the statement, Tone, cos that is already down and in the public domain.

Tony I stand by it. I wanted the two boys brought into it, yeah. We've all been sentenced.

Fred Everyone's convicted.

Tony Different after we're convicted and sentenced.

Fred It say's in here [Fido's book] that you were appealing on the grounds that you were 'precluded from telling the truth in the witness box for fear of Charles Kray, Reginald Kray and Ronnie Kray'.

Tony No. That's not right.

Fred Well, this is what the lawyers have put down to the Appeal Court. They wouldn't be able to print it if it wasn't a proper statement, would they?

Tony They've gotta put that in. It's an old excuse. Everybody used that, from Donoghue to Hart to, you name it, the King of Tibet. What crime did I commit, to try and help myself in some way?

Fred You, Chris and Ronnie thought that you could save the day for yourselves.

Tony 'Please give me a piece of the cake, give me a crumb, please do that for me. Help me a little bit.' Aren't I entitled to that? Just a crumb, that's all I want.

Fred And then you start telling the story of what happened on the night.

Tony Only to a solicitor, for my appeal. No police were present. And that has never, ever been mentioned until today, until this book. Well, that's all right. We'd all been sentenced. They [the authorities] knew the murder happened – it had to be right. There was too much against us.

Fred   There were too many witnesses.

Tony   Do I commit a fucking crime here, considering I didn't put up no defence at my trial? I denied it. I never tried to jump on the bandwagon. Never once did I have any dealings with the law from the minute they charged me until this day. I never said a word to anybody about what happened to Jack The Hat until Reggie admitted it in the book *Our Story* [published by Sidgwick & Jackson in 1988], and I was shocked when he did that.

What they're saying in this [Fido's] book is that I tried to help myself on my appeal, and it looks as if they're making out I did this at the expense of the twins. Yeah, that does make me angry. It's trying to infer that I went against them, and I didn't. I never done that. I stayed loyal to them. That day in Brixton Prison when they were talking about doing a deal, I jumped in. I said, 'I'll take the accessory to get the others out.' All I asked of them was to give me a bit of help with my appeal, and when we put it to them, we got no response. Did they not owe me? Was I not entitled to *that* (*snatching a nut from the bowl on the table*)? Do you know, I didn't get the walnut, I didn't even get a peanut. I got nothing. I'm not making them wrong, I'm not blaming them. I take full responsibility for my actions that night. I defend myself on this point. Up to the minute we were convicted, no one ever got a word out of me.

It seems to me that me and my brother stood there and took the fucking lot on the chin and never, ever defended ourselves.

Getting back to the *Titanic*, you're sitting on a boat that's going out to sea on its maiden voyage, and you've got a thousand icebergs there. And when that fucking ship went down, the captain deserted the ship and the crew went down with it. Are you with me, what I'm saying? I think you are. Who was the captain of the ship? Yeah, good question. Who was the fucking captain of that ship that night?

Fred   Well, Ronnie was the dominant one. Was he the captain?

Tony   No, I'm not gonna blame Ronnie, Fred. Because you've got to bear in mind what I said – Ronnie hit him [Jack] with a glass and told him to fuck off, so I wouldn't blame Ronnie about it.

Fred No, no.

Tony Can't blame Ronnie. Can't do that. But I just don't like what this book is inferring. It's smearing me. I don't fucking like it. I think I've explained enough. If it had've come to the death penalty, yeah, I would have swung. I know that. I didn't know that others had tried to jump on the bandwagon. No one can fucking say that about me.

Fred You didn't say anything until after the sentencing.

Tony Until after the sentencing and convictions.

Fred Well, we know it's wrong to make a statement, don't we? We should never make statements. And it did me and Charlie no good when the three of you made your statements for the appeal court. It never did any of you one bit of good either, it just dotted the 'i's and crossed the 't's for the prosecution. But I can understand the position that you and your brother and Bender were in, when you consider that you were only young fellas . . .

Tony That's not an excuse, Fred, and I accept that.

Fred The fact is, it was very daunting to be sentenced to twenty years [Bender] and fifteen years recommended sentences. You wasn't guilty of any premeditation in this case. All you were guilty of was going to a party where someone might have had a right-hander or, at the worst, got shot in the foot or the leg.

It was not fair to involve you in this sort of thing and then to take control of your representation where you couldn't defend yourselves. It's like lambs to the slaughter.

And the police withholding the two young boys' evidence . . . if that had been heard, it would never have been a premeditated murder. I can't blame you or your brother and Bender for trying to get out of it on the appeal. You stood schtum all the way through the trial, Tony, and you've always kept their name good and supported them ever since, through the last fucking thirty whatever years. You was visiting Reggie and Ronnie, and you've always stood by them. I think you need a fucking fair shake in this case, with what's come out in this Fido book. We've all got enemies and there's always people who are willing to accuse you of this or that. But, you know, who casts the first stone . . . What else can I say? As far as I know, you've always been a solid, upstanding guy and that was a mistake you made. But I can understand it. There was lots of mistakes made at the time. I mean, Donoghue made mistakes which he probably regrets now. We look back over our lives and we all think we should have done things differently.

All three of you have carried this knowledge around in your brains for over thirty years. It must have been a terrible burden.

Tony   In view of what you've said tonight, I can live with that now.

Fred   Course you can. This had to come out. You've gotta confront it head-on. I can accept what you all did, now.

Tony   Best thing that ever happened. It's a load off my mind.

10

'Allo, 'Allo, 'Allo . . . Again

Conversation in Fred's kitchen, 22 October 2000

Immediately after Carlton's January 2000 screening of The Krays, *the police began investigating Fred over his apparent TV confession to shooting and killing Frank 'The Mad Axeman' Mitchell in 1966. Fred had been found not guilty of murdering Mitchell and could not be tried again for the crime. However, he was duly arrested and told that, after thirty-four years, the police were considering charging him with perjury, depriving the coroner of a body, conspiracy and perverting the course of justice. The matter was referred to the Crown Prosecution Service and Fred had to report to the police station on several occasions to find out if the CPS intended to proceed with the charges. (They were finally dropped in December 2000).*

Fred You know, I'm still suffering over the Kray situation, ain't I? I'm still on fucking police bail. I'm hoping that they won't continue with the charges. The first I knew that the police were taking an interest in what I'd said was from newspapers hinting at it, that the police were looking at the programme, investigating it.

The police contacted my lawyers. They arrived at my address and left messages under my door saying that they'd called and that they wanted to see me.

I thought if they was ever gonna pull me, they would've pulled me when I wrote the book [*Respect*]. But I didn't expect them to pull me after the Carlton programme.

They were supposed to protect my interest, the programme makers. They had assured me their legal department was going to safeguard me, that anything that was said would not be miscon-strued, and that it would be safe to go out. I wanted a script approval, but, course, I never got it.

I did a few hours' work, which I was paid for. I'd thought, 'Oh, that's fair enough.' Didn't think no more of it.

I didn't know that it was going to be turned into a two-hour programme that was gonna go out in two parts and get seven million viewers watching it, and it was based on me and Mitchell. I didn't know that I was going to be the main focus. It was setting me up as the murderer confessing. Looking back on it, that's what I was fucking brought in to do.

The way I saw it, I was just there to fill in a ten-minute interview. I didn't know that they was gonna build the programme around me to that extent. I mean, they had a right touch and a right earner down to me, for one afternoon's work.

Tony   Since that happened to you, it's made me even more wary of the media than I was already. I've refused a lot of TV stuff. Because if they can do it to you, they can do it to me. The fact of the matter is, they can lead you down an alley and they can edit something to mean something else. Now, we all know what happened, Fred. It's well known what happened there. Everybody talked to me about it.

Fred   See, when they get the script written for the narrator, like Dennis Waterman, he's saying things and it sounds like you're saying them. They switch from one conversation, my conversation, to somebody else's conversation, the one that's been written for the narrator. And he's saying, Dennis Waterman, that I went to see the Kray brothers about Frank Mitchell, which I didn't. I said all the way through the interviews for the programme, the only person I discussed anything with was Ronnie Kray. But Dennis Waterman was coming on board saying that I went to see Charlie and Reggie, and now I'm involved with them in conspiring to murder Frank Mitchell.

Tony   Which does throw a different light on it.

Fred   You see, it's him, the words they're putting in his mouth. The scripting of his part in it was completely false to what I'd said. I was very careful in what I was saying.

Tony   I could see the editing that went on.

Fred   As I explained to the police, it's showbusiness now. The publishers and the TV people want to dress up the stories and make 'em more gory and more bloodthirsty.

Tony   Which you've got no control over.

Fred They put words in your mouth. They write about you and they put photographs in of people you've got nothing to do with. What's that magazine? *Loaded*. There's a big article in *Loaded* and there's a photograph that's supposed to be me with Christine Keeler, sitting in a club, and it's not me at all. It's Jimmy Nash. We look similar, same sort of build, but what can you do about it? The damage is done, isn't it?

Tony That's right.

Fred And it's not fair to anybody. Look at what happened to Billy Murray [the *The Bill* actor]. The *Sun* printed a picture of Ronnie Kray on holiday and the headline said he was with – look, here it is – the '*Bill* star he had hots for'. But it's not Billy Murray in the photo. It's [Ronnie's friend] Bobby Buckley.

Tony Yeah, I saw that. It's Bobby Buckley. I think we've all learnt a lesson from things like that, Fred. From what happened to you. That is dangerous and very, very wrong. Really, the media have cut their own throat with us on that. 'Cos why would we put ourselves upfront now?

11

Jamie and Patsy:
A Fine Romance!

Conversation in Fred's kitchen, 22 October 2000

In the summer of 2000, it was trumpeted in the press that actress Patsy Kensit had started a fresh relationship, with Fred's son Jamie, having separated from her husband, Oasis singer Liam Gallagher. Jamie had recently split from his long-term partner, actress Carol Harrison. However, the new friendship had cooled by the autumn.

Fred In fact, the whole thing came about through me. Patsy wanted me to go round and see her because of the separation with Liam. I was a friend of her mother and her father, years ago.

It all started with Barbara Windsor. She was sitting in the Ivy [restaurant] having a meal and Patsy was sitting at another table. During the evening, she came over to Barbara on three occasions saying that she wanted to get in touch with me and could she have my number. Being the sort of person she is, Barbara wouldn't divulge my number to her, cos she didn't feel it was right, but she said she would get a message to me. Patsy left her number with Barbara. So Barbara phoned me and asked me to ring Patsy up and have a word with her, cos she sounded very distraught.

So I rung her up. I got the address in St John's Wood and I said I would come round and see her. She did sound pretty upset.

I thought, Her husband's on tour. He was out in the States. I don't like visiting people's wives while their husbands are not there. It's like an old thing from the nick.

Tony Oh, yes.

Fred If a man is in prison, you don't visit the wife on your own. You go with another person or two people, your wife or somebody else in the family. That is part of the culture.

So I phoned up Jamie – 'I'm going to visit Patsy Kensit. You come with me in case she's on her own.'

Turns out I had no need to fear that, because when we get round there, Jim Kerr's there, from Simple Minds – her second husband – and the kids are there, there's a nanny, and there's a minder who was living in, a security guy. So the house was full of people.

She was getting a lot of stick on the phone from Liam, accusing her of this, that and the other. She played some of the tapes to me, and I said, 'You can't listen to that. There's no need for it. When he comes back to London from America, I'll lay a meet on. I'll sit him down and have a talk with him.'

Course, there's two sides to it. Always two sides to everything. I would just have had a friendly chat with him. I would've said, 'Be sensible about it. Don't abuse her on the phone and say the things you've been saying.' Cos he said some nasty things, you know. But in the end, there was no need to have the meet, was there?

Tony You quietened it down.

Fred I've got a certain sympathy for Liam, in a way, if he really loved her. The kid's frustrated and jealous, possessive, or whatever his faults are, and I consider that as being the reason why he was abusing her on the phone. You know, he was twenty-six years of age, wasn't he? He was only a young guy, and, I mean, when women set their sights on a certain person, they want them, they fucking get 'em at all costs, don't they?

Anyway, that night we all just exchanged numbers, we come outside, had a chat with Jim Kerr, and then we left.

Sometime after that, she started ringing up. She rung up Jamie on a regular basis. Finally he popped round to see her at her friends restaurant in Abbey Road. A romantic relationship developed and things were going well for about two months. And then they went out to have a meal in Sheekeys restaurant in St Martin's Court. They did it all nice and private, but when they came out, they got captured by the press.

The papers made so much out of it, but they had both just come out of relationships and they didn't want to jump straight into commitments and pressure, you know? Didn't wanna do that.

So it was just . . . they were going back over the years with all the family connections. They went to the Italia Conti school together. My daughter Danielle went to the school. She was a little bit older than Patsy. So there was this connection going back twenty, twenty-five years or so.

She, losing her mother and her father, needed a bit of security, a bit of family round her so she's got friends who are taking the place of her parents.

But from then on, it's a media story. They was there for each other, to support and help each other, a shoulder to cry on, you know.

I mean, obviously it suited Patsy to be friends with us because the divorce went through smoothly. She thought it out. I know that it suited Patsy to be around Jamie and myself at the time of the divorce settlement and the arrangements. She's got a good settlement, she's got her money and the arrangements that she wants.

I ain't benefited. Nor has Jamie. Jamie's not made no comments, no statements. And when you read the latest *OK* magazine, she's put her story together. Jamie was offered all sorts of money, forty grand, fifty grand, and he could have made money out of it, but he wouldn't exploit the situation and tell stories about their relationship.

Tony He's not said a word.

Fred She needed a bit of strength and a bit of help from us at the time. But, I mean, I ain't a fool. I know when I've been used.

Tony (*Laughing*) Course you was.

Fred I think she knew what she was doing from the very beginning. She wanted to scare Liam off, to stop him creating any problems. And who tipped off the press the night of the meal? Anything's possible. She's got very shrewd people working for her. She's been well advised, very well advised, and someone was steering her in the right direction.

Tony Not a bad move, was it?

Fred I told Jamie what she was doing.

Tony He played it very well, Jamie.

Fred   He kept schtum and he was non-committal all the time. And I'd give him credit for not doing it and then I was thinking, 'You're being used, son, and why don't you do something about it?' But he didn't do anything, so nobody can cast any aspersions on either of us. He was helping her as a friend. And they still are friends. She still phones him and speaks to him, and she's going her own way, making a film in Ireland, isn't she?

I'm still in touch with her, yeah. Yeah. I feel . . . how can I say it? I don't want her to think I don't know that Jamie and myself were used to her advantage. But we still love her and we'll take care of her, regardless.

12

Reggie's Last Battle: The End of the Krays

Conversation in Fred's kitchen, 22 October 2000

Reggie was officially released from captivity in August 2000 on compassionate grounds, after being admitted from Norfolk's Wayland Prison to the Norfolk & Norwich General Hospital in Norwich for cancer treatment. Doctors had diagnosed a secondary cancer, of the bladder. The primary cancer was never confirmed. On 22 September, Reggie moved with Roberta, his wife of three years, into the honeymoon suite in the nearby Town House hotel. There, he died on 1 October, at the age of sixty-six. Like Ronnie, he began his last journey in a horse-drawn hearse, from the English funeral parlour in Bethnal Green to St Matthew's Church. He was later buried in the family plot in Chingford. However, the 11 October funeral was sensationally boycotted by Fred, Tony and other gangland luminaries in protest at Roberta's handling of the arrangements. Dr Ken Stallard, who conducted the service, later revealed that Reggie had repented his sins and secretly converted to Christianity (although Reggie had professed to be a born-again Christian in his 1990 autobiography, Born Fighter*). And in a final, dramatic twist to the story of the Kray twins, a week after his death, the* Sunday People *published a letter, purportedly from Reggie, in which he admitted to being bisexual. It was written on Reggie's headed notepaper but not in his handwriting, implying that it had been dictated to another prisoner.*

THE MYSTERY ILLNESS

Fred Reggie rung me early one morning, cos he loved to ring early.

Tony Always early in the morning.

Fred I said, 'I saw a report, Reggie, you've been ill.' 'No, it's nothing serious,' he said. 'I've got irritable bowel syndrome.' That's what he's saying they told him. But it was in the paper that he had stomach cancer. And you'd already heard he had cancer of the bowel. So someone was trying to put a lid on it, weren't they?

Tony Covering it up, yeah.

Fred He seemed to believe himself that he had irritable bowel syndrome. And then they put out that he had a kidney infection. Of course, it wasn't that at all, was it?

Tony No.

Fred And even when they put the endoscope up his rectum, to look inside him, they never said that they suspected he had cancer. Did Roberta know then that he had cancer? Did the doctors tell her?

Tony It was a shock when they finally admitted he did have cancer, even though we'd been told about it some time before.

Fred I wasn't shocked. I thought he had it all along. I thought, They're giving us misinformation, telling us that he'd got irritable bowel syndrome and kidney infections. I think they knew what was wrong with him perfectly well. I'm always suspicious of these statements put out by the authorities. Never believe them.

Tony I believe that when Ronnie died, that had an effect on Reggie. He didn't know the effect it probably did have on him. I think it might have helped to cause the cancer.

Fred Well, the stress . . .

Tony The whole lot of it, really.

Fred When Charlie died, that was another blow. There wasn't the best of closeness between the brothers, but when Charlie got ill, Reggie was going to visit him, asking his forgiveness and apologizing for the way Charlie had been treated over the years. And Charlie was just sitting in bed and saying, 'I love you, you're my brother.' Charlie was always the scapegoat. He took it all on board and got on with it, but, I mean, Reggie had to be blaming someone. The closest to him was Charlie, and he took the blame for everything. So Reggie's anger probably could've turned inwards, to himself, when Charlie died.

Tony Cos you gotta remember, Reggie had no close family.

Fred He had nobody left. People were demanding his release. Why didn't they release him when he done the thirty years?

Tony I thought that they would release him, without a doubt, when it was confirmed that he had cancer. But he was never really released, in my eyes. He was only released to a death sentence.

Fred I never thought they would release him at all. I thought it suited the authorities for him to die in prison, because this was the scenario, the warning, that they wanted to put out to the general public, to all the young guys who want to follow in their footsteps – 'There's three Kray brothers, all died in captivity.'

Tony There's not many men who have to go through what he did. He watched his whole family die while he was in prison – the father, the mother, the two brothers, the nephew [Charlie's son, Gary]. There was no compassion for him whatsoever, which I found extraordinary.

Fred The only reason that they released him was because they knew he had only a matter of days to live. They'd been feeding him aspirin water for God knows how long before he went into hospital, to kill the pain in his stomach. I heard reports of him going off visits because he was in so much pain, and when you're getting up and walking off a visit before the time's up, there's gotta be a good reason for it. That was very unlike Reggie, cos he loved his visits. I think it was known then that he had cancer, and they was waiting for it to progress, to take him away. Course, when they did release him, the authorities knew they would look compassionate in the eyes of the public. And it would appease all the people who'd campaigned for him to be released. It solved all their problems.

Tony Which brings me back now to 1969. Did they make a secret recommendation at that time, which I believe they did, that they were never to release him?

Fred They knew that he was gonna die in prison. And he might as well have.

INSIDE THE HOTEL

Tony   I never heard from Reggie after he went into hospital.

Fred   I spoke to him on the phone one day, but I didn't visit him there. We was all kept away – by Roberta, obviously. She was in charge, in control of everything.

Wilf Pine [an old associate] phoned me. He was at the hospital with Bill Curbishley [another long-standing friend, and The Who's manager], who was doing a film, a documentary on Reg, and Wilf said, ''Ere, someone wants to talk to you,' and I knew it was Reggie. We had a conversation.

He said, 'Come and see me when I get a bit stronger, when I feel all right.' And I said, 'Yeah, we'll come down.' He said, 'Wait till I get out and I get home,' because he knew that they was gonna release him shortly at that stage.

Of course, he didn't go home, he went to a hotel. I was surprised that he left hospital at all. I thought to myself, How can he leave the hospital when you need twenty-four-hour attention from proper medical staff? I discussed that with a couple of people and they said, 'Well, they've had them Macmillan nurses coming round and looking after him and changing his dressings, and giving him the drips and the injections.' And I said, 'Well, I suppose so,' cos it would've been a nice thing for him.

Anyway, it turns out that Wilf, Bill and Reggie had been discussing who was carrying the coffin. And Reggie Kray had asked Bill Curblishley to carry it.

So Bill says, 'Oh, I hope you're talking about years to come. We're not talking about the near future, Reg, you know.' He asked, 'Who else is carrying the coffin?' Reggie replied, 'Well, Fred. Joey Pyle. Johnny Nash.'

Now, I wasn't volunteering to carry the coffin. I did it once with Ronnie. But when a man asks, you can't refuse, can you? So this was all in the phone call with Wilf Pine. And Bill Curbishley was there when Reggie asked from his own mouth, with his own words. So I said yes, I would.

Now, we were put off from going to see Reggie on several occasions. [Old pals] Joey Pyle, Johnny Nash and myself kept asking Wilf Pine, cos he was with Reggie all the time, every day. But he was being elbowed out as well, because Roberta was there with Bradley Allardyce, a young guy who made friends with Reg six years ago in prison, and his wife. And Roberta don't want us to turn up.

Tony Because of your violent past . . . allegedly.

Fred I've been friends with Reggie and Ronnie and their family for fifty fucking years, since they were sixteen years of age. But as far as she's concerned, no, that doesn't come into it, or that I fucking stood in the dock with them, was accused of murder for them and got bird with them.

Tony I stood in the dock too, and I found it very insulting that the men that'd been loyal to the twins were obviously not welcome at the hospital. Not that I wanted to go. I didn't want to see Reggie in that state. I've seen that before, with my own dad. I wanted to remember him as he was.

Fred I've never had a proper conversation with Roberta, but I think she wanted to be in control of all the situations that were going on. And she didn't want any of us having any influence at all on Reggie. Johnny Nash once got as far as buying tickets for us at Liverpool Street station. It was about the third time we'd made arrangements to go and visit him, in the hospital and then in the hotel. But there was always a message from Roberta, through Wilf Pine, to say that Reggie's not fit enough to receive visitors. But, course, she's there, Wilf's there, Allardyce is there, and his wife.

Then I had a call from Wilf Pine, and he said, 'I think you'd better get here, Fred.' So Joe, John and myself meet at half past six in the morning at Liverpool Street. Joe had a chest infection that day, but he still made the effort, made the journey down there with us, being the man he is.

Wilf Pine picked us up at the railway station in a taxi and drove us straight to the hotel.

Billl Curbishley paid all the hotel bills. He wanted to do that. Reggie had a nice garden to look out on, with a river running at the foot of it and punts and canoes going up and down there. And I thought what a lovely setting it was. If he could only have gone out in the garden to appreciate it. But, of course, Reggie wasn't in no condition to do that.

Wilf said, 'Be prepared for what you're going to see, cos he's down to about four and a half stone.' That's all he weighed.

We sort of, not gatecrashed, but we just walked bang into the bedroom. Roberta wasn't expecting us. We just arrived. And there he is laying in bed, propped up, stripped to the waist and, ahhhhh (*sighing*), what I saw – it wasn't like Reggie Kray laying there. It was just a skeletal body. There was not a bit of muscle left. It was just bone and flesh. And his little face had shrunk, and his head was like just two big eyes looking at you, you know. It was a shock.

He was highly delighted to see us. He said, 'How did you get down? Have you come by train?' And we was making conversation with him.

Roberta was just silent. She was sitting at the side of him on the bed, up by the pillow, and there was no warmth or welcome from her. Oh, no. We said to Reggie, 'This is where you bought your house for your mum and dad – you're on your old plots down here, Reg, aren't you?' And Johnny Nash said, 'It was just down the road from here.'

Tony Wisbech.

Fred 'Yeah,' Reggie was saying, 'the house was down there,' and one thing and another. So, like, he was making an effort to talk and have a conversation. He was very brave. He was facing up to it. But he kept drifting in and out of consciousness, and then he was coughing quite a bit, so Johnny Nash said to Roberta, 'Can't you get a cloth and wipe his lips? They are dry.' Cos, as you know, the bodily fluids in your eyes dry up, and your moisture in your mouth, and you need a little wet cloth to dampen them when you're like that.

And she was just stroking his head and all that, Roberta. She seemed pretty strong in what she was doing. She's not very forthcoming, not very sociable. She never said a word. Neither did Bradley. He never looked round. He was sitting on this right-hand corner, looking at Reg on the four-poster bed. And that's how they sat, him and Roberta. They were both looking mournful. They must've took it in turns to sit up with him, cos there's no day and night when a person's dying. They're awake for short periods of time and then they sleep, and they wake and sleep. But there wasn't a word said between us and them. There was no conversation.

Tony I've never spoken to Bradley in my life.

Fred He never looked at me. You know, if he was to walk in here now . . .

Tony You wouldn't even know him.

Fred I didn't look at him. I was looking at Reggie, and me, Joe and John were doing the best we could to make conversation. It was very difficult, so we were talking amongst ourselves while he was laying there, and just trying to pull him into the conversations.

And then the doctor came in. We got up to leave the room and Reggie went, 'What's up? Where are you going?' So we said, 'Well, we're going downstairs, Reg, to the bar 'cos the doctor's here to look at you. We won't be long.' 'All right, all right,' he's going. 'But come back.'

So we go downstairs and we're there for about three-quarters of an hour. We had a couple of drinks, and we needed them after that, I'll tell you. Couple of Scotches and a couple of large gins and tonics straight away. I didn't think Reggie was going to last the day. I said to the boys, 'It fucking don't look good. Good job we came here today.'

Wilf went upstairs to check on things, and when he come down again, he said, 'It's all right now. The doctor's left, so we can go back.' We just knocked our drinks back and went upstairs, and soon as we walked in the room and looked at Reggie on the bed, he was completely different. He was semi-conscious, not really aware. I mean, I've seen people dying and I knew he was fighting for his life, on his way out.

He kept gasping, deep, big gasps of air, and I knew that it was a matter of minutes, not hours. I said, 'We can't leave now, cos he's going. We're here at the death, you know.'

Roberta got up off the bed. Maybe she was scared, cos he was fighting for his breath. I went over where she'd been and I leaned on the board. I put my hand round the side of his head, just to sort of calm him down, and I spoke in his ear: 'Don't fight it, Reg. Just let go, mate. Relax. I'll see you another time, another place.' And I repeated it two or three times.

And he's going (*deep gasps*). You know, big, long pauses before the breath came out, and then he was holding it again. He knew that it was only a matter of three or four more breaths. He held one for such a long time that I looked round and I went, 'I think he's gone,' and then, all of a sudden, he went (*exhales loud breath*). It made me jump, cos I thought he was dead, and he wasn't. He gasped his last fucking gasp for air, and that was the old death rattle then, you know. And I went straight to the bathroom, and Wilf came over and said, 'He's dead.' I said, 'I know. I know he's dead.' Course, I got a little bit emotional, and then I went back out into the room and Roberta sat down on the bed and was crying, having a little sob over there.

And we just came out and went down in the bar. There were a few phone calls made, and all the activity started then. We had a few more drinks, we left the hotel and the press was all out there. They'd soon found out. Oh, yeah. Straight away.

But one thing I have to say. I was quoted as saying that Reggie asked me that day to carry the coffin. No. He didn't talk about no pall-bearing. That was done long before that, on the phone, like I told you. Bill Curbishley will substantiate that. I never spoke to any reporters outside the hotel. All I was thinking about, when I walked out, was that I was relieved and I was happy that on that day, of all days, we went down there. We were with Reggie to give him a bit of support, going to that 'undiscovered country from whose bourn/No traveller returns', as Shakespeare says. He's got a couple of his old pals who he's known for fifty years with him at those last dying moments, giving him a bit of strength to face whatever he had to face in another world.

Tony Yes.

Fred And not people he's only known for fucking two or three years. You know, Roberta had kept it to herself. She and Bradley was monopolizing all his time so that nobody else could come and see him, all his old friends. There was her, and Bradley and his wife. They was the only people who would've been there. Reggie would have died a lonely man.

Tony With people he hardly knew.

Fred At least he had three of his old pals from fucking forty and fifty years ago to help him over the last moments.

Tony I think he was hanging on until you got there.

Fred The three of us felt that. We believed that he'd waited to see us. We'd been prevented from visiting him, but when he finally did see us, he was happy about it and he decided to go. He threw the towel in. He could've perhaps hung on for another couple more days but, then again, he might not have.

THE FUNERAL AND THE TROUBLE IT CAUSED

Fred The first thing I knew about the date of the funeral was when I saw it in the paper. Nobody told me.

Tony There was no invitations to the funeral sent out. There was nothing.

Fred Roberta never personally invited me. Course, the Wednesday they picked for the funeral turned out to be the fucking day I was supposed to shape up with the police [over the proposed 'Mad Axeman' charges], and I couldn't really cancel that.

I understood I was a pall-bearer after the phone call from Wilf Pine, and that's what I believed was the case right up until after Reggie died. It was all agreed on. And if it was still on, if I was to carry the coffin, then obviously I would've got in touch with the police and said, 'I've been asked to do this and to comply with the wishes, can we postpone this appointment to another day?'

But Roberta knocked me back. She changed it completely. She changed the people that Reggie asked to carry the coffin, didn't she? She said it didn't happen, that Reggie hadn't asked, and made me out to be a liar. I found this out for the first time when she said it in the newspapers. [The pall-bearers included Bradley Allardyce, Tony Mortimer, ex-member of the pop group East 17, Reggie's lawyer Mark Goldstein and Adam Myhill, a young boxer.]

Tony Then she came out with a statement that she didn't want no one there from his 'violent past', which got on my nerves a bit.

Fred And she said something like, 'Other people have done more serious crimes, more violence and more villainy than Reg has done and got away with it.' She was referring to me.

Tony Well, I mean, what were we all doing in the dock?

Fred When we all stood in that dock at the Old Bailey, the twins wasn't the only ones that went down. There was other people that went down with them and got a lot of bird.

Tony We all stood there when Rome fell.

Fred So I boycotted the funeral. I wouldn't have gone even if I hadn't had a police appointment that day, because of her making me look like I'm a liar, and making remarks, referring to me. Am I gonna sit down in the church and watch these other people who Reggie's known for five minutes, who've not known him for forty years and stood by him, gone to prison and served a fucking ten-year sentence for helping them out?

Tony And a lot of other grief . . .

Fred Supported them all their lives. Backed them.

Tony Yeah. You can't forget what you went through with him and Ronnie.

Fred There's lots of stuff that ain't ever been told that went on between the twins and myself, and it will never be said.

Tony Where does the loyalty lie here?

Fred Where's the loyalty, you know? I said my goodbyes to him when he was in that room that day. I was with him when he took his last breath, and that was all I needed to do. And I didn't have to go through the charade of all these imposters and wannabe gangsters and complete strangers. But I told everybody, 'Don't boycott Reggie's funeral on my account. Just because I'm not going doesn't mean that you can't.'

Tony You said to me, 'You go.' And I didn't wanna. I didn't go. I mean, people were wondering who to give their sympathy, their condolences, to. Roberta? No one knew her. I spoke to her on two occasions when I met her, but I didn't know the lady. I wasn't gonna go there.

But the main thing for me was the principle. I spoke to you just after you came back from seeing Reggie, and you didn't get the welcome you should've got from Roberta and from Bradley Allardyce. That, to me, was wrong. And you've never been a liar. I couldn't support it. If you weren't going, how could I go? How could any of us go, for that matter? And I think the funeral lost a lot on that. I knew what had been said earlier, that Joey Pyle, Johnny Nash and Freddie Foreman were going to carry that coffin.

Fred Roberta wasn't carrying out his wishes. Those *were* his wishes. And if I'd gone to the funeral, I would have probably kicked off, said things that I might have regretted afterwards. So I'd rather keep away than lose my temper and upset her at the funeral.

Tony And everybody is in agreement there. They all agree one hundred per cent with what you did. Perhaps later on, we'll get round the grave together.

Fred We'll go round and see the grave without all the ballyhoo. I sent a wreath, you know. I didn't ignore it.

Then I heard that Roberta knocked everyone back at the funeral. They were all made to stand back by the security, not like Charlie's or Ronnie's funeral. Who was standing round the fucking grave? Nobody. Only [Frankie] Fraser and Marilyn.

Tony Albert Chapman done a nice thing. He threw a rose on the coffin for you and me. Albert told me that, and Keith Smart [from sixties group the Rocking Berries], from Birmingham. I felt sorry for Albert and all them who came down, because they thought you was gonna be there, Fred.

Fred Yeah, I know.

Tony It was a terrible atmosphere at the funeral, I know that. And a terrible atmosphere at the church.

Fred There was no emotion, no feeling, in the church.

Tony No tears, nothing.

Fred And they got this priest from fucking Maidstone prison who married Reggie and Roberta in the nick. If we'd had anything to do with it, we'd have got people up there to talk about him who knew him, not a fucking priest who was more concerned about talking about himself than talking about Reg, and trying to speak like a cockney, using expressions that didn't work. Now, the vicar who was at Charlie's funeral was brilliant. That man really said everything that needed to be said about Charlie. And there wasn't such a big turn-out for Reggie.

Tony Because there was a lot of bad feeling.

Fred The people turned out at Charlie's cos he was a very likeable man.

Tony I miss him.

Fred People responded to his warmth and personality, whereas Reggie was more distant and reserved. I don't think any of us really got close to him.

Tony That's right.

Fred And people knew by then that they wouldn't be seeing all the faces at the funeral. She [Roberta] ruined the whole thing. She took all the emotion out of it. People have told me every seat was numbered. You couldn't just sit anywhere. It almost felt like they could have been selling tickets, because of the people who were there, the strangers, the wannabes and the groupie types.

Tony That's what I've been told.

THE ABANDONED WAKE

Fred Janice got a phone call from Flanagan the day before the funeral. Flanagan's tearing her hair out about the wake [due to take place at Paul Jonas' Horn of Plenty pub in Stepney]. She said, 'Would you ask Fred to ring Paul Jonas and tell him that Roberta's changed the venue for the wake. They're not going back to his pub now. They're going somewhere else.' After Paul has bought all that food for a big buffet. And he does put on a terrific spread. He did it for Charlie, and it comes to thousands of pounds that food, with the extra booze that he lays on – free booze for everybody for the first two or three hours. There he is, he's put all this on, and she wants to change the venue the day before. And Flanagan wants me to tell Paul. I wasn't even going to the wake. I said, 'I'm not fucking going to tell Paul. Let Roberta get on and tell him. Not me. It's not my place.'

So it ended up there was two wakes, one with all Reggie's friends and his associates who went to the Horn of Plenty anyway. Roberta didn't turn up there. Never went. She held a separate one.

After the funeral, she went with her company in two cars to East 17's house or somewhere. Where did they come from, you know?

Tony Who the hell are they? Tony Mortimer wasn't even born when we were around.

Fred What are they doing there, even, and carrying the coffin? And there she is, she's ignored all his friends and associates who've known Reggie all his life, and supported him, and pissed off with these fucking complete strangers.

Tony Had she gone down the Horn of Plenty that night, there would've been a problem. It was going off. Tell you what, when I got there it was made plain to me that people were glad she never turned up because there would have been trouble. The atmosphere was terrible. But I'm glad I turned up. People were so pleased to see one of us there who, in a way, represented the twins' past, cos they had no one to go to. It was embarrassing. I shook everybody's hand that night.

Fred With Charlie, we stayed there all fucking day, you know, and celebrated his life, which we do – the cockney way of doing it.

Tony We done it with Charlie, we done it with Ronnie.

Fred They call it 'underground sports', cos the cockney humour comes in, and they all have a good piss-up. It's their way of celebrating a man's life, like the Irish do. They have singers and music, and they enjoy themselves.

Tony She denied Reggie that.

Fred But she comes from a different type – a middle-class family. From a schoolteacher's background, I think she is, and she's been in PR work for years. She'd been trying to pull him away from all his old associates. Maybe we stole her thunder a little bit when we arrived that day at the hotel. She wanted to be the one with him when he died, so there's that little bit of sour grapes. And I think she's jealous that there's a bond between us all. She's been around three years. She wrote letters to him, visited him and then married him. I was prepared to back her all the way, but not now, after the way she's performed.

And I don't see how it could've been consummated. He couldn't do nothing in prison, and he was in too much of a state in the hospital and the hotel. He couldn't keep any food down, he was wasted away. It was like looking at someone in a Belsen camp. Anyway, I don't believe he would have been able to love a woman in the real sense.

REGGIE'S BISEXUAL CONFESSION

Fred Why has he kept it a secret all these years and then decided to do it on his death? I didn't believe it was his letter, especially since it wasn't in his handwriting, until I heard he handed it personally to a reporter. I mean, we knew Reggie was that way in prison, until he met and married Roberta, but it didn't stop us from being his friend.

Tony See, I left Reggie in 1969, Fred. His activities after that, in prison, are nothing to do with me.

Fred They're nothing to do with nobody, are they?

Tony I've got nothing against any man's sexuality. What he done in his private life is none of my business. I knew about it, course. We all knew about it.

Fred Before the twins went to prison, I thought Reggie was the straight guy, the heterosexual. It was only after he was sent down that I thought he might be having gay relationships. For a long time, I didn't wanna believe it. No one would come and say to me that he was bisexual, cos they didn't feel right about it. It threw a different light on a lot of things, whereas I accepted it with Ronnie cos he was open. He didn't hide it. But it wasn't widely known about Reggie, and that's why I never said anything about it before he admitted it himself.

Tony I knew it for a long time. But thirty-two years is a long, long time, and sexual frustrations come out in this. It can change a person.

Fred He's been a strong man all those years, he's done his bird, and, listen, if I was doing my bird in Holloway, I probably wouldn't do it so hard as I would do in a fucking men's prison. So, you know, it's helped him through his time, being surrounded by people he finds attractive. It's like me being surrounded by birds all the time. You'd get through that all right, wouldn't you?

Tony Yeah.

Fred But the situation he found himself in, with all these handsome young boys, probably only stirred up feelings that he already had. I mean, it's either in you or it's not. It's the genes, isn't it? You just can't turn to be that way. I didn't. You didn't.

Tony It's not my cup of tea, I must admit, but I'm gonna give Reggie an excuse here. After thirty-two years, come on . . . It just wasn't a surprise to me when he made his statement to the *People*. Cos I think he wanted to straighten it up with the chaps, to say, 'Look, Fred, John, Joe . . .' He wanted it out, but not while he was alive. I think it would've changed the chaps' outlook on things. It hasn't changed my outlook, not really, because I've done a long time in prison.

Fred It's something you knew anyway. I thought he should've took it to his grave and kept his image the way it was.

Tony I agree with that one hundred per cent. It wasn't a good idea for him to confess about this. No.

Fred I wanna forget that anything like that happened. I don't wanna cast these things against his name. He's exposed himself. Now it's opened the door for all these people to come out of the woodwork and start slinging fucking mud at him.

Tony That's what he was trying to stop, by making the statement, because he knew that one of them, sooner or later, the ex-boyfriends, would come out with it.

Fred Now, there's this guy and I've been expecting him to do an article with one of the newspapers. I was told he's been hawking it around, the story.

Tony No one would buy it. I heard about it.

Fred No one would entertain it, apparently. But this guy has already given information which he's made cash out of.

Tony One way or the other, they're going to bring this out. A newspaper's asked me already about it.

Fred He had all these young, special friends around him before he met Roberta.

Tony The *People* article said that Reggie had been pulled in and warned by the prison authorities about pestering new prisoners. I think they was worried about the influence on the youngsters, I couldn't get my head round that, Fred.

Fred I'd hoped that whatever he was doing in his sexuality would be discreet.

Tony I went on a visit and I found it disgusting, shocking, the carry-on there. There was this guy running about, he had this watch on, this bracelet, and rings and necklaces, and I looked at Reggie and I thought to myself, 'Reg, come on, don't . . .' And Reg kept grabbing his hand, Fred – on a visit.

Fred How old was this guy?

Tony About twenty-five, twenty-eight, something like that. He totally dominated Reggie. The way he treated him, Fred, the way he spoke to him. Before Reggie went to prison, you couldn't have talked to him like that.

Fred Was he slagging him off?

Tony 'Get off your arse, fucking get your own tea,' and that.
    Me and Wendy was on a visit with him one day in another prison, and there was someone else there who was sitting with his hand on Reggie's leg. I wanted to chin the geezer.

Fred I do hate to feel that his image has been tarnished by the bisexual confession and by being a born-again Christian, repenting for his sins.

Tony (*Chuckling*) You can't do that.

Fred When Bill Curbishley was working on this documentary with him, he wasn't bloody well repenting what he'd done, or turning into a cry-baby wimp and a born-again Christian. It was the last footage of him, in the hotel room, having an interview. And he was cursing Jack Straw and everyone in the prison system for what they'd done to him. So he hadn't changed that much, and he's never, ever said that he regretted Jack The Hat, has he?

Tony He's always said he didn't regret it. I've always tried to protect the twins, the whole thing of it. Yes, it's caused a lot of trouble, but you've got to try and protect their name.

Perhaps we should do the right thing now, to kill it off. I resent some of the things Reggie did, because I never once heard him talk good about anyone.

Fred Or apologized to people for the shit he put them in.

Tony I put it down to thirty-two years, Fred. Don't come out with it about Christianity. That's no good to me.

Fred Nah. Bollocks, innit? We're Christians in the way we treat each other. We don't have to go to church.

Tony I'm not a religious man. At least I admit it.

Fred It's how you treat your fellow man. If I can fucking help somebody and do a favour . . .

Tony That's right. You've done that.

Fred And I've done it all my life. I don't have to go to church and fucking swear that I'm a Christian to do that. And you've done favours for people. Course you have.

Tony Because it's the right thing to do.

Fred We all meet our maker one day. The old grim reaper won't pass you by when your time's up.

Tony I'll face it.

Fred Whether you go upstairs or downstairs – but if I go downstairs, there's all my pals down there, so I'd rather not be up there with all the fucking goody-goodies.

Tony I know where me and you are gonna be, and the boys, so I'm not worried about it.

Fred Oh, fuck it, no. When you're dead, you're dead.

Tony You know something? I've gotta say this. If I'm gonna face it, I'd want you, Joey Pyle and Johnny Nash around me.

THE FALL OF THE KRAY EMPIRE

Tony   I think it's sad, very sad, that all three brothers have gone.

Fred   Oh, that's sad. In one way, it's the end of an era, but I'm relieved in another way.

Tony   And me.

Fred   That's it. Fucking done and finished. I know the books and stories are gonna carry on from now to fucking doomsday. It's not gonna go away, but let's hope we get a little bit of peace and rest from it all.

Tony   I don't think that's gonna happen. And all we ever did was try to protect the twins.

Fred   We've protected 'em all our lives.

Tony   I've lived with that, and I'm sure you have, since the day we went away. And it's a relief not to have to protect them any more.

Fred   It is a relief.

Tony   It's a weight off my shoulders. He [Reggie] ain't suffering, number one. Number two is, I haven't got to protect him. I don't have to stand up there and come out with a load of crap that I don't believe in, all this fantasy. I don't want to damage their name in any way whatsoever, and I'm sure you don't.

Fred   No. Both the twins pushed the self-destruct button in the late Sixties.

Tony   I will not diminish their credibility. But the fact of the matter is, I had my respect for Reggie and I left that behind in 1969. I don't have to talk about him no more, or be asked about his release, and what my thoughts are. My thoughts mean nothing. Because we all know that whatever we say or don't say, this is not the end of the Krays, by any means. For better or for worse, the myth and the legend will carry on.

Glossary

Aim out Eject.

Banged up In prison; locked in cell.

Barnet Hair.

Bird Jail sentence.

(The) Block Punishment block in a prison, where detention is accompanied by a huge loss of privilege.

Brief Solicitor.

Burglars Special prison officers who search convicts' cells; house-breakers.

Butcher's A look (from rhyming slang 'butcher's hook').

Cat A Category A prison status for convicts thought likely to try to escape.

Clip joint Drinking establishment where women are used to con money out of male customers.

On the cobbles Bare-knuckle fighting.

Come on top Come to a confrontation or crisis.

Connected up Knowing the right people.

Cons Convicts.

Control unit Punishment cells in a prison (see Block).

Crombie Stylish woollen overcoat.

Cut-up Share of the proceeds from a crime.

Dip your beak Mafia expression for taking a cut of the money from a crime.

Do someone up 'Stitch someone up', give them a bad deal or do something to them without their realizing it, such as spiking their food or drink.

Face Leading criminal.

Firm Gang of criminals.

Firm-handed With the gang in tow.

Flop Safe house or garage.

In the frame Implicated in a crime.

Gaff House or other establishment.

Game Unafraid.

Give 'em a clump Punch someone.

Green Goddess Army ambulance.

Growl A hostile atmosphere between two people.

The hotplate Place where prisoners collect their food at mealtimes.

Iron out Kill.

Joey Payment, reward or parcel of 'goodies'.

Jollop Medication.

Landing Long corridor in prison housing a row of cells.

Lay out Leave someone on the ground.

Liquid cosh Knockout drug.

A long 'un £1,000.

Make one with Side with.

Manor Area where a gang is based.

Mark someone's card Tell someone what's going on.

Masked up Wearing a mask.

Middled up Put into the middle of a situation.

A monkey £500.

Nick   Police station or jail.

Nonce   Paedophile or sex offender.

Oblige   Attack.

Old Bailey   Most famous criminal court in Britain.

Old Bill   Police.

On a trip   Under the influence of psychedelic drugs.

On your toes   In hiding or out of the country to avoid arrest.

The out   The world outside prison.

PO   A Principal Officer in prison.

On the pavement   Working as a robber.

Pot up   Throw a pot of excrement over someone.

Puff   Cannabis.

Punch the granny out of   Beat up vigorously.

Put it back   Take revenge.

Put down   Kill.

Put someone in it   Give someone a financial share.

Raspberry up   Cripple in an attack (from rhyming slang 'raspberry ripple' – 'cripple')

Readies   Money.

Recess   Washroom, toilet and slopping-out bay in a prison.

Richard the Third   Faeces (from rhyming slang 'third' – 'turd')

Roll over   Inform to the police.

Schtum   Quiet.

Scream   Outcry in the media.

Screw   Prison officer.

The Scrubs   Wormwood Scrubs prison, west London.

Serve up Attack so seriously that the victim requires hospital treatment.

Shape up Give support.

Shebeen Drinking club.

Shooter Gun.

Shop Inform on someone; a workshop where convicts work in prison.

Slop out Empty toilet buckets.

Smudge Photograph.

Snout Tobacco.

Spiel(er) Pub or club where unlicensed gambling takes place.

Spin Police raid.

Straighten out Sort out a problem.

Straighten out/up Punish with violence; persuade or pay money to to keep quiet or to do or say the 'right' thing.

Straightener Two men fighting without weapons or any help.

Stretch Period of imprisonment.

Suited and booted Dressed to the nines.

Sweet-grassing Allowing the authorities to discover information without telling them directly.

Tail up Follow in a car.

Tear-up Fight or other violent incident involving several people; violent scenes while escaping from police.

Tool Weapon.

A touch Money made from criminal activity.

Turned over Raided by police or by criminals.

Up Punch.

Weighed off Given a prison sentence.

Wing One of several areas, including cells, in a prison, described as A-Wing, B-Wing, etc.

Wrong 'un An untrustworthy or troublesome person.

Yard Prison exercise yard.

Yardie A member of a Jamaican criminal gang.